HUMBUG

HUMBUG

The Art of
P. T. Barnum

Neil Harris

THE UNIVERSITY OF CHICAGO PRESS
Chicago and London

The University of Chicago Press, Chicago 60637
The University of Chicago Press, Ltd., London

04 03 02 01 00 99 98 97 96 95   5 6 7 8 9

Library of Congress Cataloging in Publication Data

Harris, Neil, 1938–
  Humbug: the art of P. T. Barnum.

  Reprint of the ed. published by Little, Brown,
Boston.
  Bibliography: p.
  Includes index.
  1. Barnum, Phineas Taylor, 1810–1891.
2. Circus owners—United States—Biography.
3. United States—Social conditions.   I. Title.
[GV1811.B3H37   1981]   791.3′092′4 [B]   80-26944
ISBN 0-226-31752-8 (pbk.)

♾ The paper used in this publication meets the
minimum requirements of the American National
Standard for Information Sciences—Permanence of
Paper for Printed Library Materials, ANSI Z39.48–1984.

To Linda Harris
and S. L. P.

Contents

Illustrations

Credits

Introduction

I FIRST BECAME INTERESTED in P. T. Barnum when, several years ago, I was asked to write an introduction for his frequently reprinted autobiography. My own conception of Barnum reflected conventional wisdom: a brash huckster who had outsmarted all rivals and set up a successful circus. Central casting might well have selected W. C. Fields to play the Barnum of popular mythology; in fact it came quite close, for Wallace Beery played Barnum in Gene Fowler's 1934 screenplay.

But after reading and rereading Barnum's own writings, and reflecting on his achievements, I found that his career raised unexpectedly complex issues. Indeed, so numerous were these issues that my introduction became too unwieldy to survive that form and grew into this book.

Some of the issues involved subjects that were central to our historical experience. One, which seemed fundamental, concerned social confidence. Barnum grew up in an age of irreverence, happily exploding established rituals. Jacksonian Americans challenged notions of social order that had remained inviolate for centuries. The American Revolution had, it is true, relocated the sources of political authority, but fifty years later, during Barnum's youth, this revolution broadened. Orators and politicians now placed all authority — social, moral, aesthetic, even religious — in the hearts and minds of the ordinary citizen, the much-celebrated common man. Conservatives and academicians tried to resist this new consensus, but most Americans applauded it.

The common man faced heavy responsibilities, however. The rituals that had once comfortably protected social conventions disappeared or decayed. When credentials, coats of arms,

3

and university degrees no longer guaranteed what passed for truth, it was difficult to know whom and what to believe. Everything was up for grabs. Critics charged that the destruction of deference would encourage a generation of tricksters and confidence men, braggart adventurers who would fill the vacuum once occupied by ceremony and honor. Ordinary men, insisting upon full equality, would find themselves exploited by mercenary hypocrites.

Barnum, of course, seemed the supreme symbol of this change. Here was the independent, successful, and audacious New Man that eighteenth-century sages had been seeking. But was he a blessing or a curse? Barnum was intelligent and energetic, a devoted family man, an abstainer from liquor, an accumulator of property. But he used deceit and exaggeration, deception and disguise, to make his fortune.

But Barnum was more than merely a symbol. He was aware that a new democratic sensibility had been born, and he appealed directly to its vanities and conceits. In his early years Barnum developed techniques of advertising and exhibiting that glorified doubt and celebrated individual judgment. He placed himself in studied combat against his customers (and competitors). Barnum's mastery of showmanship had parallels with other American accomplishments, in the arts and the sciences, and his genius for hoaxing expressed certain fundamental truths about the character of American romanticism.

Moreover, Barnum was versatile as well as ingenious. He could promote high art along with vulgar amusements, and when the audiences of the post–Civil War era showed new tastes, Barnum was there to satisfy them, with three rings and thirty elephants.

Barnum was neither philosopher nor metaphysician. A hardheaded businessman, he followed no battle plan to victory. But he was self-conscious, and anxious for a claim on national gratitude. It is the intersection of private goals and public issues that makes him so fascinating. But also, for his biographer, it makes him difficult to decipher. Barnum was a public man who kept his privacy. Indeed, one is not even sure that he had a notion of privacy, so completely did he define his own needs and reactions in public terms. His inner life, if it existed, was carefully shielded. Irony and sincerity move through his rhetoric like revolving stages, and their sets are often indistinguishable.

I am most concerned with Barnum's public role, his translation of popular taste into private profit, and his insight into his own accomplishments. I have used the biographical form because it seemed the easiest way to transmit the scale and scope of Barnum's activities. Many of these feats have become familiar, and the anecdotes threaten to grow stale. But there is still room to examine the historical Barnum, to reconstruct the language of showmanship that meant so much to nineteenth-century Americans. Throughout, I try to show why Barnum's exhibits were so successful, what there was in a "Fejee Mermaid," a Tom Thumb, a Jenny Lind, or a mammoth circus that made them so enticing to their audiences. For what we confront is neither a good-natured deceiver nor an evil-minded philistine, but an intelligent, complex, and well-organized entrepreneur whose business involved the myths and values of a self-proclaimed democracy.

ONE

Early Years

PHINEAS TAYLOR BARNUM was born July 5, 1810, in Bethel, a part of Danbury, Connecticut. Western Connecticut had been home for Barnums ever since Thomas Barnum made the trip across the Atlantic in the mid-seventeenth century. Genealogical research conducted later, partly at P. T.'s request, suggested descent from Sir Martin Calthorpe, a lord mayor of London, and kinship with Francis Bacon, but Thomas Barnum was not aided by these illustrious relatives; he arrived in America as an indentured servant.[1]

Thomas Barnum, a descendant wrote to P. T. in 1882, "was no *slouch*. I should judge him," he went on with no apparent evidence, "to have been a young man with a large frame, erect and up-headed figure, and with a bright blue eye, well open and intent upon the circumstances surrounding him."[2] Physiognomy aside, this imaginary portrait had at least some basis in reality, for Thomas Barnum quickly prospered; he purchased his freedom and by 1673 was a landowner in Norwalk. Ten years later he had become one of the founders of Danbury and the possessor of a comfortable estate. The Barnums multiplied rapidly. The 1790 census showed eighty male Barnums in New England and New York, most of them living in Fairfield County, Connecticut. Ephraim Barnum, Thomas's great-grandson and P. T.'s grandfather, served as a captain in the American Revolution and accumulated an estate appraised at more than nine hundred pounds. Other Barnums gained fame in politics and hotel-keeping.[3]

But large families meant small inheritances, and P. T.'s father, Philo, was unable to make it on his own. He moved through a series of jobs, including tailoring and tavern-keeping, without stopping long enough to gather fortune or security. And his troubles were not only financial. His first wife,

Polly Fairchild, died in 1808 at the age of twenty-six. In good New England fashion, Philo remarried quickly, within six months, partly to provide a mother for his children. His second wife was Irene Taylor, descended from another old Connecticut family.

If mild adversity sharpened young P. T.s' business sense, it was also aided by Irene's father and P. T.'s namesake, Phineas Taylor. Phineas Taylor was the first person P. T. could remember having recognized, and he exerted an enormous influence on the boy. Strong-willed, crafty, Phineas Taylor would "go further, wait longer, work harder, and contrive deeper" to play a practical joke than anyone he ever knew, his grandson recalled. Jokes were played on members of the family as well as on outsiders, and P. T. himself was victimized by his grandfather's wit. Throughout his penny-pinching boyhood P. T.'s hopes were buoyed by the thought of becoming rich, and his grandfather glowingly described an inheritance, Ivy Island, which would make the boy's fortune. Though P. T. was burdened with few illusions, he dreamed fondly of reaching his maturity as a respected man of property, and more important, as a man of leisure; he hated the manual labor of farm life. When the great day came to visit his possession, however, P. T. discovered a worthless piece of swampland. His grandfather rarely, if ever, produced a more discomfited victim.

Victimization, in fact, was a way of life in the rural New England of the early nineteenth century. When the area was first settled, almost two hundred years earlier, communal harmony in all things was a religious and social necessity. "Peaceable Kingdoms," one historian has labeled the towns scattered across Massachusetts and Connecticut. But the passage from Puritan to Yankee involved psychological as well as economic changes, and the cunning Yankee type was forged in the furnace of village animosities.[4] Harmony disappeared and was replaced by compulsive competitiveness. Reviewing Barnum's autobiography in the 1850s, the Russian émigré Alexander Herzen was appalled by the commerce of roguery which enveloped rural New England, and which Barnum described without rancor. "The slightest inattention on the part of the storekeeper, and he is fooled on weight or measure; the least heedlessness on the part of the farmer and he is swindled."[5] It was a bizarre game with victory neither permanent nor assured for even the most skillful player. The nostalgia that currently shrouds many pictures of nineteenth-century communities hides a world whose poverty of recreation and scarcity of material goods forced even kinsmen to spar for advantage. Barnum never sentimentalized his past.

Along with the ploughing, raking, weeding, and cow driving that formed some of his duties on the family farm — "I never really liked to work," Barnum confessed — the boy attended the local school. He was not overly impressed by his teachers, who were better at discipline than instruction. But though Barnum disliked the schoolroom, he excelled very early at calculation, astounding his family and neighbors by his skill at arithmetic. The delicate boundary between profit and loss required a mind adept at juggling figures, and through his lifetime Barnum retained a love for statistics and a compulsion to include them in all his descriptions and reflections.

Impelled by a passion to get out of farm work, the young Barnum moved quickly into trade; he became a clerk in a local country store, driving hard bargains with his customers. Shrewdness was necessary, for payment came more often in butter, eggs, hats, and hickory nuts than in currency. Swapping stories with the local wits who gathered at the store, exploiting his employers as well as his customers, Barnum mastered the art of sharp practices. He had already been convinced of their need. "We are apt to believe," he wrote in the autobiography, puncturing another myth, "that sharp trades, especially dishonest tricks and unprincipled deceptions," are confined to the city, while country folk are honest and unsophisticated. Clerking in a country store, encountering short measurement by farmers and rag swindles by their wives, taught Barnum greater realism. By the age of twelve the boy's business experience had subverted airy generalizations about human behavior and rhetoric about public spirit.

Connecticut offered limitless opportunities to discover discrepancies between the ideal and the actual. A tightly governed society, with an established church (until 1818) and strict sabbath legislation, it tolerated human weakness when profits could be made. The wildest lottery schemes were employed to build schools and churches, and also to line promoters' pockets. Phineas Taylor was particularly successful in launching one such operation, even though he was more liberal than the official state lottery in the odds he offered purchasers. By Barnum's calculations the state offered one chance in twelve thousand for reward.

P. T.'s training in sharp dealing was early put to use; in 1825 his father died, leaving the boy of fifteen his father's debts and responsibility for four sisters and brothers under the age of seven. P. T.'s mother was forced to find work, and Barnum moved to a nearby village, where he served as a store clerk in return for board and six dollars a month. Here, in Grassy Plain, he found new challenges to his ingenuity. Trading in the store, one day, he exchanged some goods for a peddler's wagonload of green bottles. Actually, Barnum had given away trash, but he now had on hand an enormous stock of bottles, as well as an ancient supply of dirty tinware. He seized upon the idea of using these goods as lottery prizes, promising his customers five hundred winners for the one thousand tickets. Within ten days, Barnum happily reported, every glass bottle was gone and the old tinware replaced by new. The most appreciative witness of Barnum's scheme was his grandfather, who proudly proclaimed the lad "a chip off the old block."

The area around Bethel and Danbury was a center for hat manufacturing, and many of Barnum's customers were hatters; in trade, they attempted to mix their less expensive or damaged furs with some of their best. "The customers cheated us in their fabrics," Barnum recalled; "we cheated the customers with our goods. Each party expected to be cheated, if it was possible.

Our eyes, and not our ears, had to be our masters. We must believe little that we saw, and less that we heard." This type of commerce, he admitted, was not a good school for morals, but he accepted it as it was and thrived in a modest way.

Connecticut, however, was too limited an area for speculation. In 1826, aged sixteen, Barnum moved to New York to clerk in a Brooklyn grocery store owned by a former neighbor. Here Barnum observed business practices on a larger scale, attending wholesale auctions, clubbing together with other grocers to purchase goods at reduced prices. But once more, he found working for a fixed salary too confining. "My disposition is, and ever was, of a speculative character, and I am never content to engage in any business unless it is of such a nature that my profits may be greatly enhanced by an increase of energy."

In 1828, then, when his grandfather offered to help him establish a business of his own in Bethel, Barnum came home to open a fruit and confectionery store. As in most of his other businesses he began well, turning a decent profit, encountering the same kinds of wits who had filled his younger days with the crackle of competition. He even returned again to the lottery activity that had supplemented his earlier clerkship. But now he was more scientific, traveling throughout the East to learn how lottery managers made their money. He became so successful that he wrote the firm of Yates and McIntyre, which had lottery offices throughout the country, about the possibility of opening an office for them in Pittsburgh. When they suggested instead that he take over their agency in Tennessee, Barnum refused, deciding that he could make more money by buying his tickets directly from the managers of lotteries. Making as much as a thirty percent profit on his sales, Barnum soon had lottery offices scattered about most of Connecticut. Taking mail orders as well, his agents sometimes sold as much as two-thousand dollars worth of tickets a day. Lotteries were big business, but their days, like their tickets, were numbered. Concerned about fraud, state after state appointed commissions to examine lottery practices and control them more carefully; in the end, many states abolished them entirely as a type of gambling dangerous to public welfare.[6]

Barnum also went into book selling, disposing of his books at auctions. His customers, however, had moral standards lower than Barnum's own, for they ruined his chance for profits by stealing the most valuable books without even bothering to bid on them. Law students, Barnum reported, practiced the most energetic larceny, demonstrating the skills on which their future careers would rest.

During his return engagement in Connecticut, on November 8, 1829, Barnum married a twenty-one-year-old tailoress he had met earlier, Charity Hallett. Charity, like Barnum's parents, like his brothers and sisters, like his own children, remains an indistinct figure. About all we know of some of them are their dates of birth and death. "My private personal affairs I always have kept distinct from business," Barnum told his secretary in the 1880s, and he was telling the truth.[7] The autobiography describes his family only occasionally, and then smothers any individuality by invoking the conventional pieties. Barnum's public personality always dominated his private life. At his best describing contest, competition, and conquest, Barnum seemed never to know how to talk about concord, or perhaps he suspected that his audience was not interested. Whether his married life was happy or unhappy, whether he was disappointed in or proud of any of his children, whether he maintained relationships with his sisters and brothers, he did not bother to disclose.[8] About all we know is that he remained married to Charity until her death in 1873. Indeed, the only time Barnum wrote in detail about his relatives was to mention their deaths, which he invariably accepted with fortitude and religious faith.

That his was a religious and God-fearing nature Barnum consistently emphasized throughout his lifetime. But his religious life, like his secular activities, was highly individual. Phineas Taylor had been a Universalist, and his grandson took after him in rejecting the dominant Congregationalism of the day. Connecticut was among the last New England states to retain an active church establishment, forcing her citizens to pay taxes to support the churches, normally Congregational, and holding in force well through the nineteenth century the most rigid sabbatarian legislation in the United States.⁹ Many Connecticut towns refused to permit travel on Sunday. In later years Barnum would become friendly with some of the most famous ministers in America, men like Henry Ward Beecher and Edwin H. Chapin, but his attitude toward the local Congregationalist clergy was usually hostile. His autobiography lovingly described the tricks played on bigoted and self-righteous ministers, whose pomposity and pedantry often provided the key to their downfall. Anecdote after anecdote recalled some ridiculous scrape which Barnum or his grandfather managed to arrange. On one occasion his grandfather, by an elaborate scheme, managed to get a minister to New York on the sabbath with only half a beard on his face and a sermon to give. Connecticut's belief that clergymen "were considerably more than human" was only another illusion, Barnum wrote, for "we have all learned, with pain and sorrow, that the title 'Rev.' does not necessarily imply a saint." Dignity, learning, and fame were no protection to local bigots if Barnum took after them.

On some occasions Barnum's anger was so roused that he could not keep within the limits of practical joking. As a Jacksonian Democrat in a conservative state, he brooded about aristocratical combinations and overzealous Christians. He knew there were some in Connecticut who wanted to go back to the good old days when church consociations had fixed the community's manners and morals. An excited Barnum established a weekly newspaper "which should oppose all combinations against the liberties of our country." On October 19, 1831, the first issue of the *Herald of Freedom* appeared. Several times during the three years of his editorship, irate targets of his newspaper had him prosecuted for libel, but the most serious incident occurred when he accused Seth Seelye, a prominent local dignitary and a deacon of the church, of charging an orphan usurious interest rates. Seelye, father of a future president of Amherst and also a future in-law to one of Barnum's own daughters, took him to court. Judge David Daggett, who would, in the Prudence Crandall case the following year, deny free Negroes American citizenship, seemed to demonstrate a similar hostility to Barnum. That "lump of superstition" charged the jury "as though he were the attorney for the prosecution," Barnum insisted, "and was believed to experience personal satisfaction in pronouncing the sentence." The sentence was a hundred-dollar fine and sixty days in jail. Barnum began his term in a spirit of defiance. "The same spirit governs my enemies that burnt to death Michael Servetus by order of John Calvin," he wrote Gideon Welles from Danbury jail.[10] But the benefits far outweighed the costs. Subscriptions to the *Herald of Freedom* multiplied as prosecution transformed Barnum from an obscure country editor into a backwoods Voltaire. The cry of "Freedom of the Press" aroused neighboring libertarians to expatiate on Barnum's martyrdom, indifferent to the fact that his cell was papered and carpeted and served as a meeting place for many friends.

But most impressive of all was Barnum's release from jail. A round of celebrations, parades, and dinners greeted the hero. Sixty carriages and forty horsemen escorted him home to Bethel, while a band played throughout the entire three-mile trip. Theophilus Fisk, a New Haven editor, reflected the mood of the occasion when he celebrated the work of the newspaper. "Great engine of knowledge," he cried, "pause not in thy career of glory till the world shall hear of deliverance to its utmost verve! Speed on thy pathway of light till the sleeping earth shall rise in the strength of a giant refreshed with wine!"[11] No demonstrations or celebrations Barnum organized in later years quite matched the headiness of this greeting.

But why Barnum should have invited martyrdom, however brief, why he should have spent so much time on an editorship that could return him little financial profit, is difficult to determine. The direction of his first twenty years had been toward effecting a coldly realistic truce with life. His boyhood had not been filled with days at the swimming hole, but with sharp, if ritualized, conflict with his customers and competitors. Even in his seventies Barnum remembered the harsher side of the early nineteenth century. People were just as eager for money than as they were in postwar America, he recalled, "and a great deal more vulgar, unscrupulous, and foolish in their endeavors to get it." Nevertheless, despite his genius for calculation and his lack of illusions, Barnum undertook his local crusade.

The answer lay in that strange combination of cynicism and idealism that prompted so many other Yankees to work toward reforms. The cynicism was bred by observation and history: self-interest was the mainspring of human action, for theories of altruism were belied by daily experience and the lessons of the past. The idealism was nourished by a sense of new possibilities to manipulate this same self-interest: a frank recognition of the role of human selfishness and the creation of mechanisms to exploit it benevolently. Eighteenth-century Americans, notably the Constitution-makers, had also acknowledged the clash of private interests as the motive power of society, but they had been unwilling to accept its full logic. Many still hoped for a reign of virtue and dreamed of eradicating combinations of private interests. Jacksonians, however, moved beyond their fathers. They legitimized the pursuit of personal gain in their political parties, their hostility to establishments, and their liberal attitudes toward incorporation; they made ambition and improvement the keynotes of civilization.

Barnum was a true Jacksonian Democrat; his loyalty to the Democratic party lasted almost to the eve of the Civil War, despite his increasing antagonism to the institution of slavery. He was always willing to fight for the right of fighting itself, to compete against competitors, audiences, or self-styled experts. But the terms had to be fair. His boyhood taught that cunning and alertness were necessities to the man on the make, but shrewdness could go only so far. Actual dishonesty and broken contracts invited retribution, and a sharp trader avoided such risks. He relied instead on his own intelligence and sense of proportion. That was all he needed, without special license or official privilege. And if that was all Barnum needed, no one else deserved more. Clergymen and showmen, like merchants and farmers, would have to defend themselves in open markets, subject to both criticism and competition.

Barnum's world view was complemented by his personal makeup. During a long life his periods of active business speculation alternated with bouts of aggressive moralizing and philanthropy. His youthful zeal for civil liberties was followed by participation in temperance crusades and advocacy of abolition. He toyed with the women's rights movement and after the Civil War took up the cudgels against corporate monopoly. Whether his reforms and charities were natural products of his show-business activities or expiations of the controversial advertising practices that accompanied them is difficult to say. Probably a little of both, for Barnum learned early that crusading was good for business; it brought publicity and identified the entrepreneur with objects higher than the quest for profits.

But despite his intelligence and energy, Barnum reached the age of twenty-five without spectacular success. His store suffered from his journalistic diversions, and also from the dishonesties of customers who refused to pay their debts. Not for the last time the man whose name was permanently identified with sharp business practices found himself taken in by promises. Dunning was a disagreeable business, particularly to someone who preferred to be known for amiability and expansiveness. In January 1833, Barnum sold out his interest in the store and the following year severed his connection with the *Herald of Freedom*. In 1833 Connecticut outlawed his final source of income, lotteries, and there seemed little to do but start out again. So in late 1834 Barnum took his family to New York City, there to seek his fortune anew and begin the first phase of the showman's life.

2

New York City, when Barnum took up residence there, had just recently replaced Philadelphia as America's metropolis. Aided by superb natural shipping facilities, aggressive merchants, and the newly completed Erie Canal, which linked the seaport to a rich hinterland, the city typified the pace of Jacksonian change and the scale of new problems. A quarter of a million people, of every race and color, made up New York's population in 1834, but they still occupied what was little more than an overgrown village. Houses, offices, theaters, and warehouses huddled together in close quarters; the bustle and traffic of the streets were complicated by antiquated municipal institutions that couldn't cope with the dirt, crime, and fires. And official interference often compounded these problems.[12]

The growth of wealth and population made for new career possibilities. Retail merchants, real-estate speculators, newspaper editors, ship builders, and railroad managers reaped the rewards of rapid exploitation. The formula was to discover an avenue to fortune and quickly follow it up.

Barnum arrived in the city with little education, less money, and high ambitions. He did not yet know what he wanted to do with his life, but he wanted to get ahead. A whole generation of young men confronted the novel but anxious experience of free choice: family traditions and time-honored formulas were threatened by new opportunities. Thousands like Barnum, migrants from the countryside without capital or specialized training, knew only that they had to succeed. Inventors, entrepreneurs, manufacturers, and confidence men advertised in the columns of the city's newspapers for bright young men. "Fortunes equalling that of Croesus, and as plenty as blackberries, were dangling from many an advertisement," Barnum remembered. Applicants were invited to cellars and dark attics, where temporarily impoverished capitalists asked them for money and ingenuity in distributing patent medicines, new microscopes, or directories providing vital information sure to be purchased by every citizen. The promises were large, the investments small. Barnum answered the advertisements and heard the lyrical forecasts.

But beyond meeting an array of curious types and making a few useful contacts, he gained little from these explorations. Invariably his prospective fortune "depended firstly upon my advancing a certain sum of money, and secondly, upon my success in peddling a newly discovered patent life-pill." "A student of human nature," Barnum was more interested in the effect these schemes had on others than enticed himself. His family had to be fed, however, so he opened a boarding house and acquired an interest in a grocery store. He appealed to his old neighbors to visit him while in New York and was able to turn a decent profit.

But he remained unsatisfied. His life's work had to be personally fulfilling as well as income-producing, and grocery-keeping remained simply an extension of his earlier jobs. It "was clear to my mind that my proper position in this busy world was not yet reached. I had displayed the faculty of getting money, as well as getting rid of it; but the business for which I was destined . . . had not yet come to me." His language reveals that Barnum still sought a calling; even if the vocabulary of religious thought was being rapidly diluted, its operative concepts, like the divine blueprint justifying man through his work, remained in force.

Barnum did not have to wait long. Less than a year after his arrival in the city he became involved in his first great entertainment feat, one that would be identified with him permanently: the Joice Heth affair. Although he had done many things — farming, trading, editing, lottery-managing — Barnum had no formal experience with showmanship up to this time. He did possess a sense of dramatic possibility, a gift for rhetoric, and an ability to exploit his opportunities. Imagination proved the critical weapon for gaining success with Joice Heth; imagination and an instinct for public excitement.

In the summer of 1835 Barnum heard a curious story from a

fellow New Englander, Coley Bartram. Bartram told him he had just sold out his interest in a slave named Joice Heth, who was believed to be one hundred and sixty-one years old and claimed to have been George Washington's nurse. The combination of biological abnormality and patriotic appeal should have ensured an unbeatable attraction. Yet Bartram and his partner, R. W. Lindsay, had been exhibiting her to the paying public without very much success. Bartram, in fact, had sold out to Lindsay, who was himself anxious to get rid of his property.

Barnum was fascinated and went down to Philadelphia, where Lindsay was exhibiting his slave. "I was favorably struck with the appearance of the old woman," Barnum wrote. "So far as outward indications were concerned, she might almost as well have been called a thousand years old as any other age," although Barnum resisted this temptation to exaggerate. Partially paralyzed, totally blind and toothless, Joice Heth was nonetheless very spirited, talking about her years with "dear little George" and lapsing into occasional hymns. As proof of her incredible story Lindsay offered a bill of sale from Augustine Washington, dated 1727, to a relative in Westmoreland County, Virginia. The bill of sale seemed as old as the slave, and Lindsay explained that the document had only recently been discovered in a Virginia record office by Joice Heth's owner, John Bowling, who thereupon sold her to Lindsay for exhibition purposes. Lindsay's price was three thousand dollars, but Barnum bargained him down to one thousand dollars. He returned to New York, gathered up what cash he had, borrowed more, sold out his interest in the grocery store, and on August 6, 1835, became Joice Heth's sole owner. At last he was launched as a manager of entertainments.

On arranging this, his first exhibition, Barnum did not try hard to authenticate his property. He was charged at the time and for years afterward with deliberately contriving the details of Joice Heth's background. Critics insisted that Barnum himself had drawn up the old Augustine Washington bill of sale before staining it with tobacco juice to make it appear antique. Although he later admitted much about his early career, Barnum never conceded that he had fabricated this episode. The story he gave in the first edition of his autobiography, in 1855, was the one he stuck to, with few variations, for the rest of his life. He may have had some suspicions, but when Barnum came across an exploitable commodity he did not create unnecessary difficulties for himself. He had examined what purported to be documentary proof, and he knew he owned a potential sensation. That was enough. The pattern of this transaction endured for the rest of his career. Barnum's genius lay not so much in the invention or manufacture of curiosities as in their discovery, purchase, and advertisement. Joice Heth, after all, had been exhibited before Barnum ever got hold of her. The story of her age and employment was the same before he put her on display as afterward. The difference was that Barnum made a profit, and that was because of his publicity techniques.

The first task was to arrange for exhibition. Barnum decided to hold his first show in rooms owned by William Niblo, the proprietor of a large New York saloon, Niblo's Garden. Barnum then hired a lawyer, a Yankee like himself, Levi Lyman, to assist in planning the campaign. Lyman wrote a brief pamphlet about Joice Heth, illustrated it, and sold it to visitors, turning a small profit on his own. Barnum printed Joice Heth's portrait on handbills and filled New York with posters advertising his new attraction. The promises were great and the language extravagant. Joice Heth was "the most astonishing and interesting curiosity in the world," the first person "to put clothes" on George Washington, the "most ancient specimen of mortality" Americans were ever likely to encounter. He persuaded newspapers to discuss the exhibit in their stories and editorials, harping on the slave's strange appearance, her defiance of time, and the skill with which she answered questions about her life with Washington and the glorious days of the Revolution. Her self-assurance at public interviews was so great that Barnum used it as proof of her genuineness. She never

contradicted herself, she spoke long and well on religious subjects, and she knew an astonishing number of church hymns. If
Joice Heth was an imposter, Barnum asked, who taught her all
these things, including many unknown details about the Washington family? "She was perfectly familiar with them all before
I ever saw her," he insisted.

The New York show was successful, and Barnum took Joice
Heth on a tour of New England, stopping first in Providence
and then in Boston. He began to demonstrate the countless
variations he would master in his numerous publicity cam-
paigns: the quick discovery, the barrage of rapid and unusual
information, the maximum exploitation of the local press, the
planted lie and the indignant denial — all these he utilized almost immediately. It was during Joice Heth's tour that Barnum first realized that an exhibitor did not have to guarantee
truthfulness; all he had to do was possess probability and invite
doubt. The public would be more excited by controversy than
by conclusiveness. The only requirement was to keep the issue
alive and in print. Any statement was better than silence.

When attendance at Boston began to fall off, Barnum wrote
a letter, which appeared in a local newspaper, suggesting that
Joice Heth was a fraud, a "curiously constructed automaton,
made up of whalebone, india-rubber, and numberless springs,
ingeniously put together, and made to move at the slightest
touch, according to the will of the operator." Automata were
popular attractions in the early nineteenth century: Johann
Maelzel was showing his famous automatic chess player in Boston at just the time Barnum was exhibiting Joice Heth. The
crowds who had seen the slave once immediately returned to
check out their possible deception; newcomers who had somehow managed to avoid Barnum's ticket seller were attracted by
the debate.

Having demonstrated his ability to put over one attraction,
Barnum began to look for more; Joice Heth's novelty could not
last forever. While on tour in Albany he was so impressed by a
juggling act he engaged "Signor Antonio" for a one-year con-

23

tract at twelve dollars a week plus expenses. "I did not know exactly where I should use my protégé, but I was certain that there was money in him." The first thing Barnum did was improve on reality, for even genuine curiosities could use expert help. Antonio he now called Signor Vivalla, because the real name did not seem sufficiently foreign (Barnum would repeat this technique in later years). Then he turned once again to the newspapers, announcing that Vivalla was an extraordinary artist who would astound his audiences. With Barnum onstage assisting, Vivalla did just that and was soon launched on a successful tour of the eastern cities. Once again, Barnum had taken someone else's exhibit and turned lackluster receipts into impressive profits.

There were further tricks up Barnum's sleeve. In Philadelphia another juggler, named Roberts, sent some friends into the audience to hiss Vivalla's performance. Curious rather than angry, Barnum investigated further and introduced himself to Roberts, who insisted proudly that he could do everything Vivalla did, and more. Wasting no time, for he sensed a superb opportunity for public excitement (and private gain), Barnum announced next day that he would present a thousand-dollar reward to any man who could duplicate Vivalla's feats in public. Roberts accepted the offer, sending a card, but when Barnum visited him to make the arrangements, Roberts proved reluctant to undertake the trial. Barnum's terms required Roberts to perform every trick Vivalla did in order to collect the money. Knowing that he could not meet the terms, Roberts refused to participate. Barnum was equal to this sudden change of events, however. Turning a potential rivalry into a partnership, he offered Roberts thirty dollars if he agreed to perform according to his instructions. Getting Roberts's consent, he brought the two jugglers together and arranged the details of a rehearsed competition.

Meanwhile, the newspapers busily promoted the contest into a test of American skill, for Roberts, a native, was challenging a foreigner. Under Barnum's inspired supervision the excitement grew, and the night of the trial saw a crowded theater divided into intense partisans of the two jugglers, hissing and cheering contrapuntally. After forty minutes of work Roberts surrendered, as the rehearsals had indicated. But to keep his profitable arrangement going, Barnum had Roberts challenge Vivalla to imitate *his* tricks. The following night the two "rivals" met again, witnessed once more by an enormous house attracted by the bitter competition. The antagonists, of course, were happily at work making money, and Barnum was taking his share of the receipts.

When he discussed this episode in his autobiography, Barnum softened his account by explaining that this was the way such things were frequently contrived in theaters. People were brought to great excitement entirely by arrangement. The entertainment offset the humbug; few theater managers would even be hurt by his revelations, "for the public appears disposed to be amused even while they are conscious of being deceived." He implied that he would have filled his theaters even if the partisans of the jugglers had known the whole contest was an act.

While Vivalla and Roberts were entertaining the public, Joice Heth had died. Barnum had promised a surgeon that he would permit a postmortem, and the physicians examining the body were astonished by the absence of "ossification"; they insisted that Joice Heth could not have been more than half of her pretended age. Richard Adams Locke of the *New York Sun* published the report in an editorial excoriating Barnum for his part in the whole episode. The showman was accused of imposture and deceit.[13]

Barnum's associate Lyman, however, was unwilling to let the affair drop there. He somehow persuaded publisher James Gordon Bennett of the *Herald* that Joice Heth was still alive, closeted in Connecticut, and that the body examined by the physicians was not hers at all. Lyman convinced Bennett that it was the *New York Sun* that had been hoaxed, and on February 27, 1836, Bennett's *Herald* published its own version of the autopsy, charging that it was all a trick. A thoroughly confused but intrigued public then saw Bennett sheepishly take back his account, only to be tricked once again. This time Lyman told him a fantastic story about Barnum's having discovered Joice Heth in Kentucky, extracted all her teeth, and taught her the whole Washington story from beginning to end. Apparently insatiable for ridicule and humiliation, Bennett published this "final" account in the fall of 1836, only to discover that he had once again been taken. Quite understandably, the publisher conceived a hatred for Barnum and all his work, although years later he would once again be bested by the showman and suffer spectacular losses.

Lyman's stories, however, were not filling Barnum's pockets, for his chief attraction was gone and Vivalla's receipts had begun to decline. Barnum decided to join forces with a larger organization. He arranged with Aaron Turner, owner of a traveling circus, to put Vivalla in the show. Barnum himself would act as secretary and ticket seller, and in return would receive both a salary and a share in the profits. Moving his family back to Bethel, Barnum began the life of the road. He never explained why he did not simply seek other exhibits that he could display under his own auspices, instead of becoming a junior partner; subordination was never to his liking. But his experience as an impresario may have revealed that there was much more to know and the opportunity to travel with a circus troupe throughout the country offered obvious educational advantages.

Turner himself also attracted Barnum. In his passion for practical joking he resembled that fabled Connecticut grandfather, Phineas Taylor. Turner's victims included his partner. In Maryland Barnum was almost lynched by an angry mob who had been told by Turner that he was a clergyman (Barnum was wearing a new black suit) just acquitted of murder. There was obvious irony in Barnum's being mistaken for one of his favorite targets, a hypocritical cleric, but the humor was lost on him as the crowd tried to force him to ride a rail. Saved at the last minute, Barnum asked his partner why he had bothered to misinform the citizenry. Turner's answer was worthy of Barnum himself. "Remember, all we need to insure success is *notoriety*. You will see that this will be noised all about town . . . and our pavilion will be crammed tomorrow night." And Turner was right. This, of course, did not stop Barnum from exercising his own ingenuity and catching Turner himself out several times. The whole circus seemed a re-creation of the Connecticut country store, a tightly knit group that lived by taking in one another's mental washing, in this case by hoaxing, punning and practical joking. It was as if Barnum had returned to his old environment for the additional nourishment he needed for permanent success. The Turner circus, in the six months he accompanied it, brought Barnum much more than the twelve hundred dollars profit he took away with him.

In the early winter of 1836, with Vivalla and a blackface singer and dancer, Barnum struck out on his own tour of the southern states. For almost two years he faced the dangers of life on the road, going through crisis after crisis, his company alternately disappearing and reappearing, local authorities pressing him with lawsuits and threats of punishment, financial backers and partners cheating him, highwaymen and Indians threatening his safety. He went into partnership along the way with some remarkable men, including Henry Hawley, one of the most ingenious liars in the country, whose feats of persuasion set a high standard for any advertiser. Toward the end of his tour Barnum sold all his equipment and bought a steamboat, presenting entertainments along the Mississippi.

But troubles continued to multiply and he disbanded his company in the spring of 1838. He arrived back in New York in June, "thoroughly disgusted with the life of an itinerant showman," though he was certain he could succeed in the trade. He hoped for "a respectable, permanent business," and advertised that he had twenty-five hundred dollars to invest. He was back again where he had started, looking for an opportunity, but this time with a little more capital. Almost one hundred propositions poured in from "brokers, lottery-policy men, pawnbrokers, inventors"; even a counterfeiter joined the parade. From the plenitude of offers Barnum unerringly chose a bad one: he decided to invest his money in a firm headed by a German named Proler. Proler manufactured cologne, paste-blacking, and bear's grease. After a promising start in which Proler handled the sales and manufacturing ends and Barnum dealt with the retail outlet on Broadway, debts grew and Proler sailed for Europe leaving his ex-partner with a worthless note for twenty-six hundred dollars and some formulas. Barnum's excursion into bourgeois respectability was over.

In late 1840 Barnum returned to the entertainment world and organized a new entertainment troupe, traveling through the South and West with a Negro dancer, Master Jack Diamond. Most of the tour was unprofitable but Barnum recouped some of his losses in New Orleans by running a dancing match between Diamond and another performer. According to Sol Smith, a St. Louis theatrical manager, Barnum was up to his old tricks again: Barnum, Smith wrote, got up a phony dancing match for a pretended wager of five hundred dollars and introduced another dancer, his face blacked, to be beaten by Diamond.[14] This variation on his old Vivalla technique yielded Barnum almost five hundred dollars.

Another experience in New Orleans, while less remunerative, was more valuable. In March 1841, Fanny Elssler, the Viennese dancer who was making a sensationally profitable tour of the United States, arrived in New Orleans to give some performances. Good tickets were going for nearly five dollars, sold at a New Orleans auction by her manager, who had created great public interest in his performer. Impressed by the technique (and the profits) Barnum filed the information away for future use: culture could pay.

But troubles lay ahead. Jack Diamond deserted Barnum, and the showman headed north. Here accounts differ. Barnum insisted that one of his former employees hired an imposter to resemble Jack Diamond, and when Barnum threatened to expose him had him thrown into jail for failure to pay an old contract. But an attorney later claimed that it was Barnum who was the imposter, getting a white dancer, blacking his face, and taking him along "Master Diamond's" well-advertised route several days in advance, reaping both the profits and the advantages of his rival's advertising. Judge Robert Cooper Grief, presiding over the Pittsburgh trial, called both plaintiff and defendant vagabonds and angrily dismissed the case and discharged the prisoner.[15] If this jailing was briefer than Barnum's Connecticut experience, it was also less glorious.

In Pittsburgh Barnum decided to become a sales agent for *Sears' Pictorial Illustration of the Bible.* The itinerant life he had been leading was too unpleasant to continue, so back in New York he opened an office and organized subagencies to distribute the book for him elsewhere. Despite the thousands of copies his agents sold, Barnum was left with little money; he insisted that his employees had cheated him.

Even while he was selling Bibles, Barnum did not abandon the entertainment world entirely; he leased a local theater, the Vauxhall Saloon, and made a small profit there. Because of his Bible interests he prudently leased the theater under a brother-in-law's name. Barnum himself was big enough for religion and the theater, but his clientele would not have understood.

It was now almost seven years since Barnum had left Connecticut. They had not been barren years: he had demonstrated imaginative advertising skills, led two separate national tours, successfully publicized curiosities after their owners had given up on them, and even made some money. The Joice Heth business alone had given him considerable notoriety, if not reputation. But in the end he was left with neither capital nor a permanent position. Public amusements stimulated his best talents, but even with his sense of the popular he remained at the mercy of fads and circumstances. Audiences tired of some exhibits; other attractions grew difficult or died off before they could return a decent profit. Barnum needed an institution that could offer a permanent base of operation and continuing income. Without it he would remain a free-lance pieceworker, capable of sudden successes but cut off from the wealth and respectability he hungered for. There were dozens of touring managers, like Aaron Turner for example, whose lives resolved into wonderful anecdotes but who never achieved fame or stability. Reflecting his Connecticut background, Barnum's goals remained the traditional signs of success: a fine home, servants, a carriage, local respect. He needed money to ensure this success and he was willing to work hard to get it. Discipline was never his problem if the right situation came to hand; so lethargic when it came to manual labor, his energy was inexhaustible in the planning and administration of exhibits. But there seemed no jobs that would allow Barnum to exploit his shrewdness and audacity and also permit him to become a respectable businessman.

Then, in mid-1841, he learned that Scudder's Museum, a quiet little enterprise on Broadway and Ann streets, was up for sale. The opportunity had arrived.

TWO

The American Museum

RETURNING TO NEW YORK in 1851 after an extensive European trip, Henry Tappan, soon to become president of the University of Michigan, rhapsodized about institutions like the British Museum. *"Museums — a place for the Muses —* fit appellation for such a place as this." Supported by the government, the British Museum attracted scholars from all over the world, its treasures of art and science carefully cataloged and displayed. In New York, alas, mourned Tappan, the word "museum" brought up far different ideas, "a place for some stuffed birds and animals, for the exhibition of monsters, and for vulgar dramatic performances — a mere place of popular amusement."[1]

P. T. Barnum was one of those responsible for Tappan's disgruntlement; by 1851 Barnum's American Museum had become the most popular institution of its kind in the country. But American museums had a long and honorable history before Barnum's involvement with them. Indeed, the vulgarization of the museum and its transformation from a place for scholarship and rational instruction to an amusement center symbolized the larger shift from Jeffersonian republicanism to Jacksonian democracy.

In the heady days of the Revolution many Americans turned to the popularization of science as a means of increasing public enlightenment and stimulating the collection of indigenous natural curiosities. It was a time when the glories of increasing human knowledge could be shared among scientists, artists, and politicians. Nature was a work of art, its smooth and varied operations a testament to the benevolence of the Creator. The more men learned about their role in Creation and the wonders of the natural world, the more would they respect and honor truth and virtue, for what were truth and virtue but distillations of divine wisdom? Particularly was this true in America, where Nature was still fresh, unspoiled, and marvelous. Nature appears to the American "in magnitude," wrote Thomas Paine.[2] "The mighty objects he beholds, act upon his mind by enlarging it, and he partakes of the greatness he contemplates."

No one was more active in this movement to encourage virtue and patriotism through knowledge of Nature than Charles Willson Peale. Painter, inventor, natural philosopher, and enthusiast, Peale founded a museum in Philadelphia in 1784 to hang the paintings of his prolific family and parade the curiosities he was receiving from friends across the country. Peale's Museum soon featured mammoth bones from Ohio, mineral specimens, stuffed birds and animals, skeletons, plant life, portraits of famous Americans, and other items demonstrating the richness of the New World environment. Many of the great figures of the American Enlightenment participated with Peale in planning and administering his museum: Benjamin Franklin presented some specimens, Thomas Jefferson deposited items from the Lewis and Clark Expedition, James Madison, Robert Morris, Alexander Hamilton, and Edmund Randolph joined its Society of Visitors.

Housed until 1802 in the home of the American Philosophical Society, Peale's Museum made strenuous efforts to achieve scholarly exhibits. Natural history collections were arranged according to Linnaean principles, where possible, and some specimens were placed in replicas of their natural habitats. Peale hoped to have his museum publicly owned and supported, as an institution of national importance, and appealed for aid in bringing together objects that might be helpful "in advancing knowledge and the arts." The whole display was designed as a "world in miniature," a "Great School of Nature." "Can the imagination conceive anything more interesting than such a museum?" Peale asked in 1800. "Or can there be a more agreeable spectacle to an admirer of the divine wisdom! Where, within a magnificent pile, every art and every science should be taught, by plans, models, pictures, real subjects and lectures."[3] In 1802 the Philadelphia Museum moved to Independence Hall, further cementing the bond between patriotism and natural science.

Peale soon had imitators. As western migration revealed more natural wonders and as American towns developed metropolitan ambitions, other museums were founded, in Boston, New York, Albany, and Baltimore.[4] Popular interest matched intellectual justifications for studying the varieties of nature. Frequently, lecture rooms within the museum buildings permitted the public to gain more concentrated access to scientific knowledge. Distinguished naturalists and men of letters reported on recent discoveries and commented on the significance of the exhibits so conveniently located nearby.

But competition and growth were the keynotes of American progress, and as the nineteenth century progressed, museums faced new difficulties. Privately operated for profit, they were challenged by the increasing number and variety of urban amusements. Giant panoramas of cities and historic events, small circuses, theatrical troupes, and touring artists competed for clients. In the first decades of the century dozens of theaters were built in the major cities, large, elegant, and impressive, even if their fragility was revealed by the fires which destroyed them with astonishing regularity.

Museum owners tried desperately to keep up, but the taxonomic and contemplative spirit of their exhibits could not compete with the more active (if narrower) diversions that competitors offered.[5] The great Philadelphia Museum itself acknowledged the need for change. Rubens Peale, administering the institution for his father for some years after 1810, quietly discarded its more prosaic exhibits in favor of curiosities. Charles Willson Peale, who accepted the changes (although he later tried to restrain some of them), had once refused to permit oddities to dominate the collection, showing them only on demand. Rubens Peale replaced his father's missionary zeal with a bureaucrat's temperament. "He was running a business, not a 'temple,'" Charles Coleman Sellers, biographer of the elder Peale, concluded. But even Rubens Peale refused to fake exhibits; he displayed a "great sea serpent" only after the Linnaean Society of New England had approved it.[6]

The museums continued to enjoy one advantage, however, in this era of increased competition, and it proved to be the basis of their transformation. American Protestantism had long cherished antipathies toward the theater on religious, social, and economic grounds. During the Revolutionary period, a number of American cities still possessed ordinances prohibiting all theatrical presentations. The economic and political crisis was sometimes used to justify what were basically religious prejudices. In time, the ordinances fell into disuse or were repealed. Nevertheless, a large number of Americans, in urban areas as well as in country districts, conceived of theatergoing in terms not very different from their Roundhead ancestors: lewd plays and volatile audiences were a threat to morals and salvation. Like their European counterparts, American theaters were frequently rowdy and sometimes violent, patronized by gamblers, prostitutes, drifters, and rambunctious youngsters, in addition to any respectable elements who happened to attend. The stage was attacked as a nursery of vice and good Christians were warned, on peril of their eternal lives, to avoid its contamination.

Despite religious prejudices, the theater grew. All the same, many people, eager for recreation, would be reluctant to enter the doors of Boston's Tremont Street Theater or New York's Park, no matter how elegant their appointments nor how earnestly their managers defended their respectable productions and peaceful customers. Museum lecture rooms, on the other hand, were not theaters but could do what theaters did: mount dramatic entertainments or present variety acts under the guise of education and public enlightenment. However transparent, the fiction was effective, and museum owners lost no time exploiting their advantage. European visitors were mystified but impressed. "A walk through a room full of stuffed birds and beasts, boasting of little to interest anybody, served as a kind of *penance* for what is to follow," one Englishman suggested.[7] The devil lurked only in playhouses; museums were out of his territory, and so safe for ordinary folk.

Not all museum managers exploited these popular prejudices successfully. The entertainments, however moral, also had to be interesting, and surrounded by curiosities to entice the passerby off the street. And not every museum manager understood the importance of his lecture room. Some played it straight, retaining in quiet but unprofitable dignity the original ideals of the museum founders, while others, striving for greater entertainment, had no notion how they could begin.

New York City, when Barnum returned in 1841, had several museums, as well as half a dozen theaters. The city was on the eve of what could only be termed an amusement explosion. Population growth itself was only partly responsible for the increase in places of entertainment; qualities peculiar to the city's environment made it extraordinarily profitable, at least potentially, to amusement managers. Writing in 1851, ten years after Barnum took over his museum, a New York playwright named William K. Northall wondered "if there be a city in the world of the same size and population which can exhibit a theatrical prosperity equal to New York." Even Paris paled beside it. The reason, Northall concluded, lay in the prevalence of boardinghouse life, a product of mobility and the absence of servants. Instead of setting up their own households, thousands of New Yorkers, deterred by high costs, took up residence in boardinghouses. Boarders might be polite to each other, Northall wrote, but there was little warmth in their relationships. Cold rules protected comfort and self-respect, for boarders tended to be heterogeneous in occupation and origin. "There is no bond of union among the lodgers of a boardinghouse; and scarcely anything short of a murder or a suicide has sufficient interest to cause one boarder to feel an interest in what may be occurring to the gentlemen in the next rooms. With such unsympathising materials," nothing like a united family circle could be formed. So boarders were thrown on their own resources for amusement, and "public places of entertainment offer the readiest means to these poor undomesticated animals."[8]

Whether or not Northall was right (and visiting Europeans continually commented on the dangerous effects boarding-house and hotel life would have on the American family), New Yorkers seemed insatiable in their zest for variety and amusement. By the 1840s the city was not only America's largest but also its most heterogeneous and, by reputation, its wickedest, filled, according to the exposés that found their way into print, with gamblers and seducers, criminals and confidence men, who took advantage of foreign immigrants and country bumpkins. The glitter of the city's restaurants and theaters was already becoming proverbial.

Such an environment posed particular problems to a theatrical manager. He faced, among certain classes, religious inhibitions; among others, a zest for novelty that quickly became jaded; and among all, lack of patience with amateurish efforts, fit only for unlettered backwoodsmen unused to anything better. The successful showman had to achieve the appearance of morality and yet seduce the sensation-seeker; outright wickedness and simple lewdness were not permitted, yet somehow a group of hard-boiled urbanites had to be cajoled into spending their money, on a regular basis.

Theater managers came and went. They had good seasons and bad, and some of them, Noah Ludlow and Sol Smith in St. Louis, Thomas Barry and Moses Kimball in Boston, William Mitchell and Stephen Price in New York, succeeded in establishing permanent reputations. But they were always on the edge of poverty: plays might not please, actors grew unpopular, financial panics cut down customer interest. Barnum was the only one who grew rich and nationally famous. And his fortune was founded when he took control of Scudder's American Museum.

The museum stood at Broadway and Ann streets, near the

churches, hotels, restaurants, and stores that gave New York what urbanity it possessed. John Scudder, the founder, had gathered an impressive collection, but since his death the museum had been allowed to run down. Because it was losing money, the owners decided to sell it for fifteen thousand dollars. After several inspection visits, Barnum saw great possibilities. He was convinced that "only energy, tact, and liberality were needed, to give it life and to put it on a profitable footing." Despite the fact that he had almost no money, he decided to purchase it.

He approached the owner of the museum building, Francis Olmsted, and asked for credit. With the recommendations of Barnum's friends and a piece of unencumbered real estate — the hitherto despised Ivy Island — as collateral, Barnum succeeded in gaining Olmsted's support. But when Barnum came with his offer, the owners of the collection announced they had sold it to the neighboring Peale's Museum for the asking price, fifteen thousand dollars. Astounded but not defeated, Barnum discovered that the directors of Peale's Museum Company were speculators. The museum had been founded by Rubens Peale in the 1820s, when the Peale family was active in several cities. But the Peales had been forced to sell out. The later owners intended to sell a large amount of stock in their new enterprise, pocket the profits, and abandon the collection. But they would be unable to pay for Scudder's until they had unloaded some of their shares on a gullible public.

Barnum moved quickly. He sent letters to newspapers attacking the directors and charging them with fraudulent intentions. Aware that such publicity could destroy the market for their stock, the frightened directors invited Barnum to a conference and offered to hire him as manager of the two museums at a handsome salary. Barnum's tactics had caused some delay in their plans, but the directors were not worried. They assumed Scudder's would wait beyond December 26, the previously announced deadline, for payment, because they knew of no other buyers.

Barnum, meanwhile, had gotten the owners of Scudder's to promise to sell it to him for twelve thousand dollars if the new directors did not pay the balance they owed on December 26. Barnum merrily went his way. The directors "thought they had caught me securely. I *knew* that I had caught *them*." And on December 27, 1841, with the directors blissfully ignorant of the arrangement, Barnum became the proprietor of Scudder's American Museum. It had taken cunning to acquire the institution, but it would require even more to make it successful.

In the seasons before Barnum took it over, Scudder's Museum had deteriorated. The lecture room presented variety entertainment at night, with occasional matinees, but its performers failed to make much of an impression. Advertisements described contortionists, a lady magician, a banjoist, O'Connell the Tattooed Man, an exhibition of laughing gas, a comic dancer named Oakey, a lecture on animal magnetism, an elaborate painting of Rheims Cathedral, and a number of other oddly assorted curiosities, some on permanent exhibition, others hired for temporary display. Peale's Museum, Scudder's rival, had many of the same exhibits: lectures on animal magnetism and phrenology, a ventriloquist, O'Clancy the Irish giant, and a daguerreotypist. With repetitive shows and weak publicity, museums could not hope to compete with theaters like Mitchell's Olympic and the Park, or the variety shows at Vauxhall Gardens and the Tivoli Garden, to say nothing of the concert halls and panoramas.[9]

Two courses were open to Barnum. The first lay through advertisement and reorganization; the second was in acquiring his own special reputation. He took both, turning first to his entertainments. Increasing the number of performances in the lecture room, he scoured the country for "industrious fleas, automatons, jugglers, ventriloquists, living statuary, tableaux, gypsies, albinos, fat boys, giants, dwarfs, rope-dancers, dioramas, panoramas, models of Niagara, Dublin, Paris and Jerusalem . . . Punch and Judy . . . fancy glass-blowing, knitting machines . . . dissolving views, American Indians" — anything that might divert the stream of Broadway pedestrians into the building. Some of the attractions had appeared earlier in Scudder's, but Barnum sought novelty and continual change. In the first few years of ownership he moved his performers about, running them in different combinations and then serially, experimenting and innovating. In the fall of 1843, for example, visitors could see Harrington, "the great Magician and Ventriloquist"; a "mysterious Gypsey" girl; Mr. Nellis (born without arms); a popular monologist and impersonator, Dr. Valentine; a tattooed man; H. G. Sherman, a ballad singer; dioramas of European landscapes and Biblical scenes; an albino lady; a model of Niagara Falls with running water; and a host of other curiosities and performers.

Obtaining exhibits in such number was not easy; Barnum had to make arrangements with colleagues in other cities, most notably Moses Kimball, the successful manager of the Boston Museum.[10] Kimball had opened his establishment in June 1841, not so many years before. Born in Newburyport in 1809 Kimball, like Barnum, had worked on newspapers before he entered the museum business in 1839, buying most of the old New England Museum's collection of portraits, stuffed birds and animals, and pieces of statuary. In 1843 Kimball added a theater, which ensured his museum's popularity, and three years later opened a handsome new building. By the early 1850s an observer would note that the Boston Museum was being patronized "by a large class who do not frequent theaters, but who have a nice perception of the difference between tweedle-*dum* and tweedle-*dee*. We have noticed, however, that many who make a first attempt at countenancing theatricals at the Museum, may shortly after be found at the regular theaters."[11] Kimball, like Barnum, helped stimulate a taste for drama by lacing his entertainments with a liberal dose of moralizing.

Just getting under way in the early forties, Barnum and Kimball wrote each other almost weekly, sending exhibits and promises back and forth, sharing information about the idiosyncrasies (and salaries) of their performers, and competing for the larger gate. "My business averaged about seventy dollars per day last week," Barnum reported in January 1843, "so yours is not better than that." One of Barnum's agents was out exhibiting a diorama in Newark, another was operating in the South. "I *must* have the fat boy or the other monster, something new *in the course of this week*," Barnum begged his colleague. He didn't want Yan Zoo, a Chinese giant, unless "he can perform on an eight foot stage and will come for fifteen dollars per week for two weeks with the privilege on my part and he pay his own expenses."[12] The rivalry between the two managers was a gentle one, and they cooperated on many ventures. Kimball lacked Barnum's sense of publicity, but he was often skillful at locating curiosities that his New York friend could then puff into fame and profit.

The situation quickly grew more complicated as Barnum secretly took control of his major rival, Peale's Museum. Peale's, or the New York Museum, was even more run-down than Scudder's and did not have a chance against Barnum's aggressive management. It was still relying on daguerreotypists and lecturers on animal magnetism and phrenology. Henry Bennett, its English-born manager, began to consider closing his establishment down, but Barnum realized that rivalry brought greater profits than monopoly. Privately purchasing the entire collection for seven thousand dollars, Barnum engaged Bennett as his own agent; the public was as blissfully ignorant of any arrangement as it had been during Vivalla's juggling "contests." Peale's New York Museum reopened in late January 1843, ostensibly parodying some of the American Museum's exhibits but actually working to publicize them. In the six months which were left it, the New York Museum would offer pale imitations of Barnum's acts, never seriously interfering with the American's business but occasionally causing some excitement.

The cost was small: a rent of twenty-five dollars a week; nine dollars for gas and fuel; and ten dollars and fifty cents for a doorman, sweeper, and advertisements.[13] So Peale's required little more than forty dollars a week to run, Barnum told Kimball, exclusive of any acts he decided to hire. And the acts Barnum settled upon were sure to find him a hard bargain-driver. Performers might receive as little as five to ten dollars a week, with an occasional benefit thrown in (when they took home a portion of the gate). The most difficult task for Barnum, in the early years before he had accumulated some capital, was gauging how much money he could afford to expend on an attraction. He determined to be tougher than Peale, who paid too much for his performers and never went out and advertised them properly. Barnum demonstrated his ability by paying off his last debts to Olmsted in April 1843, only fifteen months after purchasing the museum.

He was helped by a great find. For if, in 1843, Barnum needed "a fat boy or the other monster" from Kimball to fill out his program, Kimball was even more anxious to obtain an exhibit from Barnum, perhaps the most profitable exhibit item that the showman ever stumbled upon: General Tom Thumb.

Tom Thumb was one of the sensations of the nineteenth century, and Barnum's discovery of the five-year-old midget in Bridgeport, Connecticut, coming as it did less than one year after he bought the American Museum, must have seemed providential.[14] Charles S. Stratton, when Barnum met him in November 1842, was one inch over two feet, and weighed only fifteen pounds. Since his birth on January 4, 1838, the boy had gained fewer than six pounds.

But his size alone was not what made Stratton so appealing. Dwarfs had been the playthings of monarchs since the days of the Pharoahs, and European showmen had been exhibiting them for centuries. Henry VIII made Will Sommers, an English dwarf, his court jester, and during the following century Archibald Armstrong made his way at the courts of James I and Charles I. "Count" Boruwlaski, a Polish dwarf, won the favor of Maria Theresa and the French royal family, made European tours, and died in England after having gained the support of

The young Barnum starting out at thirty-four

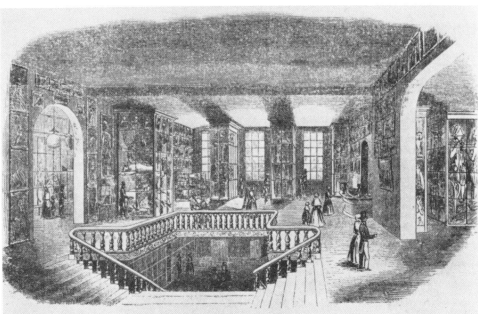

INTERIOR VIEW OF THE FIRST GRAND HALL OF THE MUSEUM.

The American Museum in its glory, 1851–52

The American Museum by a critic, 1851

Moses Kimball

Tom Thumb in action

members of the nobility. Other dwarfs entertained crowds at raree-shows that appeared at English fairgrounds, along with other monsters — giants, genetic freaks, pig-faced women, armless men.

These oddities served two functions. The more intelligent, who were retained at courts, emphasized their masters' power and domination, much as the royal menageries testified to wealth and status. They were exotics, adding color to princely retinues. And the true monsters, items at side shows, fed public curiosity (and cruelty). Gaping crowds of onlookers made sport with them, often taunting the creatures whose ties to humanity seemed so fragile. In eras when popular superstition fed ancient fears and anxieties, the monsters were demonstrations of the power of divine wrath, unfathomable punishments for unknown crimes. Or else they were products of witchcraft and signs of malevolence. Terror and repugnance mixed with curiosity, and continued to do so long after scientific explanations succeeded superstition.

Charles Stratton, however, fit neither category. He was just the sort of oddity suited to an optimistic and benevolent society bent on showing Nature's bounty, not her nightmares. Despite contemporary labels, Stratton was not a dwarf; he was a midget. A malfunctioning pituitary gland had left him tiny but normally proportioned, lacking the deformities or misshapenness many associated with stunted growth.[15] He was the furthest thing possible from a monster. Pert, intelligible, able to mimic, sing, and dance, General Tom Thumb (the name Barnum gave him) would become the perfect man-child, the perpetual boy, appealing to all ages and conditions. Crowds identified with him, rather than against him. Anyone who had ever dreamed of never growing up, anyone whose childhood fantasies included visions of glory, could identify with Tom Thumb and the fantastic costumes, posturings, and impersonations that Barnum provided him with. In time ponies, uniforms, and carriages, all in miniature, would adorn Charlie Stratton. Children delighted in seeing one so small mock the pretensions of the mighty; adults also found irresistible the combination of innocence and pomposity. Even at the beginning, without the variations and trappings that later evolved, the midget drew enormous crowds. Within months his manager realized he had a sensation on his hands.

To be sure, midgets had been shown in America before Tom Thumb. Calvin Phillips, born in Massachusetts in 1791, was exhibited in New York in 1810, but he died only two years later. "Major" Stevens of Hoboken was another celebrity, but by Tom Thumb's time he had grown to more than four feet. Tom Thumb's success rested not only on his size but on his truly childlike benevolence, and on Barnum's careful advertising.

The Strattons were Connecticut Yankees but they could not match Barnum's shrewdness. Sherwood Stratton was a poor carpenter; his wife, Cynthia, worked in a local inn. They seemed made to be exploited. The agreement, which was signed in New York, December 22, 1842, was not generous to them.[16] Charles was to be indentured to Barnum until January 1, 1844, and exhibited according to Barnum's directions; his father would labor for Barnum "at his trade of carpenter or any other respectable employment." Charles and his mother would get four dollars a week plus board, while Sherwood received three dollars. The whole family, therefore, would receive only seven dollars a week, besides board and travel allowance. One month before the contract's expiration Sherwood would get an additional fifty dollars. Nothing was to be paid Charles if he was sick more than one week, but the board and lodging was to be "good, respectable and comfortable."

Barnum knew he had made an unbelievable bargain. He hired a friend, "Parson" Fordyce Hitchcock, to tutor the boy and travel with the Strattons, keeping them from the envious eyes of other showmen who might "try to hire them away." In New York, with Sherwood Stratton serving occasionally as the ticket seller, Barnum took in several hundred dollars on some of the days when Tom Thumb appeared in his lecture room;

two hundred and eighty dollars on February 4, he told Kimball triumphantly.[17] But the audiences were uneven: the day before, receipts had fallen to ninety dollars. Barnum decided to test the water by sending Tom Thumb on tour. He hoped to clear at least one thousand dollars in Philadelphia and Baltimore, and he was not disappointed. The only one disappointed was Moses Kimball, who had been promised the midget as a stellar attraction in Boston, but kept on receiving postponements from Barnum. With the tour so successful, interruptions seemed foolish. "In keeping Tom Thumb longer South than I expected, I keep him out of my own Museum as well as yours," Barnum explained. "If he lives, you shall have him, and at a time when you can make more money than he now could for you." As for raising excitement, Barnum insisted it would be easy with Tom Thumb, especially the first time he was put on show. With the lack of feeling that he often displayed in business matters Barnum then asked Kimball, "Do you want a pretty good size bald eagle skin? I bought two yesterday — shot on Long Island."[18] Kimball's reply has been lost to history.

In fact, Tom Thumb did not return to New York from his travels until May 1843. Despite Barnum's gift of a watch, the Strattons were restless during the long southern tour. Barnum feared they might be enticed by some other showman, and told Kimball he would "blow the concern to hell" before allowing anyone to gather the "fruit which I have shaken from the tree."[19] But a few days in the American Museum helped business and spirits wonderfully. By May 24 receipts were up to more than one hundred and fifty dollars, and Barnum was offering advice on handling Tom Thumb to Kimball. "First introduce him to some of the tip top families or have them come in and see him on the first day while I am there." Above all, "fail not to *circulate documents*."[20]

As with so many other attractions, Barnum succeeded with Tom Thumb where others could have failed. He understood that even his most popular exhibits required extensive advertising. Biographies of Tom Thumb, as well as lithographs, were printed up by the thousands and distributed in cities where he was shown. Advertisements doubled his age (a small five-year-old was so much less impressive than a small eleven-year-old) and changed his place of birth (from Connecticut to England). Newspapers printed glowing descriptions both in their advertising and their news columns. Barnum had early learned the art of pleasing editors.

Even after Tom Thumb's initial fame no opportunity was lost to gain further attention. After his New England trip, when Tom Thumb returned to the American Museum, Barnum revealed that he had permitted an actor, John Lefton, to have the general one night for his benefit. "I am to take General on the stage and show him off," Barnum told Kimball, "and have somebody in the boxes call out to have him *passed around* which I shall decline but express my *regret* at being obliged to do so, as he must return at once to the American Museum, but that they can see him shake hands and converse with him at the Museum any day during the week! Lefton gives me fifty dollars," Barnum chuckled, "and will not detain him thirty minutes."[21]

Despite Barnum's anxiety about the financial ambitions of the Stratton family (within the year he had raised Tom Thumb's weekly salary to twenty-five dollars), the midget gave Barnum little trouble and learned his act quickly. Barnum, moreover, seems to have held real affection for him, an affection nourished by the steady profits his exhibition brought.

This relatively carefree attitude could not be extended to many of Barnum's other early exhibits, however. Both animals and men gave continual trouble. Just before his fall season in 1843, Barnum's orangoutang got sick. "D — n the luck," he wrote Kimball, "I have puffed her high and dry — got a large transparency and a flag ten by sixteen feet painted for her — besides newspaper cuts." Now he cursed the beast for her expense and trouble.[22] There was a goat that Barnum had set great hopes on, "but he *shits* so I can do nothing with him," he admitted ruefully to Kimball. "I fear the same objection would spoil the pony business."[23] And then there were the Indians that Barnum advertised as brutal savages just brought back from killing white men in the Far West. They seemed threatening enough during performances, and once indeed Barnum feared for his own scalp, but "the lazy devils want to be *lying down* nearly all the time and as it looks so bad for them to be lying about the Museum, I have them stretched out in the work shop all day." Despite the money they brought in, Barnum had only contempt for them as persons. "D — n Indians *anyhow* they are a lazy shiftless set of brutes — though they will *draw*."[24]

Finally, the indiscretions of employees complicated Barnum's plans. In March 1843, the *Spirit of the Times*, a Philadelphia journal, exposed Miss Darling, Barnum's female magician "whose fame and beauty has agitated all the thrones of Europe." Barnum had made it appear that she had just arrived from Europe when in reality, charged the *Times*, Miss Darling was a Miss Mills, who had robbed her father, run off with a scoundrel, and become an inmate of the Worcester Insane Asylum.[25] "Now how the hell to keep anything from the damned traitors except to do all the work and performing myself I don't know," Barnum groused to Kimball. He blamed Dr. Valentine and other performers for leaking the Darling story but he added that "she is no 'bitch' and I really believe she is honest and that it is a *charity* to help her."[26] The fact that Grace Darling was drawing more than sixty dollars a night helped Barnum's opinion, of course, for he admitted that an act of charity "is rather pleasanter when it is profitable."[27]

The exhibits, exciting as they may have seemed to Barnum, were not enough to guarantee attendance, and he devoted himself to developing methods of attracting public attention. "It was my monomania to make the Museum the town wonder and town talk," he explained in his autobiography. "I often seized upon an opportunity by instinct, even before I had a very definite conception as to how it should be used, and it seemed, somehow, to mature itself and serve my purpose." Such invisible hands seemed to guide his reaction to a man who entered the office one morning and begged for work. Barnum hired him for a dollar and a half per diem and asked him to take five bricks and place them at various points on Broadway, then walk from one to another, exchanging them, and keeping silent. Within thirty minutes, Barnum reported, hundreds of New Yorkers were gathered to watch this strange behavior. Every hour the "brick man" would go into the museum, followed, of course, by citizens who had to pay the admission fee to satisfy their curiosity. "This trivial incident excited considerable talk and amusement; it advertised me; and it materially advanced my purpose of making a lively corner near the Museum." This was the most convincing kind of advertisement for Barnum: it employed novelty, demonstrated ingenuity, and achieved free publicity.

But when he could not manufacture incidents himself, Barnum did not hesitate to spend freely on more conventional publicity. "I fell in with the world's way; and if my 'puffing' was more persistent, my posters more glaring, my pictures more exaggerated, my flags more patriotic and my transparencies more brilliant," this was not because of fewer scruples but more energy and ingenuity. The front of the American Museum was soon covered with brightly colored banners of the wonders to be seen inside. Drummond lights, the first in New York, glared brightly from the roof, illuminating Broadway "from the Battery to Niblo's." A band played music on the balcony, announcing "Free Music for the Millions." At first the public was delighted. But there was method to Barnum's generosity. "I took pains to select and maintain the poorest band I could find — one whose discordant notes would drive the crowd into the Museum, out of earshot of my outside orchestra." Always justifying his contrivances, Barnum argued that the music should have been poor. "When people expect to get 'something for nothing' they are sure to be cheated, and generally deserve to be, and so, no doubt, some of my out-door patrons were sorely disappointed." His Connecticut boyhood had taught him the foolishness of relying on simple generosity as a sufficient motive for action; self-interest was an appropriate governor, and those who did not realize it were helplessly naïve or hopelessly greedy. But, as soon as the "out-door patrons" parted with a quarter and entered the friendly confines of the American Museum, then they would indeed get full value: hours and hours of entertainment, instruction, and moral up-lift. Or such was Barnum's reasoning. Once dreams of getting something for nothing were forgotten, then the customer could begin enjoying. His education had begun.

The attractions and the novel advertising yielded immediate gains. In the three years before Barnum took over the museum, receipts had averaged about eleven thousand dollars annually. In the first three years of Barnum's management, the annual average tripled to more than thirty thousand dollars and showed a steady increase from year to year. And Barnum's in-come was supplemented by interests elsewhere: out-of-town exhibitions of Tom Thumb, receipt-sharing with owners of other museums to whom he sent his own attractions, and vari-ous other investments in public taste. "I trust that ere long, the richest men in America will be *we Museum chaps*," he wrote Kimball from Paris; and within a few years he was making his wish look like a prophecy.[28]

Exhibits, entertainers, and advertising helped make the mu-seum a financial success. By the mid-forties New Yorkers were boasting about it in their guidebooks, and it quickly became a shrine for foreign tourists and visiting country folk. An air of activity and purposeful energy hung over the establishment. For by developing a unique public reputation, Barnum was able to transfer to the American Museum something of the awed fascination that his countrymen felt for him. A visiting Englishman sensed this aura in 1850. Barnum's name, he in-sisted, was the museum's greatest attraction: "Barnum is not an ordinary showman. He is not one who will be handed down to posterity only on the strength of the objects which he has exhib-ited. . . . He stands alone. Adopting Mr. Emerson's idea, I should say that Barnum is a representative man. He represents the enterprise and energy of his countrymen in the 19th century, as Washington represented their resistance to oppression in the century preceding."[29]

So closely was the showman associated with museums that visitors assumed that any such institution must belong to him. "The enterprising Barnum possesses in this city (and in what city does he not possess) a museum," Thomas Fitzgunne wrote from Boston.[30] Moses Kimball would have been horrified to see the ease with which Barnum's reputation had spread into his own empire. Barnum did operate an aquarium in Boston and he had bought out Peale's in Philadelphia, but his major base remained New York.

Barnum's growing fortune obviously helped his reputation. Outward prosperity proved inner intelligence in Jacksonian America. But there were many Americans richer than Barnum who had also begun from the bottom up. Wealth formed only a part of Barnum's appeal. Contemporaries sensed that he was a representative American not simply because of his enterprise and energy, but because of a special outlook on reality, a peculiar and masterly way of manipulating other people and somehow making them feel grateful for being the subjects of his manipulation. Unlike Charles Willson Peale, Barnum did not develop his museum to fill a national need and increase public enlightenment. He accepted its profit-making function candidly and pursued any feature or oddity that might attract customers. Advertisement and display rather than scholarship and comprehensiveness were his strong suits.

But if Barnum had abandoned the grandiose ideals of an earlier generation of naturalists and museum owners, he turned the merchandiser's pursuit into an art form of its own. His objectives may have been prosaic and self-interested, but his methods, exquisitely sensitive to popular feeling, were innovative and daring. The energies that Americans of the Revolutionary era hoped to harness to the cause of public virtue now dictated their own personal aims. Ambition had become an end in itself, resourcefulness and ingenuity were more important than traditional skills and standards of value. More than a mere show manager, Barnum was remarkably self-conscious about the basis for his success. From the first moments of his career — carting about the fabled Joice Heth — he became aware of his ability to gull others, to make them pay for the opportunity of being fooled. It was not simply as an entrepreneur but as a master of imposture, an expert on disguise, that Barnum gained his early reputation. So completely did he explore the possibilities exaggeration offered, and so shrewdly did he broadcast his own discoveries, that his technique deserves a more dignified label — an aesthetic — for it embodied a philosophy of taste.

The American Museum housed, on the surface, a random assortment of odd curiosities and a collection of interesting performers. But despite Barnum's eclecticism there was a certain unity to its exotic trappings, an approach to reality and to pleasure. The objects inside the museum, and Barnum's activities outside, focused attention on their own structures and operations, were empirically testable, and enabled — or at least invited — audiences and participants to learn how they worked. They appealed because they exposed their processes of action. Adding an adjective to the label, one might term this an "operational aesthetic," an approach to experience that equated beauty with information and technique, accepting guile because it was more complicated than candor. Deception, hoaxing, humbugging, cheating, these were some of the words Americans commonly associated with Barnum, during his lifetime and ever since. In the 1840s, by a series of memorable acts, Barnum acquired his fame, and in so doing raised important questions that transcended the amusements he so carefully exploited.

THREE

The Operational Aesthetic

A T THE END OF AUGUST 1843, New York newspaper advertisements announced a "Grand Buffalo Hunt, Free of Charge," to take place on a Thursday afternoon in Hoboken. A Mr. C. D. French, "one of the most daring and experienced hunters of the West," had captured the animals near Santa Fe at considerable risk to life and limb. Strong fences would protect the public from the savage beasts, who would be lassoed and hunted as part of the entertainment. What the newspaper advertisements did not say was that the buffaloes were feeble, docile beasts, hardly capable of movement, much less of violence. Barnum had purchased the herd for seven hundred dollars when he saw it earlier that summer in Massachusetts and had stowed it away for several weeks in New Jersey. Knowing that the spectacle might not be all the audience anticipated, Barnum wisely decided to make admission free. What he did not disclose was an arrangement with the ferryboat owners who would transport the public from Manhattan to New Jersey; his profits were to come from a percentage of the fares.

The great day finally arrived, and boatloads of spectators crossed to New Jersey. There were to be several shows, and by the time the first batch of spectators had seen the hunt, a second batch was passing them on the Hudson. The returnees called out from their boats that the hunt — a debacle in which the frightened animals fled to a nearby swamp — was the biggest humbug imaginable. Instead of being disappointed, however, the expectant audience, in the words of a witness, "instantly gave three cheers for the author of the humbug, whoever he might be."

Barnum told the whole story in his autobiography. He understood that American audiences did not mind cries of trickery; in fact, they delighted in debate. Amusement and deceit could coexist; people would come to see something they suspected might be an exaggeration or even a masquerade. Any publicity was better than none at all, and if the audiences did not get all they anticipated, they had a pleasant outing in New Jersey for the price of a boat ride.

The principle of the Hoboken hunt — the national tolerance for clever imposture — was one Barnum relied on again and again in his early museum days. As he was building up his cabinet of natural curiosities, he couldn't resist making his exhibits a bit more enticing than literal truth permitted. In the 1840s museum visitors could examine the wooden leg that Santa Anna had lost on a Mexican battlefield, captured, presumably, by American troops; a woolly horse, supposedly brought back by John Fremont from the Rocky Mountains; and a mass of other spurious but colorfully described oddities.

The most famous put-on of all, or the one on which Barnum exercised his most vigorous ingenuity, was the "Fejee Mermaid." The origin of the mermaid is shrouded in mystery, but according to Barnum — not the most reliable but the only witness — he encountered this oddity in the summer of 1842. Moses Kimball owned the mermaid, having purchased it from a sailor, and he offered to share exhibition profits (and costs) with Barnum. Before parting with any money Barnum referred the matter to a naturalist, who pronounced the object manufactured. When Barnum asked the naturalist why he gave this verdict, he replied, "Because I don't believe in mermaids." With only faith at stake, Barnum decided to ignore the advice. But he realized that more objective observers might take a bit more convincing.

On June 18, 1842, Barnum and Kimball signed an agreement.[1] For twelve dollars and fifty cents a week Barnum was to lease the mermaid and hire a manager for it (at no more than eight dollars a week, or one quarter of the net profits). Promising "to take all proper and possible care of said curiosity and not allow it to be handled or in any manner injured or abused," and agreeing "to exert himself to the utmost without regard to trouble or expense to bring it before the public," Barnum would share the profits with Kimball. Thus, Barnum never became literally the owner of the mermaid, a fact he would use to advantage in the controversy that followed.

The campaign of preparation was long and tortuous. In the early summer of 1842 letters were sent to New York newspapers from various southern cities — Montgomery, Charleston, Washington — mentioning a British naturalist who had with him a remarkable mermaid owned by the Lyceum of Natural History in London and said to have originated in the "Fejee [Fiji] Islands." This "Dr. Griffin," as he was known, was in reality the redoubtable Levi Lyman, who had proved of such assistance in the Joice Heth episode and who was hired as the mermaid's manager under the contract's terms. In Philadelphia "Dr. Griffin" actually permitted several editors to view the incredible find. Barnum, of course, had written the various dispatches, which were postmarked from southern cities by friends.

The mermaid itself, as Barnum agreed, was hardly an object of beauty. It consisted of the body of a fish and the head and hands of a monkey. "The animal was an ugly, dried-up, black-looking, and diminutive specimen, about three feet long. Its mouth was open, its tail turned over, and its arms thrown up, giving it the appearance of having died in great agony." Even if it had been manufactured, as Barnum suspected, the object was a superb piece of craftsmanship, for it seemed impossible to see where the fish and the monkey had been "joined." For the moment, however, emphasis was on its natural origins, and after putting "Dr. Griffin" up at a New York hotel, Barnum arranged for reporters to call and examine the curiosity. They were convinced it was genuine, and "while Lyman was preparing public opinion on mermaids at the Pacific Hotel, I was industriously at work (though of course privately) in getting up wood-cuts and transparencies, as well as a pamphlet, proving the authenticity of mermaids." Barnum then made the rounds of the New York papers, offering free use of a mermaid woodcut, explaining that he had it made in hopes of exhibiting the mermaid but that "Dr. Griffin" would not permit its exhibition. On Sunday, July 17, 1842, each editor, convinced he had an exclusive, printed the woodcut, and Barnum distributed ten thousand copies of the pamphlet on mermaids through the city. With the public aroused, "Dr. Griffin" supervised an exhibition at Concert Hall on Broadway, the clever Lyman lecturing his audience on the Great Chain of Being and other scientific theories that could account for Nature's whims in producing such a beast. And then, after a week of this show, the mermaid was brought to the American Museum and therein presented "without extra charge."

At the time, Barnum was well pleased with his coup. In the first four weeks of the mermaid's exhibition, museum receipts almost tripled. Obviously, the careful campaign of publicity, the dignified appearance of "Dr. Griffin," the reports from other cities, the transparencies, pamphlets, and newspaper puffs had produced results. Moreover, prompted in part by the growth of racism, debates about the immutability of species and the divine plan were vigorous. A number of Americans, arguing for the perpetuation of black slavery, challenged belief in the unity of mankind. The races of mankind, men like Dr. Josiah Nott insisted, had been created at separate times and formed distinctive species. The Mosaic description in Genesis was ignorant and incorrect, said Nott, and belief in the equality of man, an assumption of Jefferson's generation, was ill-founded.[2] Into this atmosphere of controversy, any bizarre product of Nature that might bear on biblical narrative or the relationship among species was bound to find a large audience.

In later years, as dignity and philanthropy figured more importantly among Barnum's objectives, he grew reticent about the mermaid episode. The fraud was so transparent, no matter who had originally manufactured the article, and the campaign of deception was so elaborate, that it took the most artful rationalizations to justify it. Even then, Barnum had to take care.

Faced with newspaper indignation and a certain level of public clamor, he curbed his publicity plans. Accepting Lyman's objections, he discarded an enormous flag depicting an eighteen-foot mermaid that was meant to wave in front of the museum. Exaggeration could go too far, Lyman warned. And the advertising changed in tone. In 1843 Barnum suggested a more cautiously worded description of the mermaid, emphasizing the problematic rather than the assured. Writing Kimball, he proposed to present the mermaid as "positively asserted by its owner to have been taken alive in the Fejee Islands, and implicitly believed by many scientific persons, while it is pronounced by other scientific persons to be an utter impossibility." "Who is to decide," an advertisement asked piously, "when *doctors* disagree?" But whether the mermaid was "the work of *nature or art* it is decidedly the most stupendous curiosity ever submitted to the public for inspection. If it is artificial the senses of sight and touch are ineffectual — if it is natural then all concur in declaring it *the greatest Curiosity in the World*."[3]

The new emphasis may have reflected Barnum's reaction to a stormy southern tour made in 1843 by his uncle, Alanson Taylor. In early February of that year, Barnum had been delighted at Taylor's success in exhibiting the mermaid. "Wasn't it lucky to [get] rid of slow-moving, lazy-boned Lyman?" Barnum crowed to Kimball. Taylor was not only Lyman's superior as a lecturer "but far exceeds him in point of *industry* and perseverance. He is as faithful as the sun."[4]

But Taylor's triumph was brief. On February 13 Barnum wrote his friend in Boston that "the bubble has burst. Poor Taylor has gone through everything that a mortal could stand," and the mermaid was on its way back to New York.[5] In Charleston Taylor had become caught up in a vigorous and sometimes vicious local controversy that also involved rival newspapers, the *Courier* and the *Mercury*. The angry debate contributed to Barnum's notoriety and utterly ruined his uncle. Soon after Taylor's arrival in Charleston a Lutheran clergyman and naturalist, a collaborator of John James

Audubon (and a critic of Nott), the Reverend John Bachman, wrote to local newspapers denouncing the mermaid as a fraud. Using the pseudonym "No Humbug," Bachman charged the whole thing was calculated to extort money from a deceived public.[6] Taylor thereupon denounced the letter writer, using as his pseudonym "The Man Who Exhibits the Mermaid," and soon after, a group of distinguished Charleston scientists and naturalists, led by Lewis R. Gibbes, a professor of mathematics, and J. Edwards Holbrook, a professor of anatomy, joined in supporting Bachman.[7] They argued that the mermaid was simply the body of a monkey sewn together with a fish and done with very little regard to anatomical accuracy, since there were present two chests and two abdomens.

But Richard Yeadon, editor of the *Courier*, now attacked the scientists. He had visited the mermaid, touched it, and was convinced it was real. "We take the position," he wrote, "that neither 'No Humbug,' nor his certifiers . . . with all their learned and scientific appendages and paraphernalia — no, not even if, like Dr. Peter Pangloss in the play, they could add to their names and professional titles those of L.L.D. and A.S.S., are entitled to authority in this matter, because they have all denounced as an imposture that which neither has submitted to the test of a scientific examination, nor even seen with the naked eye."[8] Since Taylor, the exhibitor, refused to permit certain kinds of examination, this was begging the question rather boldly, and the furious naturalists protested Yeadon's assault on science. Few were willing to give the time and patience necessary to become naturalists, Bachman wrote. If the public considers such studies of no value, "if they enjoy the joke, whilst men who are ashamed of their names hurl their missiles at them from all quarters; if they chuckle and say, 'see what another lashing these naturalists have received,' let it be so," Bachman went on, but don't expect scientists to continue to respond to questions about natural curiosities.[9]

The controversy followed Taylor from city to city, and unlike such disputes in the North, cost him profits and attendance. Barnum wrote Kimball, who remained the nominal owner of the mermaid, about suing Bachman for libel and employing Yeadon as an attorney. Such a suit would stir up intense excitement, Barnum argued, and "it might breathe the breath of life" into the mermaid's nostrils. Of course Kimball, as the owner, would have to bring the suit in his own name. The shrewd Barnum agreed only to "join in that speculation," not to initiate it. Yeadon was asking for money, and Barnum thought a little advance might help keep his feelings on the right side.[10]

In the end, however, although rumors of the proposed lawsuit found their way into southern papers, Barnum and Kimball decided the risks of loss were too great. Yeadon did not feel confident enough of victory and said he could win the lawsuit only if Barnum and Kimball owned "a *genuine* specimen." "Now my dear Moses," Barnum wrote angrily, "every devil among the scientists would *swear* that its existence is a *natural impossibility* — and would they not raise suspicions too strong in the minds of the *cannaile* [sic] for us to use *them* to advantage."[11] The lawsuit was dropped.

In other parts of the country such controversies were more profitable. Barnum had realized the value of disagreement earlier when he spread rumors that Joice Heth was an automaton. He acted on it again when he arranged for someone to prosecute him for imposture on the grounds that the American Museum's bearded lady was a man. With great unwillingness, or so it seemed, Barnum arranged for a medical examination, and crowds poured in for a closer look. This time his triumph was total, as he had both truth and profits on his side. But as usual, truth was more expendable than cash receipts.

The frequency with which Barnum repeated this pattern of planted objections, denials, and countercharges raises some questions concerning his audience. Barnum's success was so great and so long-lasting, everywhere but in the South, that there had to be more to it than the simple collection of curiosities on which other entrepreneurs had already given up. To explain it, at least two questions must be answered. First, why were Americans apparently so credulous, why could they be fooled so easily, why did they flock to see mermaids, woolly horses, and other anatomical monstrosities that seem in later days to be so patently false? Why did they accept commonplace objects — wooden legs, articles of clothing, minerals and weapons — as sacred relics associated with famous men and historic events? And second, why did Americans *enjoy* watching shows and visiting exhibits that they suspected might be contrived, why did they flock to witness impostures that they knew about? In other words, why the apparent naïveté about deception, and why the pleasure in experiencing deception after knowledge of it had been gained?

These questions are related to a larger issue, for P. T. Barnum was not the only entrepreneur to fool Americans in the early nineteenth century. Ever since Washington Irving and James K. Paulding had published *Salmagundi; or, The Whim-Whams and Opinions of Lancelot Langstaff, Esq.*, in 1807–08, New York City had been popularly known as Gotham, the legendary town of fools, and the name appeared to have some basis in fact. In the three decades before the Civil War, New York was the setting for several tremendous hoaxes that Barnum had no hand in. One of the most memorable became known as the Moon Hoax, an episode engineered by Richard Adams Locke of the *New York Sun*.[12]

The *Sun* had been founded in 1833 by Benjamin H. Day as a penny daily. It concentrated on human interest stories, and Day was one of the earliest practitioners of what would become an established tradition in American urban journalism. Readers of the *Sun* discovered, in the summer of 1835, that the internationally known British astronomer Sir John Herschel had gone to the Cape of Good Hope to experiment with a new and powerful telescope. The articles, supposedly reprinted from the *Edinburgh Journal of Science*, went on to say that Herschel's success had been beyond his wildest dreams, for with the telescope he had managed to penetrate the secrets of the moon. And Herschel's discoveries were far more interesting, or at least more astounding, than the actual voyage that would be made over a century later. The moon, it turned out, contained trees, oceans, pelicans, and most exciting of all, winged men. The *Sun* "quoted" Herschel's minute description. "I could perceive," he wrote, "that their wings possessed great expansion and were similar in structure to those of the bat, being a semitransparent membrane expanded in curvilineal divisions by means of straight radii, united at the back by the dorsal integuments."[13]

This was, to be sure, hard reading, and so was the extremely detailed description of the telescope's design. The *Sun* sold its papers madly, however, and while running the article reached a circulation of almost twenty thousand, larger, it asserted, than any daily newspaper in the world. Thousands of Americans believed the story absolutely, and there followed some of the rituals that seem inevitably to be born of these jokes. Some Baptist clergymen immediately began prayer meetings for the benefit of their unconverted brethren in the moon. A number of scholars at Yale went over the material to substantiate the accuracy of the episode. At last, to much general embarrassment, Locke confessed his authorship, and the discoveries turned out to be an important chapter not in the history of natural science but in the history of hoaxing.

Having achieved one success, the *New York Sun* did not rest on its laurels for too long. In 1844 the same newspaper relayed astonishing news from South Carolina. Mr. Monck Mason had crossed the Atlantic in his balloon, the *Victoria*, making the voyage from England to America in seventy-five hours. Once again, the description was careful. The size and weight of the flying machine were specified, and so was the design of the screw, "an axis of hollow brass tube, eighteen inches in length, through which, upon a semi-spiral inclined at fifteen degrees, pass a series of steel-wire radii, two feet long, and thus projecting a foot on either side." The technical analysis could not be matched by anything so astonishing as moon men, but the newspaper dispatch did celebrate the joys of flying over water: "The immense flaming ocean writhes and is tortured uncomplainingly. The mountainous surges suggest the idea of innumerable dumb gigantic fiends struggling in impotent agony. In a night such as is this to me, a man *lives* — lives a whole century of ordinary life — nor would I forego this rapturous delight for that of a whole century of ordinary existence."[14] This marvelous conquest of nature could not last as long as the Moon Hoax, alas, because it took only a short time to establish contact with the Charleston post office and find that no Atlantic crossing had taken place. It was all the product of the fertile imagination of Edgar Allan Poe.

Poe himself, in "Diddling Considered as One of the Exact Sciences," noted the prevalence of deception on both a large and a small scale. "A crow thieves; a fox cheats; a weasel outwits; a man diddles." The successful diddler was ingenious, audacious, persevering, original, and entirely self-interested. Poe described some of the successful variations. A camp meeting would be held near a free bridge. "A diddler stations himself upon this bridge, respectfully informs all passers-by of the new county law which establishes a toll of one cent for foot passengers, two for horses and donkeys, and so forth and so forth. Some grumble but all submit, and the diddler goes home a wealthier man by some $50 or $60 well earned."[15] This scene was not the product of Poe's imagination but actually took place, one of the innumerable devices by which Americans tricked each other.

At first glance, America appeared an unlikely setting for either the successful hoaxer or the successful diddler. According to foreign travelers and native critics alike, one of America's besetting vices was an aggressive individualism that disinclined the citizen to trust anyone or anything, a cynical suspicion of idealism and pure motives. Frances Trollope, Harriet Martineau, and Charles Dickens found the typical American a hardheaded, hard-bitten realist, shrewd, cautious, suspicious, sparing in speech, narrow in sentiment, refusing to credit surface appearances and demanding proof for any statement, particularly any statement impugning American greatness.[16] "The want of warmth, of interest, of feeling, upon all subjects which do not immediately touch their own concerns," Mrs. Trollope wrote of Americans, "is universal, and has a most paralyzing effect upon conversation. All the enthusiasm of America is concentrated to the one point of her own emancipation and independence."[17] The only unity of feeling and purpose she could find involved the dollar. However industrious and prosperous, the New Englanders, for example, were invariably "sly, grinding, selfish, and tricking." Dickens concluded that the great flaw of American democracy was a "universal distrust," which led Americans to ascribe mean, suspicious motives to the most beneficent actions. As a result, complained European visitors, social life in America was hard and crass, barren of grace, relaxation, elegance, and good humor.[18] "I never saw a population so totally divested of gaiety," wrote Mrs. Trollope. "There is no trace of this feeling from one end of the Union to the other. They have no fetes, no fairs, no merry-makings, no music in the streets, no Punch, no puppet-shows."[19]

One explanation for the prevalence of hoaxes in the competitive materialism of American life focused on the proximity of the frontier — an untamed natural world fraught with obstacles and dangers. Constance Rourke, Richard Chase, and Kenneth Lynn have pointed to the relationship between the hoax and the western tall tale, with its characteristic boasting and exaggeration.[20] A practical joke, Richard Chase wrote, "creates a situation which appears dangerous, horrible, or uncanny, and then disperses the sensation of terror with the sudden revelation that the whole thing is a hoax. It is the exercise of what Freud called 'anxiety' — the imaginative creation of danger, a psychic exercise designed to reduce the stature of real danger or to keep the senses alert."[21] The practical joke survived in a skeptical society because it was a way of reducing a hostile and threatening environment to human scale by manipulating its elements and so demonstrating control over them. The tall tale, the put-on, the travel lie, were social conveniences, and even the most hardheaded Yankee peddler could participate in their creation or enjoyment.

But this explanation does not account for the popularity and effectiveness of practical joking in eastern cities, physically and spiritually hundreds of miles away from the frontier. A full explanation for the effectiveness of the pranksters must take account of the advanced technical and material conditions of American life. By the 1830s and 1840s portions of the United States were as advanced in those areas as any part of the Old World; innovations like the railroad and the telegraph were greeted with enthusiasm and constructed with rapidity. American mechanics and toolmakers competed with European rivals. There was widespread interest in and support for scientific progress.[22] Physical improvement had become inextricably connected with the genius of American civilization. Visiting the United States in the 1830s, Harriet Martineau was fascinated by the Moon Hoax. She argued, however, that its success was misleading. Americans learned of real scientific advances more quickly than they were taken in by frauds. In any other nation, she went on, the Moon Hoax would have fooled a far larger proportion of the population than in America, because Americans were becoming scientifically educated and alert to the possibilities and varieties of technological change.[23]

In emphasizing American scientific literacy Harriet Martineau got hold of the right issue, but from the wrong end. American experience with science and technology was crucial to the hoaxing attempts, but this experience led not to less credulity but to more. A vital factor in the success of the hoaxes was national skepticism itself. Men accustomed to examining the truth or validity of every person, idea, object or act presented to them — as Americans proverbially were — became easy targets for pseudoscientific explanations, for detailed descriptions of fictional machinery, for any fantasy that was couched in the bland neutrality of a technological vocabulary.

Men priding themselves on their rationalistic, scientific bent, familiar with the operation of novel machines, aware of the variety of nature, tended to accept as true anything which seemed to work — or seemed likely to work. The coming of steam, of railroads, of telegraphs indicated the futility of declaring anything impossible or incredible. Nothing mechanical was beyond the range of Nature's imagination. "Who shall now describe the circle within which human ability must confine itself?" cried a Boston cleric of the period, awestruck at man's new power over Nature.[24] And the same note was sounded by Joseph Atterley, who published his *Voyage to the Moon* in New York in 1827. If travelers sometimes imposed on human gullibility, he argued, they were also attacked when speaking the truth. "Credulity and scepticism are indeed but different names for the same hasty judgment on insufficient evidence." He reminded those refusing to credit anything that contradicted "the narrow limits of their own observation," that Nature had more secrets than they could possibly imagine.[25]

Atterley's warning about resistance to new revelations was well taken, even among Americans coming to expect the unexpected. Marcus Aurelius Root, a prominent Philadelphia daguerreotypist, recalled that in 1839, when Philadelphia newspapers reported on Louis Daguerre's epochal discovery, Dr. Bird, a distinguished professor of chemistry, was asked what he thought of "this new method of copying objects with the sunbeam." Dr. Bird was discouraging. In a lengthy reply the doctor "pronounced the whole report a fabrication — a new edition of the famed 'moon-hoax' — such a performance being, in his view, an intrinsic impossibility."[26]

But men like Dr. Bird were in a minority. Not only was the predisposition to accept the mechanically probable or the organically possible a result of changing technology and the growth of natural science, it was also a peculiarly patriotic position in Jacksonian America. At a time when the advantages of a common school education were being extolled by reformers, when the common sense of the average citizen was proposed as a guarantee for the republic's future, many avid democrats assumed that any problem could be expressed clearly, concisely, and comprehensibly enough for the ordinary man to resolve it. Secret information and private learning were anathema. All knowledge was meant to be shared. Contemporary pamphleteers delighted in ridiculing experts and specialists; the expert turned out frequently to be a pedantic ignoramus, easily fooled himself; the learned doctor was often a victim of scientific nonsense and deserved to be overruled by intelligent laymen. "When *doctors* disagree," Barnum had phrased it in his mermaid advertisement, then it was up to ordinary men to decide for themselves.

This emphasis on individual learning and confidence in popular majorities made Americans inveterate lecturers and lecuture-goers. "I honestly believe," wrote Edward Hingston, the English biographer of the popular humorist, Artemus Ward, "that if the good people across the water had fewer individuals in their midst who feel themselves effervescing with information, and under such high pressure that they must impart it without delay, there would be a less number of lecturers." As things stood, however, "everything is lectured upon, from the destinies of humanity down to the proper method of making a pumpkin-pie." Educated as he was to know a little of everything, Hingston continued, it was no wonder "that the American schoolboy, peppered with science, and salted with history, should be a sciolist, with a strong inclination to teach."

The American was eager to impart whatever he knew, politely but volubly. "Every American believes himself to be the repository of extensive information; within him is the pent-up source of knowledge; his amiable spirit of benevolence prompts him to let it flow forth for the enlightenment of his benighted fellow-citizens, and the outer world of darkness generally." There were two sins outside the Decalogue regarded as major transgressions in America, Hingston concluded. "One is to grow old; the other is not to know."[27]

Technological progress and egalitarian self-confidence combined to make many Americans certain of their own opinions — and so, easy prey for the hoaxers. And these traits were supplemented by the sheer exhilaration of debate, the utter fun of the opportunity to learn and evaluate, whether the subject was an ancient slave, an exotic mermaid, or a politician's honor. Barnum's audiences found the encounter with potential frauds exciting. It was a form of intellectual exercise, stimulating even when literal truth could not be determined. Machinery was beginning to accustom the public not merely to a belief in the continual appearance of new marvels but to a jargon that concentrated on methods of operation, on aspects of mechanical organization and construction, on horsepower, gears, pulleys, and safety valves.

The language of technical explanation and scientific description itself had become a form of recreational literature by the 1840s and 1850s. Newspapers, magazines, even novels and short stories catered to this passion for detail. Manuals on almost every conceivable activity poured forth from American presses. Carl Bode has listed their variety: "How to render olive-oil soap. How to build a staircase with curving balustrades. How to make a rocking chair. How to cut marble. How to make iron. How to breed poultry. How to (or rather, officially, how not to) counterfeit bank notes." Without vocational schools or effective systems of apprenticeship "the main method of independent technical instruction became, by default, the how-to-do-it book. It taught embryo craftsmen how to make the material things America insisted on wanting."[28] It also, of course, taught amateurs how to evaluate as well as how to build. Architectural writers like Samuel Sloan, Ithiel Town, and Orson Fowler (who also published phrenological diagrams) put out books giving details of construction and calling upon their readers to read diagrams and blueprints.[29] Some, like C. W. Elliott, in his sentimental novel of 1845, *Cottages and Cottage Life*, interrupted the progress of the tale with maps and floor plans to let readers know the dimensions of the homes of the protagonists.[30]

Nowhere was the zest for operational description better satisfied than in the sea novels that figured prominently on American reading lists of the Jacksonian era. The complexity of the great sailing ship, the varied activities of the crew, the complex task of coordinating the rapid raising and lowering of the sails to meet the challenges of weather and position, formed a staple for the novelists. Richard Henry Dana's descriptions in *Two Years Before the Mast* appealed both to experienced travelers and a much larger group that relished learning how the ship functioned. "We had got the light sails furled," Dana wrote, and "the courses hauled up, and the topsail reef tackles hauled out, and were just mounting the forerigging when the storm struck us. In an instant the sea, which had been comparatively quiet, was running higher and higher. . . . We were longer taking in sail than ever before; for the sails were stiff and wet, the ropes and rigging covered with snow and sleet. . . . By the time we had got down upon deck again, the little brig was plunging madly into a tremendous head sea. . . . At this instant the chief mate, who was standing on the top of the windlass, at the foot of the spencer mast, called out, 'Lay out there and furl the jib!' . . . I was near the mate, but sprang past several, threw the downhaul over the windlass, and jumped between the knightheads out upon the bowsprit. The crew stood abaft the windlass and hauled the jib down, while John and I got out upon the weather side of the jib boom, our feet on the foot ropes, holding on by the spar, the great jib flying off to leeward and 'slatting' so as almost to throw us off the boom."[31] Page after page recreated the physical world of the sailor, and the landlubber who wished to get through the novel had, perforce, to learn the vocabulary and master the sets to follow the drama properly.

The novels of Herman Melville contained, in addition to the depiction of sailing and harpooning operations, immense and erudite discussions of anatomy, geology, and physiology. Floods of data, anecdotes, measurements, whaling lore, manipulated more skillfully by Melville than by any contemporary writer, overwhelmed the reader in his passage through the book. Such detail satisfied the same relish for acquiring knowledge that led to travel literature, how-to-do-it manuals, and almanacs of useful information.

This delight in learning explains why the experience of deceit was enjoyable even after the hoax had been penetrated, or at least during the period of doubt and suspicion. Experiencing a complicated hoax was pleasurable because of the competition between victim and hoaxer, each seeking to outmaneuver the other, to catch him off-balance and detect the critical weakness. Barnum, Poe, Locke, and other hoaxers didn't fear public suspicion; they invited it. They understood, most particularly Barnum understood, that the opportunity to debate the *issue* of falsity, to discover how deception had been practiced, was even more exciting than the discovery of fraud itself. The manipulation of a prank, after all, was as interesting a technique in its own right as the presentation of genuine curiosities. Therefore, when people paid to see frauds, thinking they were true, they paid again to hear how the frauds were committed. Barnum reprinted his own ticket-seller's analysis. "First he humbugs them, and then they pay to hear him tell how he did it. I believe if he should swindle a man out of twenty dollars, the man would give a quarter to hear him tell about it."

Others agreed. An English tourist in the American Museum reported his own experience. "'Is it real or is it humbug?' asks an astonished visitor, and Mr. Barnum replied with a smile, 'That's just the question: persons who pay their money at the door have a right to form their own opinions after they have got up stairs.' "[32] Charles Godfrey Leland, a writer and poet who worked temporarily for Barnum on an illustrated newspaper and who genuinely admired the showman, also recalled the cleverness with which Barnum hinted at deception. "When he had concocted some monstrous cock-and-bull curiosity," Leland noted in his *Memoirs*, Barnum "was wont to advertise that 'it is with great reluctance that he presented this unprecedented marvel to the world, as doubts had been expressed as to its genuineness — doubts inspired by the actually incredible amount of attention in it. All that we ask of an enlightened and honest public is, that it will pass a fair verdict and decide whether it be a humbug or not.'" The enlightened public, Leland wrote tartly, paid its quarters and decided it *was* a humbug, "and Barnum abode by their decision and then sent it to another city to be again decided on."[33]

There is one final reason why American audiences responded to Barnum's techniques and so enjoyed practical joking. The practice of humbugging solved some special problems of the mass sensibility, problems particularly acute in America, where cultural ambitions outstripped cultural achievements. Concentration on whether a particular show, exhibit, or event was real or false, genuine or contrived, narrowed the task of judgment for the multitude of spectators. It structured problems of experiencing the exotic and unfamiliar by reducing that experience to a simple evaluation.

Many Americans, however much they admired and respected the realm of art, feared its mysteries.[34] They were uncomfortable encountering masterpieces because they could neither analyze nor justify their reactions. Art exhibitions, when they were organized with theatrical settings and sentimental appeals — Hiram Powers's sensationally popular "Greek Slave," for example — were crowded with onlookers. And patriotic appeals aided the art unions of the forties and fifties in distributing thousands of lithographs of landscapes and genre paintings. But these were, on the whole, exceptional experiences. No great public galleries existed for the public to stroll through, no historic buildings featured ancient murals and statuary. Instead, paintings and sculpture stood alongside mummies, mastodon bones and stuffed animals. American museums were not, in the antebellum period, segregated temples of the fine arts, but repositories of information, collections of strange or doubtful data. Such indiscriminate assemblages made artistic objects take on the innocent yet familiar shape of exhibition curiosities. Contemplating a painting or a statue was not so different from studying Napoleon's cane or wood from Noah's ark; in every instance, a momentary brush with a historical artifact stimulating reflections on its cost, age, detail, and rarity.

The American Museum then, as well as Barnum's elaborate hoaxes, trained Americans to absorb knowledge. This was an aesthetic of the operational, a delight in observing process and examining for literal truth. In place of intensive spiritual absorption, Barnum's exhibitions concentrated on information and the problem of deception. Onlookers were relieved from the burden of coping with more abstract problems. Beauty, significance, spiritual values, could be bypassed in favor of seeing what was odd, or what worked, or was genuine.

Barnum insisted again and again that what gave pleasure to democratic audiences was good, that his own art was, in its way, as satisfying and important as high culture. His career suggested that art could not be confined to the narrower, classic categories evolved by critics over the centuries. The entertainer who relieved public tedium and brought momentary excitement and happiness to masses of men deserved the thanks of humanity, Barnum insisted. He legitimized his humbugging and exaggerated advertising by pointing to audience satisfactions. What pleased the American masses was, by definition, good. The crowds thronging his enterprises were ordinary citizens, possessed of the virtue and intelligence that good Jacksonians, like Barnum, held as an article of faith. What counted were results. Barnum spoke out continually and bitterly against Protestant clergymen who condemned entertainments in general and his own shows in particular. He argued that in tightening the area of experience open to man, religious leaders were encouraging their own downfall. Without appropriate moral relaxation, humanity could not survive the rigor and routine of mundane existence. Men were meant to laugh and frolic for at least part of the time, and the successful entertainer was really a philanthropist who ministered to a basic human need.

In his attack on formal categories, in his assault on self-styled or academically certified experts, in his expansion of the sources of human pleasure, Barnum was related, in a fashion, to men who abhorred his vulgarity and exaggeration, who insisted on total honesty as a condition of communication, and who served a much smaller and more select audience: the Transcendentalist writers and prophets of the 1840s and 1850s. Men like Emerson, Thoreau, and Horatio Greenough differed almost totally in life style, metaphysic, and ultimate commitment from Barnum, but they engaged in an aesthetic enterprise not so very far from his in purpose and technique. Transcendentalist critics were also taking the task of judgment away from juries of classically trained experts. They also condemned traditional constraints placed on beauty and pleasure and extended the task of evaluation to the mass audience. Fitness, simplicity, universality — these were the qualities which Transcendentalist seers found in every great work of art. And they were qualities which could be understood by popular majorities. "I now require this of all pictures," wrote Emerson, "that they domesticate me, not that they dazzle me."[35] If all matter possessed equal value in the eye of God, then true art could not be confined to the art academy or the concert hall. Trees were more glorious than Corinthian columns, wrote Thoreau.[36] And Emerson repudiated the boundaries between the sacred and the profane. "Beauty must come back to the useful arts, and the distinction between the fine and the useful arts be forgotten."[37]

Indeed, the Transcendentalist deprecation of art, when compared to nature, led to an emphasis on literalism and imitation which came perilously close, at times, to trickery. "If we searched deeply enough," wrote George William Curtis, a close friend of many Transcendentalists and a frequent visitor to Brook Farm, we would find that the best critic of art was the man whose "life has been hid in nature; and therefore the triumph of art is complete when birds peck at the [painted] grapes."[38] In other words, when the illusion has been acted upon, and when the spectator has been induced to believe he beholds another reality, instead of its shadow.

Obviously, these connections can easily be overemphasized. Nevertheless, there are parallels between the Transcendentalist emphasis on materials and function and Barnum's appeal to a delight in problem-solving and information-collecting. In fact, the pleasure taken in observing process may be the basis for the American vernacular tradition itself, that continuity of design which, John Kouwenhoven has argued, connects American technology, architecture, and industry.[39] The characteristics of "economy, simplicity and flexibility" in our machinery, design, and craftsmanship may have developed not simply from the physical needs of a rapidly growing industrial society but from the sheer pleasure in creating objects which exemplified their own operations. P. T. Barnum, along with Eli Whitney, Samuel Colt, and Frank Lloyd Wright, fits into the long association between Americans and mechanical innovation.

Interest in demonstrating process also stimulated American concern with principles of design. The man who most eloquently transformed problem-solving into a basis for beauty was Horatio Greenough, a sculptor whose neoclassic statuary is now largely forgotten. But his theoretical writings make him a startling precursor of modern functionalist philosophies.[40] The best designers of artistic objects, Greenough suggested, were engineers. They achieved beauty because it was not their conscious aim. For beauty was not an independent status or a collection of categories. It rested entirely on relationships. That which was beautiful in one context was deformed in another. Beautiful design was that which worked most efficiently and evinced its operations most clearly. The relationship between the forms employed and the functions they served was the basis of beauty.

The sailing ship, for example, the same ship that American novelists loved to describe, perfectly illustrated Greenough's conception of beauty. Outlines and component parts told observers just what role they played in the operation of the whole.

"Obedient as the horse, swift as the stag," the ship at sea had an organization second only to that of an animal. "What academy of design, what research of connoisseurship, what imitation of the Greeks produced this marvel of construction?" Greenough asked scornfully.[41] Beauty was the promise of function, and any ordinary layman could evaluate it.

The American nation was "the advanced guard of humanity; because it is one vast interrogation. Never affirming but when there is need of action, in its affirmation conceding that the minority represents a sacred human want not yet articulate to the aggregate ear, it gives peace and good will in proportion to the universality of the wants to which it ministers."[42] Structural coherence, functional efficiency — these were criteria which ordinary men, who refused to be blinded by the dictates of pedants and codifiers, could demand in the objects that surrounded them, as well as in the political constitution that governed them.

On the surface, of course, Barnum and Greenough were in direct opposition, at least philosophically. Barnum's genius lay in embellishment and adornment of word and gesture. His task was to entice and impose. Greenough was the deadly enemy of decoration as false beauty, an attempt to compensate for defects in plan and incompleteness. But what did join them was the realization that men took instinctive pleasure in uncovering process. Greenough postulated that design in the first instance should appeal to this sense of structure, while Barnum arranged his hoaxes and exhibits to encourage debate about which processes were real. One opposed adornment as unnatural; the other employed it as worthy of study in its own right. Thus, an interest in exposure, a revelation of fundamental but hidden relationships, was common ground for both Barnum and Greenough.

The exposure of sham was the negative image of the practical joke, and both appealed to the same sensibility. Many deceivers were also exposers, since the two processes fed public fascination for information and detail. Barnum, for example, after he had described his own deceptions, published in 1865 a large tome entitled *Humbugs of the World*, in which he listed some of the memorable tricks practiced on credulous humanity since the beginning of time. Witch-hunting, the South Sea Bubble, religious imposters, stock frauds, mediums, magicians, imposters, all figured in his story, which he piously insisted was written to release men from superstitious bondage and naïveté. Richard Adams Locke both exposed the Joice Heth affair and created the Moon Hoax. And Edgar Allan Poe, in addition to authoring the balloon hoax, uncovered the secret of Maelzel's automatic chess player and so broke down an illusion with as much energy and imagination as he used trying to create one.

The public's taste for exposure also had political implications. Some abolitionist literature owed its popularity more to the titillation of uncovering disguise than to real sympathy for the slave. *Uncle Tom's Cabin*, and even more directly the book on which Harriet Beecher Stowe relied for her facts, Theodore Dwight Weld's *Slavery as It Is*, claimed to present the "real truth" that lay hidden behind the great plantation houses and the genteel lives of the southern slave-owners. Corruption was covered by gilded culture, sin and wickedness by polished manners and handsome dress. In his collection of documents revealing the character of American slavery, Weld referred explicitly to the most obvious popular instrument of exposure: the jury system. He told his readers they were being impaneled "to try a plain case and bring in an honest verdict." He described his task as one of demasking. Slaveholders, Weld wrote, were trying to "bandage our eyes with thin gauzes."[43] Northerners were being "gulled" and "hoaxed" by southern professions of kindness and sincerity. Abolitionists and antislave politicians insisted that southern legislators were trying to disguise their true interests and real purposes, and gradually the term "conspiracy" came into favor as an indication of the sweeping and dangerous nature of southern aims. No more thrilling or enticing word could have been used, and none could have stimulated more interest in political behavior.

Conspiracy charges were widespread in the Jacksonian era. Mormons, Catholics, and Masons were all suspected of devious, dangerous, and even criminal behavior. David B. Davis has demonstrated the social functions that isolation of enemies served in heterogeneous America. But the thrill of reading about conspiracy, being fed clues in newspapers and pamphlets, and rendering a verdict as part of the "enlightened public" transcended the desire for social unity and the suspicion of outsiders.[44] What was secret deserved exposure. One Bostonian informed a British visitor that the destruction of the Ursuline convent by a mob in 1834 simply expressed the public's wish to see what lay within the walls, because it lay within.[45]

Not surprisingly, the passion for revelation was less popular in the South than elsewhere, and equally significant is the fact that the operational aesthetic itself was less powerful there as well. There, technological and industrial changes seemed least appreciated; there, the smallest proportion of the population was exposed to revolutionary physical improvement or accustomed to tinkering with machinery. Moreover, the mechanic himself, along with the laborer, enjoyed less status there than elsewhere because of the taint placed by chattel slavery upon manual labor. Appropriately enough then, some Southerners frowned not only on abolitionists and Transcendentalists, but on Barnum. In one memorable magazine review, Barnum and Mrs. Stowe were brought together as twin examples of northern perfidy: one a mountebank, the other a Transcendental pretender. Both were examples of the dangers of unleashing public curiosity and of the destructiveness of the democratic sensibility.[46] The desire for information, for confessions and for hidden truth, was dangerous in a closed society, and southern critics were right to spot the connection between political ideology and tastes in amusement.

But it was in American fiction that the taste for exposure and problem-solving most convincingly appeared. The preeminent practitioner of the art was Edgar Allan Poe, with his famous studies of criminal detection.[47] This period witnessed the birth of the modern detective story, and in C. Auguste Dupin, the hero of "The Purloined Letter," "The Murders in the Rue Morgue," and "The Mystery of Marie Roget," Poe created one of the archetypes of detective fiction, the detached, powerful, analytic intellect who solved crimes of the greatest mystery by logical method and intensive empathizing. In "The Murders in the Rue Morgue," Dupin proves even before he discovers the evidence that the true killer of two women in a Paris apartment had to be an orangoutang, and much of the story deals with the steps which lead him to this conclusion. Poe begins the tale by apostrophizing the analytical intellect: "As the strong man exults in his physical ability, delighting in such exercises as call his muscles into action, so glories the analyst in that moral activity which Disentangles. He derives pleasure from even the most trivial occupations bringing his talent into play. He is fond of enigmas, of conundrums, hieroglyphics; exhibiting in his solutions of each a degree of acumen which appears to the ordinary apprehension praeternatural."[48] This was also a description of the person who delighted in the competitiveness of Barnum's exhibitions, who sought to measure his wits against a master hoaxer, who enjoyed the intellectual exercise of disentangling the true from the false, the spurious from the genuine.

Reason alone, to be sure, was insufficient for the great detective. In "The Purloined Letter" the Paris police, "persevering, ingenious, cunning, and thoroughly versed in the knowledge which their duties seem chiefly to demand," fail to discover a stolen document they know to be in the hands of a government minister. Dupin is more successful because he measures the minister as a man and a mind before deciding what he could have done with the letter. The police consider only "their *own* ideas of ingenuity; and, in searching for any thing hidden," refer "only to the modes in which *they* would have hidden it." When the cunning of the felon differs from their own, the felon foils them. "They have no variation of principle in their investigations."[49] Problem-solving of the highest sort, then, was not simply a rarefied strategy of logical rules; it demanded insight into personality and character, a knowledge of the ways of the world, a willingness to burrow into the temperament of other men and uncover the springs of action that push them forward. Dupin, like Barnum, never made the mistake of assuming that all men reflected his tastes and proclivities; he acted only after observation and generalization permitted him to categorize the possibilities and vary his techniques.

Poe's artistic intentions, certainly, were complex, and his tales of mystery touched on interests not directly related to the operational aesthetic. Yet his stories exerted an immediate appeal and enthralled his readers because of their controlled problems; his audience joined with the protagonist to discover the intricacies of the puzzle and enjoyed the lengthy expositions that demonstrated the true facts. In the popular 1845 edition of Poe's tales, Evert A. Duyckinck, the editor, selected the three detective stories as part of his total of twelve, leaving out others that Poe considered among his best.[50] For many, Poe's mystery tales actually came to symbolize mental training, and they served this use even in political campaigning.

In 1860, shortly before the presidential election, William Dean Howells wrote a brief but influential campaign biography of Abraham Lincoln. Howells faced the problem of proving that this little-known western lawyer, poorly educated, with few intellectual pretensions, was really quite intelligent, and equal to the burdens of the office he sought. Howells turned to Lincoln's reading habits to make his point. Having a mathematical bent of mind, he wrote, Lincoln was naturally pleased "with the absolute and logical method of Poe's tales and sketches, in which the problem of mystery is given, and wrought out into every-day facts by processes of cunning analysis."[51] In the isolation of the rural Midwest men could sharpen their wits by studying the clever reasoning of C. Auguste Dupin. Lincoln allowed no year to go by without reading some Poe, added Howells to clinch his argument.

Poe's fascination with cryptography also satisfied the taste for problem-solving. In various issues of *Alexander's Weekly Messenger* for 1840, and in the summer of 1841 in *Graham's Magazine*, Poe published a series of ciphers with some solutions to them. Wide public interest was aroused, and readers sent codes in for Poe to solve. In a three-month period in 1840, fifteen articles on ciphers appeared in *Alexander's* and thirty-six ciphers were published or referred to. Poe did not explain his methods at this point, but waited until he published "The Gold Bug." Here, W. K. Wimsatt, Jr., has written, "in dramatized form, with the romantic adjuncts of invisible ink, a golden scaraboeus, a skull and a buried treasure," Poe revealed his method of translating ciphers, "for which fireside cogitators had long awaited. It was a master stroke of selling strategy," stimulating the interest of readers with tempting glimpses of cryptographic methods, but satisfying them only in his finished tale.[52] That Poe's analysis contained important errors was less important than the impression he made on his contemporaries as a man of great analytic power, whetting their appetite for its continual demonstration.

It was entirely appropriate then that Poe, like Barnum and Locke, was both an exposer and a deceiver. Common to both modes was the interest in problem-solving. Poe devoted a popular essay to revealing the fraud behind Maelzel's chess player, a widely seen automaton that played chess with delighted customers and appeared to be entirely mechanical. Though Poe cribbed his information from other writers, he proved that the machine concealed within it, shielded by a complex system of sliding panels, a crouching man who made the actual chess moves. Rather than a brilliant piece of invention, the chess player was only an ingenious deception.[53]

The pervasiveness of the operational taste also explained the profusion at this time of large amounts of information, sometimes in statistical tables, sometimes in long lists of data. In large enough quantities, information gave the illusion of problem-solving by presenting previously unknown facts. Even if the reader missed the author's artistic intent, he could take away with him vivid details that frequently served other functions within the context of the novels and poems. And operationalism was served also by the "Is it fact or is it fiction?" question Americans asked, not only of such Poe stories as "The Facts in the Case of M. Valdemar" but of exotic travel narratives, like Melville's *Typee*. As the nineteenth century progressed, increasing numbers of American writers worked with science-fiction themes, using mechanical inventions — sometimes described in great detail — or fabulous medical experiments to lend verisimilitude to their themes. Hawthorne, Poe, and Melville were joined by Fitz-James O'Brien, Edward Bellamy, and William Dean Howells.[54]

Interest in science fiction and in details of operation was not, of course, solely American. The aesthetic characterized other industrializing and urbanizing societies in the latter part of the nineteenth century. C. Auguste Dupin was a predecessor of the much more popular Sherlock Holmes, and in science fiction few Americans came close to matching the work of Jules Verne in France.[55] But the interest appeared in America so early, and so intensively, because the implications of technology were complemented by a concern with popular verdicts and diffused competence. Civic culture encouraged the spread of information and skill at making decisions.

Barnum never analyzed in detail the reasons for his success and the popularity of his vast practical jokes, but he understood in practice how they worked. He determined, then, to give as many details as possible of his operations. In Europe, by contrast, showmen faced different audiences. Robert-Houdin, the great French magician, wrote in his own memoirs that it was useless to portray in any detail the machines he developed and repaired. "If my readers were only mechanicians," Robert-

Houdin wrote, "how willingly would I describe to them all my trials, attempts and studies. . . . But as I fancy I can see my readers turning over my pages to seek the end of a chapter that is growing too serious, I will check my inclination."[56]

Barnum never checked his revelations; he accepted what Robert-Houdin rejected: that perfection and absolute conviction in exhibits made them less valuable. Spectators required some hint of a problem, some suggestion of difficulty. When Robert-Houdin displayed his first automaton, its quiet perfection worked against it. Some spectators said it was too simple. Robert-Houdin then decided to tamper with the machinery to produce a whizzing sound. The public now valued his work more, and "admiration increased in a ratio to the intensity of the noise. . . . 'How ingenious! What complicated machinery!'" audiences cried. But, said Robert-Houdin, to "obtain this result I had rendered my automaton less perfect; and I was wrong. . . . Eventually, I got over my susceptibility, and my machine was restored to its first condition."[57]

Barnum, however, was less interested in craftsmanship and more in profits. He catered to public taste and rarely challenged it. But his ambitions drove him to extend the orbit of his triumphs and to gain a reputation that was more than local. As his museum prospered and his advertising grew more daring, Barnum's sense of mission became stronger and his urge to travel returned. The New World was too small a field to display his genius; Europe's turn came next.

FOUR

International Triumphs

B<small>Y JANUARY</small> 1844, Barnum's museum operations were solidly established. He had been in business for only two years but already he had begun to accumulate some capital and could think about larger schemes which, if riskier, also promised greater rewards.

In this era Americans still considered the ultimate accolades to be European. Though the Old World was dominated by her monarchies and class system, she continued to be the arbiter of fame. Barnum could not claim true greatness until he had demonstrated his ability to enthrall critics more severe than any America possessed.

He had been showing Tom Thumb for twelve months in America. The public continued to flock to his shows, and newspaper editors waxed eloquent. Tom Thumb is "magnitude in miniature," wrote James Watson Webb of the *Courier and Enquirer*, "*multum in parvo;* not exactly an abridgement of human nature, [but] one of Nature's Indices, in which the principal features of the race may be looked at with one glance."[1] The little fellow was "a sort of mental and physical concentration, a chemical synthesis, in which manhood has been *boiled down.*" Here was "the cube root of all creation!" Tom Thumb was a museum in himself, a display piece for the race. And his cheerful spirit testified, as a later critic put it, to the goodness of his Creator and the exquisiteness with which "nature performs all her work."[2]

In his year of American performances Tom Thumb had been taught to sing and dance; he played with children invited onstage (to further dramatize his size) and fought mimic battles with Barnum's giants. Strutting before audiences in a Yankee Doodle suit, or clad in tights as "Cupid" or "Hercules with the Nemean Lion," he won wide sympathy from young and old. "His large imitation gives him the power to do what he sees done," ran a later phrenological analysis of Tom Thumb's head, and "his large self-esteem, love of approbation, firmness, hope, and imitation inspire him with ambition, pride of feeling." Moreover, the analysis continued, "neither veneration nor marvellousness is present, so that he will be perfectly at home in the midst of superiority and greatness."[3]

Barnum did not yet have the advantage of the phrenologist's report, but he was impressed by his ward's braggadocio and self-assurance. In America these traits were admired and enjoyed, but in Europe they might play a more important function: with more to criticize, Tom Thumb could assume the comedian's role, innocently deflating the pretensions of the great while running no risk of their anger. He could become a court jester for the multitudes, a caricaturist who would lampoon the aristocracy and simultaneously request their patronage.

On January 18, 1844, the little general sailed for England on the *Yorkshire*, and thousands crowded the docks to see him off. Barnum continued to maintain the fiction that he was English, suggesting that this was merely a homecoming trip, but Americans knew better. "Our little countryman will astonish the citizens of the Old World!" crowed one New York newspaper.[4] Americans, who had boasted of size, capaciousness, and scale, appreciated the conceit of demonstrating their superiority on both ends of the spectrum: they had outdone Europeans in littleness as easily as they had in magnitude.

But Barnum faced a considerable task. English showmen had been exhibiting dwarfs, alongside other curiosities, for centuries. In Liverpool, where the entourage landed, an English waxworks owner thought he was being generous when he offered Barnum ten dollars a week to show Tom Thumb, and another Englishman advised him to keep his admission fee down to a penny, "the usual price for seeing giants and dwarfs in England." Barnum, however, set his sights a great deal higher. He had a plan in mind. "Luck," he wrote in the autobiography, "is in no sense the foundation of my fortune; from the beginning of my career I planned and worked for my success. To be sure," he admitted, "my schemes often amazed me with the affluence of their results, and . . . I sometimes 'builded better than I knew.' " Such was the case in London. To get British audiences excited, Barnum did not employ the techniques that had made Joice Heth and the Fejee Mermaid so appealing: like C. Auguste Dupin he was capable of variation. His intention was to have Tom Thumb become the petted darling of the English peerage and the royal court; the approbation of majesty would surely bring the patronage of the masses.

To start, Barnum took a mansion on Grafton Street in the West End, "the very centre of the most fashionable locality." Distinguished noblemen had been previous occupants, and Barnum's neighbors included "half a dozen families of the aristocracy and many of the gentry." Letters of invitation were sent to assorted editors and peers, and Barnum wisely refused admittance to those without invitation, even when they drove up in "crested carriages." They would be sure, however, to receive invitations for another visit. As interest in meeting Tom Thumb grew, Edward Everett, the American minister, promised to use his influence to get Tom Thumb introduced to the queen. Baroness Rothschild and a wealthy banker, Mr. Drummond, invited Barnum to bring Tom Thumb to their homes. "The golden shower had begun to fall," Barnum noted.

And shortly after Barnum opened Tom Thumb at the Egyptian Hall, the long-desired communication came: the queen would receive them. Closing up shop for the evening, Barnum and Tom Thumb, carefully instructed in court decorum, made their way to Buckingham Palace. The general was brash, clever, and engaging. He made an immediate hit and devised a hilarious exit, alternately running and "backing out" of the royal presence and fighting with the queen's poodle. Barnum immediately arranged for the court journal to contain a lengthy description of the interview, and in fact managed to write it himself. As he foresaw, the visit increased his audiences.

Two more visits to Buckingham Palace followed, in which Tom Thumb met the Prince of Wales and royal relatives from abroad and received various presents from the queen's own hand. "The British public was now fairly excited," Barnum wrote contentedly.

For four months the Egyptian Hall was crowded, the daily receipts averaging five hundred dollars (Barnum was still giving Tom Thumb a salary, by this time paying him fifty dollars a week). All the elements of celebrity accompanied the box-office success. Dishes and dances were named after Tom Thumb; sales of his biography brought thirty pounds a day; notables vied with one another to entertain him.

Barnum, of course, made the most of it. The gifts of the queen and members of the royal family were placed on exhibition. Tom Thumb's witty sallies were immediately publicized: when he met the Duke of Wellington while dressed in the uniform of Napoleon, the duke asked him what he was thinking of and the general replied, "I was thinking of the loss of the battle of Waterloo." This exchange, said Barnum, "was of itself worth thousands of pounds to the exhibition."

The money was intensely satisfying, but so was the association with an aristocracy for which Barnum professed contempt but actually admired. The palaces and great homes he visited, the gilding and gold of the drawing rooms, made a lasting impression. He rolled off the titles of his patrons with satisfaction; none could doubt his respectability after this. The general was petted by "some of the first personages in the land, among whom may be mentioned Sir Robert and Lady Peel, the Duke and Duchess of Buckingham, Duke of Bedford, Duke of Devonshire, Count d'Orsay, Lady Blessington, Daniel O'Connell, Lord Adolphus Fitzclarence, Lord Chesterfield, Mr. and Mrs. Joshua Bates, of the firm of Baring Brothers & Co.," and so on and on. The whirl of London society caught Barnum up, and his triumphs (along with his profits) exceeded all expectations.

Success stimulated Barnum; it did not intoxicate him. He managed to arrange for a successful tour of the British provinces and also to engage in many other ventures. His letters to Moses Kimball testify to a bewildering rate of activity. By the end of July 1844, writing from Norwich, Barnum reported that he had hired a group of bell ringers at an enormous price. But being English was not exotic enough for American audiences. "I have made them 'Swiss,' procured *Swiss dresses*, got out a lithography representing them in *Swiss costume* and have sent the stone by this steamer *directed to you*." Neither Kimball nor himself could drop a hint about the business, Barnum warned, for "the public are to suppose the 'Ringers' go to America *on their own hook*, and *you* must help us to prepare the public by means of lithograph." Barnum hoped for a furor "equal to the *Ole Bull* excitement" and advised Kimball to open the ringers in New York and then go on to Philadelphia, Baltimore, and Boston. He had a heavy investment in them, having advanced them their passage money and over three hundred dollars besides. "If *I* was in America," Barnum added longingly, "I would make a fortune on them."[5]

There was more to come. Besides the "Swiss" bell ringers (who caused a bit less excitement than Barnum had hoped for), he asked Kimball if he was interested in showing a glassblower he discovered in London and announced he was sending out a state robe that had been worn by Queen Victoria. It was genuine, "true on my honor, so help me God!" and he thought it might make twenty thousand dollars in three years of showing. Barnum further advised Kimball to label the item secondhand wardrobe to avoid paying ruinous duties. "I dare not tell *how* I got it — but I got it honestly and *paid for it*."[6] Tom Thumb was in excellent health, and more important, "don't grow a hair." There were "at least 20 General Tom Thumbs" exhibiting in various parts of England, seeking to capitalize on Barnum's success, but they didn't worry the showman; they only paved "the way for the approach of the 'Conquering Hero.'"

Presumably Barnum's concerns, added to his own, were too much for Kimball to bear, for Barnum was soon sympathizing with a breakdown in his health and hoping that a vacation would help. The Boston Museum was taking in more than six hundred dollars a week, and that was cheering. "As for my own part," the irrepressible correspondent wrote, "the more business I have the better I like it. I now have got the Indians under full blast, and what with them, and Tom Thumb, my automaton writer exhibiting at the Adelaide Gallery, the Bell Ringers — Am. Museum and Peales — Giants, dwarf, etc., I guess I have about enough on hand to keep *one* busy."

But this was still not enough to absorb Barnum's energies. He told Kimball that he was thinking seriously of buying out the Adelaide Gallery in London and running it in conjunction with a nephew of George Catlin, the American artist who was exhibiting his Indian paintings in London at just this time. The chances for making it successful seemed good, and Catlin's nephew could send him various novelties from the Adelaide for the American Museum. "Besides he is *at home* with the *press* and could *glorify in advance* anything sent to America."[7] The investment would be only six thousand dollars, with a prospect of clearing twenty thousand dollars. Despite the inducements, Barnum did not after all buy out the Adelaide, but the fact that he even considered the possibility indicates his ability to coordinate a schedule that would have driven many contemporary managers wild and yet remain alert to novelty and expansion.

Not every foreign speculation was successful, of course. Still in England in 1846, Barnum announced he would be showing an "animal" at the Egyptian Hall, allowing "the sagacious public to decide" whether it was human or not, which he called the "What Is It?" He feared he would be found out in the matter, and in fact it proved "*rayther* too big a pill for John Bull to swallow." "Still," Barnum added contentedly, "he has a most capacious throat and stomach!"[8]

With Tom Thumb's tour successfully launched and audiences continuing to appear, Barnum made a brief trip back to America, successfully browbeating the museum building's owner, Olmsted, into giving him a new lease (Barnum threatened to move to another place) and gathering his own family up for a return to England. Back in Britain he found that Tom Thumb was doing better outside of London than in the metropolis. (In Dublin, for example, he took in thirteen hundred dollars in one day, and the following day receipts were three hundred and twenty dollars for only two hours of showing.) The impatient Strattons, however, were insisting on a new contract, and after January 1, 1845, instead of Tom Thumb working for salary, the profits were divided between the Stratton family and Barnum. The first month under this arrangement, Barnum reported, his profits were averaging eight hundred dollars a week, and he was counting on clearing twenty-five thousand dollars annually. "You may well say it is a 'fairy business,'" Barnum exclaimed. "The Strattons are crazy," he went on, "absolutely deranged with such golden success. At first they were inclined to take airs, carry high heads, and talk about what *we* were doing but when Mrs. Stratton began to be too inquisitive about the *business* and to say that *she* thought expenses were too high and that I spent too much for printing etc. I told them both *very decidedly* that *I* was the *manager* and that unless the *whole* was left to my direction I would not stay a single day." The Strattons thereupon retreated and were down to "their *old level*," Barnum told Kimball. Barnum's affection for the family did not, of course, increase. "I can do business with blockheads and brutes when there is money enough to be made by it, but I can't be tempted by money to associate with them, nor allow them to rule," he concluded.[9] Naturally, none of these differences ever penetrated the pages of the autobiography, only the overwhelming success of the European tours.

And the success was indeed incredible. Barnum made plans for a conquest of the Continent and went to Paris to begin his arrangements. He met the great French conjurer Robert-Houdin and purchased an automaton from him. On a second trip his business was even more successful. The French government taxed the exhibition of natural curiosities at twenty-five percent of their gross receipts. Even though the tax went to support municipal hospitals, Barnum thought the imposition unfair because theaters paid a tax of only eleven percent. He decided to compromise. Visiting the license bureau he dazzled the chief with an offer of two thousand francs for a two-months' license. Whatever the size of his audiences, this would be Barnum's total payment. The official was convinced Barnum's "dwarf" would never draw and thought he would come out ahead by paying one quarter of the receipts to the hospitals from his own pocket and keeping the two thousand francs for himself. Like most bureaucrats who dealt with Barnum, he was destined to be disappointed; Barnum, in fact, never paid the tax, for he succeeded in getting Tom Thumb's appearances classified as "theatrical" entertainment and so subject to the lower tax.

In Paris Barnum followed the pattern that had proven successful in London, except that with the court contacts he had already obtained, he could telescope the whole procedure. On the day after his arrival, even before Tom Thumb began his exhibitions, Barnum received a command to appear at the Tuileries before King Louis Philippe, his queen, and other members of the royal family and the French court. The visit went so well that Louis Philippe presented Tom Thumb with an emerald brooch and agreed to Barnum's request that Tom Thumb's tiny carriage be permitted to drive at the Longchamps display in the section reserved for the court and diplomatic corps. This, along with the court visit, gave "Général Tom Pouce" all the publicity Barnum wished and ensured tremendous houses.

Even before the opening "all Paris knew that General Tom Thumb was in the city," wrote Barnum. "The French are exceedingly impressible; and what in London is only excitement, in Paris becomes furor." Statuettes, songs, paintings, and lithographs kept Tom Thumb before the public. The receipts grew so large that Barnum was forced to hire a cab to take his "bag of silver home at night." Father Stratton was making more than five hundred dollars a week as his share, and Barnum told Kimball that "Bridgeport will be quite too small to hold him on our return, and as for his wife, she will look upon New York or Boston as dirty villages, quite beneath her notice." A French play, *Le Petit Poucet,* was written especially for Tom Thumb, and he appeared in it nightly, in addition to his "levees" during the day, when he donned his many costumes and did his impersonations. Three more visits to the royal family followed, two at the Tuileries and one at St. Cloud, where Tom Thumb did his imitation of Napoleon by special request. Barnum was again elated at having so many of the "elite" and "aristocracy" patronize his entertainment and buoyed also by French displays of support in the current Anglo-American diplomatic disputes. "The French are ready to join America if a war should take place," he told Kimball.

The Parisian triumphs behind him, Barnum left, in the summer of 1845, for a tour of the provinces. Rouen, Orléans, Nantes, Bordeaux, Toulon, Nîmes, Marseille, all got a glimpse of the general, who was carried on the French highways by a three-vehicle retinue "in grander style than a field marshal," providing free publicity wherever it went. Along the way Barnum battled with municipal officials and theater managers about the tax laws, invariably coming off best. In Bordeaux the manager claimed fifteen percent and the hospital another twenty percent of gross receipts. So, Barnum wrote Kimball, "I have given them a touch of *Yankee.*" In the middle of the city of Bordeaux stood the independent village of Vincennes, with its own mayor. "I have therefore arranged to exhibit the General in a magnificent saloon in *Vincennes,*" wrote Barnum, "where I pay the Hospice ten francs per day, and as there is no *theater* in that commune, I don't pay a d—d sou for the Theater!" Because of their refusal to compromise, the theater managers and hospitals of Bordeaux got nothing. The lesson, Barnum wrote in his autobiography was "not to attempt to offset French Shylockism against Yankee shrewdness." "I'll raise hell here for ten or twelve days and no mistake," Barnum wrote again, in the privacy of his correspondence. "There's plenty of money here and I'll get a good bit of it." And the vineyards made "a man's mouth water," fifty- and one-hundred-acre spreads "all loaded with grapes."[10] Barnum had not yet become a temperance lecturer.

In France, Barnum exploited another incident. When the entourage was attacked by bandits and robbed, Barnum quickly spread the rumor that Tom Thumb had been kidnapped and was being held for an enormous ransom. Actually, the bandits were captured and Tom Thumb was entirely safe, but the story added to public excitement and increased interest both in France and in Belgium, which was Barnum's next stop. In Brussels Barnum picked up some Waterloo "relics" for speculation.

The Strattons provided continuing amusement, and Barnum recounted some of their adventures in the dozens of articles he was writing for the *New York Atlas*. In Belgium Sherwood Stratton said he was surprised to hear Dutch spoken; he never knew that the Dutch traveled so far from home. "I asked him where he supposed their 'home' was. He said — '*in the western part of the state of New York!*' Wasn't that rich?"[11]

And then it was back to England for stands of several weeks in London and long tours of the provinces. Albert Smith, a British showman, wrote *Hop-o'-my-Thumb* for the general to play in, and this proved as popular as the French play.

During the years 1844–1847, when Tom Thumb was in Europe, Barnum made frequent trips back and forth across the Atlantic, purchasing and selling museums and museum collections in various cities, making certain that the American Museum was maintaining its own flow of profits, gathering new exhibits, and investing his considerable fortune. The strain occasionally got to him. In August 1846, he wrote Kimball from Brighton about some business matters and then briefly philosophized, with some uncharacteristic pessimism: "Oh Moses this is a d—d mean world and fortunate is he who can succeed in extracting honey from such a flower whose root and every petal is bitterness. And yet *we* belong to this same d—d mean world, and are ourselves made of much the same material as all the rest, viz. *selfishness, selfishness, selfishness. I* plead guilty to this general crime and can only give as my excuse that it is a part of *human nature.*"[12] Normally Barnum did not permit such thoughts to bother him, but he had moved so fast in the previous four years that he sometimes brooded about what his success actually meant. He was tired of traveling, he wrote Kimball in October, and wished he "could be contented, and stop this roving life."[13] But whatever the spiritual cost, Barnum's wealth and international position were beginning to produce an almost universal recognition of his talent. He was able to catalog "almost everybody who was anybody" among his acquaintances, and by the time he returned home for good, in early 1847, he found audiences as interested in seeing him as they were excited by his exhibits.

At this time also, Barnum began to think of settling down and acquiring the possessions which befitted a man of his wealth and success. After some thought he decided upon Bridgeport, Connecticut, as a permanent residence, attracted by its convenient location and scenic setting on Long Island Sound. Ordinary housing, of course, suited neither Barnum's zest for magnificence nor his sense of advertising. There was no reason why his style of living could not feed his reputation for uniqueness and so aid the enterprises he managed. While traveling in England he had been impressed by the oriental magnificence of the royal pavilion at Brighton, built by the prince regent, later George IV. He determined in 1846 to build an American version and commissioned drawings. Work began on a seventeen-acre site in Bridgeport while he was still in Europe, and it continued until the housewarming in November 1848.

Iranistan, as the new home was called ("Eastern Country Place" was Barnum's definition), immediately became one of the sights of New England, a fantastic multiturreted oriental palace surrounded by gardens and fountains, filled with rosewood, marble, velvet, and lace.[14] Its Middle Eastern opulence astonished eyes used to the severities of Georgian homes or the restrained asymmetry of Italianate villas. The minareted pleasure dome was immediately reproduced on Barnum's stationery and provided him with what he hoped for: a standing testimonial to stylish extravagance, a foretaste of the thrills that awaited paying visitors to his entertainments. The advertising possibilities also justified the great expense — more than one hundred and fifty thousand dollars — and Barnum rationalized his own desires for personal opulence, for the gold and silver and silk that he loved to surround himself with, by emphasizing their box-office return. How different was all this visual and tactile sensuousness from the colorless austerity of his Bethel boyhood! Barnum was still in his thirties when building Iranistan, and his appetite for glitter was at its most intense. Architects and landscape gardeners criticized the inappropriateness of the display, but American visitors found it all a tribute to art and beauty, made more, not less, effective by its profusion and redundancies.

The quest for respectability and position that ownership of a great house aided was further evidenced by changes in the American Museum's management. Through the late 1840s the museum was visited primarily for its increasing collection of curiosities, along with the variety shows presented in its lecture room. Tom Thumb's carriage and his royal presents; Calvin Edson, the thin man; a moving diorama of Napoleon's funeral; giants, monkeys, crocodiles, burlesque operas, all dominated the institution until about 1849. The advertisements continued their lurid way. "Major Littlefinger," a midget even smaller than Tom Thumb, "holds the same relation to the Lilliputians that the little finger does to the thumb," swore Barnum. Baby shows with swarms of anxious and quarreling mothers competing for prizes alternated with special scoops like Colonel Fremont's woolly horse, still another fiction created by Barnum in the spring of 1849, which was extremely profitable.[15] At periods his reciepts averaged well over two thousand dollars a week.

But Barnum was also growing more involved with the legitimate theater. In February 1848, he wrote Kimball asking if he thought *The Drunkard*, one of the great melodramas of the Jacksonian era, would do well in New York and inquiring about the number of characters in it. In the same letter Barnum seemed to indicate some desire for a change of emphasis. He was training John Greenwood to handle the daily management of the museum and complained about the publicity he was still receiving because of the Fejee Mermaid. "I get all the curses for humbugging the public with the critter."[16]

By 1849, with a new ten-year lease on the museum and plans for enlarging the lecture room, Barnum was able to move. Engaging F. C. Wemyss, an English-born theater manager who had operated theaters in Philadelphia, Pittsburgh, and Baltimore, to manage the lecture room, Barnum witnessed its transformation into a theater and stock company. Novelties, comedians, and curiosities like the English Druids, the Hoosier Giant, and the Mammoth Lady, still entertained the crowds, but only on certain days. At night, and for selected matinee performances, the new company put on melodramas like *The Drunkard*, which achieved the first uninterrupted one-hundred-performance run in New York. By October 7, 1850, *The Drunkard* had reached one hundred and fifty performances, and the "Swiss" bell ringers were reduced to performing between acts. C. W. Clarke, the actor, was cast in the role of "the Drunkard" so often that he became known as "Drunkard" Clarke; others who would appear in the company included T. H. Hadaway, Emily Mestayer, and Harry Watkins, all distinguished American actors and actresses. Clarke himself would take over the museum's amusements for a time, to be followed by Harry Watkins in 1856.

The American Museum performed as its staple fare melodramas like *The Soldier's Daughter*, *Charlotte Temple*, *Passion and Repentance*, and *Rosina Meadows*, farces of high excitement with robberies, rescues, and seductions; honest virtue eventually triumphed over many challenges. In 1853 H. J.

Conway's adaptation of *Uncle Tom's Cabin* played in the American Museum, directed by C. W. Clarke. Unlike the novel, this version had a happy ending; tragedy was never emphasized at the American Museum.

When, during the financial depression of the fifties, Barnum was having trouble filling his seats and began to turn once again to freaks and sensations, Harry Watkins promised to write plays that would draw the public to the house. *The Pioneer Patriot*, Watkins's version of a *New York Ledger* story did just that, and Barnum urged more adaptations on Watkins. The showman, as always, was careful with his money. When Watkins asked for payment for the plays, Barnum was astonished. He thought, wrote Watkins, "he had a good thing in me, getting the work of three men for the salary of one. As the play had to be written in one week, he proposed to leave me out of the bill for that week, and to consider my labor as author equivalent for not acting." When Watkins persisted, Barnum grandly offered an additional twenty-five dollars for his trouble. "His *liberality*, however, instead of developing my gratitude, excited my indignation," Watkins continued, "and I gave the 'Great Showman' my opinion of his offer." Watkins hunted up a playwright who would furnish the play for forty dollars. "It was an evil day when I put my pen to paper," Watkins concluded, for he had converted friendly employers into enemies.[17] But if Barnum thought forty dollars was full value for a dramatist's labors he was "ignorant of the difference between muscle and brains." The smiling, affable, and optimistic face Barnum displayed for the world covered a shrewd and tight-fisted bargainer, lavish with funds only when he was certain of a profitable return, anxious when his profits dipped, and committed to no brand of entertainment, only to success.

Despite the lean years of the late 1850s, for almost two decades the American Museum offered a generation of New Yorkers (whose ranks included the young Henry James) a rich and heady sampling of American melodrama, exciting and didactic at the same time. Occasionally the melodramas were leavened by scriptural dramas like *Joseph and His Brethren*, "interlarded with farce to extort laughter from the clownish 'barren spectators and groundlings,'" wrote one English visitor, Walter Thornbury. Barnum's object in this "sort of mystery play, with its garbled text and vulgar perversions of Scripture," Thornbury went on, "is to catch the quiet country people — the simple New Hampshire farmers, the Connecticut pedlars [*sic*], and the Boston persuasionists, who have the old puritanical horror of the ordinary theatrical performance." These visitors, caught by the "scriptural piece" sound, paid their extra quarter "without offending public opinion at home."[18]

Barnum's foray into legitimate theater, while it undoubtedly raised the reputation of the museum and gave the showman éclat by association, also provoked criticism from admirers of the theater. William K. Northall wrote, in 1851, just as Barnum was stabilizing his stock company, that he should abandon his hypocrisy and disguises about acting: "If the stage be distasteful, in his judgment, to the habits and morals of the audiences who visit his establishment, why not eschew them altogether, not wheedle the public into his trap, and thus oblige them to patch up their damaged consciences with the paltry excuse that it was the museum and not the play they went to see?" asked Northall. The habit of calling each force a moral affair he termed a "miserable trick." There was not a theater in New York that did not teach morality as pure as the museum's. It was fine for Barnum to be temperate, "but we do object that he should be continually thrusting this solitary virtue of sobriety under our noses, and insist upon us, who were never intoxicated, submitting to the same bondage of security as himself. . . . Theatres and museums were never intended to be schools of ethics. . . . The stage, to be respected, must be careful not to offend good manners or violate the moral principles which govern every well regulated community; but they have no more to do with the promulgation of ethical doctrines than they have with the teaching of astronomy."[19]

Northall's critique would be elaborated in years to come by

others who found Barnum's moral claims exaggerated and dangerous to the artist's independence. Not a play or performer could come under Barnum's sponsorship without moral purposes being proclaimed. The American Museum itself sanitized the surroundings in which the plays were produced — no liquor was sold on the premises, no prostitutes crowded its galleries — but Northall's examination of its pretensions to greater morality was justified. Despite his development of one of the city's best repertory companies Barnum never took up the cudgels for an independent theater or defended it as such against the attacks of the censorious. His museum itself, his exhibits and his circus, he was always willing to protect; but the "lecture room" retained its title until the American Museum finally was destroyed in 1868.

Barnum's search for respectability was well served by the Tom Thumb tours and his popular repertory company. He had demonstrated his versatility by pleasing audiences on both sides of the Atlantic, knowing how and when to vary his publicity techniques and exhibits. The operational aesthetic was only one of many methods of capturing popular interest. It worked better in America than it did abroad, as Barnum's experience with the "What Is It?" in England proved. The showman possessed an amazing talent for adaptability. As he moved from audience to audience he sensed their changing requirements. Subtle differences marked Tom Thumb's American appearances, with their emphasis on innocent brashness, from the mock heroics and caricatures of his European shows and his condescension to the wealthy and noble.

Tom Thumb, however, was simply a curiosity, and the repertory theater concentrated on melodramas. They were both far from traditional high culture. For an entertainment entrepreneur, interested in profit and respectability and anxious to avoid challenging the community's moral code, music offered great possibilities. Concert artists symbolized the best that European culture had to offer, and recitals could be attended without fear of recrimination. And it was here, ironically enough, in the cultivated realm of fine art, and not in his museum or his Tom Thumb tours, that Barnum made his fattest profits. In September 1850, when the Swedish Nightingale, Jenny Lind, gave her first American concert at Castle Garden, there began an unprecedented conquest of the American public, and Barnum became a household name. But it was not managed without adroit planning.

FIVE

The Swedish Nightingale

BARNUM GOT THE IDEA of bringing Jenny Lind to America in October 1849. Describing his decision in the autobiography, he emphasized its boldness. "It was an enterprise," he reminisced, "never before or since equalled in managerial annals. As I recall it now, I almost tremble at the seeming temerity of the attempt. . . . I risked much but I made more."

The boldness may perhaps have been overemphasized, for he was certainly not the first to bring over a great artist. During the 1840s a procession of European performers made their way across the Atlantic. In 1840 Stephen Price brought over the Viennese dancer Fanny Elssler, whose success Barnum had noted in New Orleans. She had a triumphal two-year stay, her artistry complemented by a powerful sex appeal.[1] Elssler shoes, stockings, garters, fans, cigars, shaving soap, bootjacks and bread were displayed by the shops. One critic termed the enthusiasm she provoked "elsslermaniaphobia." In her one hundred and ninety-nine performances throughout the country she earned a fortune. In Boston she received five hundred dollars a night from the manager of the Tremont Theater, but she brought in more than triple that amount at the box office some evenings. Fanny Elssler was followed in the next few years by Ole Bull, the Norwegian violinist, the pianists Leopold de Meyer and Henri Herz, and the tenor, Manuel García, whose daughter, María Malibran, became one of the world's great sopranos.[2] None of these artists matched Fanny Elssler's success, but they indicated how rapidly knowledge of the rich American market was spreading in Europe.

Not even Fanny Elssler could equal Jenny Lind. In arranging for her trip (without ever having heard her sing) Barnum knew he was displaying more than a mere singer: Jenny Lind's life story was made to order for American adulation. Her biography could have been written by Samuel Smiles (or Horatio Alger) and subtitled: "A Struggle Against Difficulties."[3] She had been born in Stockholm in 1820; her mother, a divorcée, refused to marry Nikla Lind, who had fathered Jenny. Her childhood was passed in a series of households, complicated by her mother's angry moods and bad temper. But her love for song attracted passersby, and one day the singing of the little girl of nine was heard by a dancer at the Royal Opera House who brought Jenny to officials at the Royal Theater School. So anxious were the teachers to enroll the girl that they offered funds to board her. Finally overcoming her mother's fear of the perils and temptations of theatrical life, Jenny entered the Swedish Royal Theater School in 1830, the youngest student it had ever accepted. During the next few years she learned acting and dancing skills, along with voice training. And she began to appear on the stage of the Royal Theater, singing a wide range of parts. In 1837 she sang her first leading role in opera, Agatha in *Der Freischütz*, and caused a sensation. Within two years she was appointed court singer by the king of Sweden and made a member of the Swedish Royal Academy.

The early successes proved deceptive. Still only twenty, the intensive singing and training of the previous years began to affect her voice. In Paris Manuel García, the greatest voice teacher in Europe, told Jenny that she had no voice left and advised her to return to Sweden. Only one chance remained, said García, and that was total rest for six weeks and another try. When Jenny returned, García found the voice stronger, and consented to give her lessons. It meant starting out again, working very hard on the fundamentals of breathing and scales, surrounded by a city she neither liked nor admired. But a year's study with García helped bring back her voice, and she returned to Stockholm in 1842, to star in Bellini's *Norma* at the Royal Theater and earn a wild ovation from the audience. Jenny was now a national treasure; her acquaintance with Scandinavian artists and writers like Fredrika Bremer, the novelist, and Hans Christian Andersen broadened her musical insight and her reputation. Andersen, in fact, wooed Jenny Lind with fairy tales such as "The Snow Queen" and "The Ugly Duckling" and frequently proposed marriage. Despite these proposals, and others, Jenny remained unmarried and unsure of her ability. Audiences frightened her, and until 1844 she confined her singing to Scandinavia.

In 1844 she became known to a larger public. Giacomo Meyerbeer had heard Jenny sing in Paris while she was studying with García; despite an uneven performance he had been impressed with her voice. He wanted Jenny to premiere his new opera, *Camp in Silesia*, which was to be the opening production for the new Berlin Opera House. Although this meant she would have to learn German and face a foreign audience in one of Europe's musical capitals, Jenny accepted the proposal. Before she could appear, however, another soprano claimed a prior right to appear in the role. Instead of opening in Meyerbeer's work, Jenny Lind appeared in *Norma* on December 15, 1844. This was her introduction to the non-Scandinavian musical world. The Berlin audience was stunned by her voice and forced her to repeat certain passages before it would permit the opera to continue. Command performances at court, gifts from Prussian royalty, and a contract with the Prussian Royal Opera followed very quickly.

The next half-dozen years were filled with unprecedented triumphs. Operas and concert halls were not large enough to hold the crowds that demanded entry. In university towns students crowned her with laurel and unhitched the horses from her carriage that they might draw it themselves. Princes and empresses waited on her. Along with her musical reputation, Jenny Lind's charities and evident modesty enabled opera lovers to applaud a heroine whose spotless private life entitled her to unambiguous loyalty. Contemporary composers, most particularly Felix Mendelssohn, idolized her and wrote some of their most memorable music for her to sing. Clara Schumann insisted that Jenny Lind was "the warmest, noblest being" she had ever encountered among artists.[4] In Leipzig, in Vienna, Frankfort, and Hanover, her sensations were as great as they had been in Copenhagen and Stockholm.

The excitement created on the Continent was mild compared to what happened in London. After several years of complex negotiations, complicated by contractual disputes and Jenny's fears of displeasing British audiences, she opened in the Italian version of Meyerbeer's *Robert de Normandie*. Even before she appeared at Her Majesty's Theatre, May 4, 1847, the crowd was in an uproar; the delays in arranging her London premiere had intensified public excitement, and the mob scene on opening night was unprecedented. Some of the spectators were thrown off their feet. The audience included Queen Victoria and Prince Albert, Mendelssohn, George Grote, Fanny Kemble, and many other notables. At the end the queen dropped at Jenny's feet a bouquet presented to herself, and the audience went wild. Jenny Lind had become and would remain the greatest musical sensation of the nineteenth century. So universal was British enthusiasm that it soon became satirized in magazines and newspapers. Dances, dogs, children, china, cigars, flowers, and fruits were named after her; bishops, peers, and statesmen sought her acquaintance; the queen loaded her with gifts.

Although Jenny's modesty and deportment added to her attractiveness, her primary appeal, to connoisseurs and the masses alike, was her voice. A few, like Carlyle and Thackeray, found it disappointing, and others criticized her musical taste, but there was overwhelming agreement that her high register was superb, demonstrating an ability to produce beautiful tones, at any volume, without forcing. She could manage vocal crescendos and decrescendos better than any singer alive, and her overall technique was unparalleled. The years of discipline and training enabled her to control not only the sounds she produced but the words themselves. What was most impressive, this technical mastery did not obscure her ability to create an atmosphere of emotional intensity, normally one of pathos and sweetness, which invariably elicited tears and raptures from her audiences. The early association of her talents with Nature rather than Art; the sobriquet "Swedish Nightingale," which the English applied; the frequency with which "warblings" were applied as a description of her singing, revealed the conviction that technique itself had been absorbed by some magical process and subordinated to overall artistic effect. Her performances seemed natural rather than artificial, the spontaneous expressions of a great talent.

Along with the concert and opera performances came benefits for hospitals and orphanages and a deepening preoccupation with piety and religion. It was ironic that Jenny's engagement to an Englishman, Claudius Harris, broke up because his family insisted that she pledge never again to sing on a stage. Jenny had already decided to abandon opera entirely but she would not accept preconditions for marriage. On May 10, 1849, she gave her last operatic performance, singing in *Roberto il Diablo*; many in the audience wept.

Such, then, was the performer whom Barnum intended to bring to America. She had already caused a sensation wherever she sang in Europe, without the aid of any of the devices normally employed to publicize his exhibits. Barnum's first problem, though, was to attract the singer, for she was already contemplating permanent retirement. His solution was to make his financial offer so enticing that it would be difficult for Jenny to refuse. The profits would enable her to settle huge sums on her favorite charities. As his agent Barnum sent over an English musician he had employed in America, John Hall Wilton, and he gave Wilton a variety of offers to make. After considerable difficulty Wilton managed to see Jenny in Lübeck. Barnum's top offer was a guarantee of one hundred and fifty thousand dollars for one hundred and fifty concerts, in addition to paying salaries and expenses for Jenny's companion, a secretary, an orchestra director, and a male singer. Barnum hoped he would be able to get away for less, but Jenny Lind did not sell herself cheaply. She insisted that the conductor had to be Julius Benedict, and his fee was five thousand pounds; the male singer, a baritone, Giovanni Belletti, would receive half that amount. Jenny also would require travel and hotel expenses for herself, a companion, a secretary and a maid, along with a manservant and carriage in every city she visited. Finally, Barnum was to deposit with a bank the total for the salaries and expenses of the entire group before it would leave Europe. The amount came to one hundred and eighty-seven thousand five hundred dollars — in present-day figures, something between one and two million dollars — which Barnum somehow had to raise.

When Barnum realized the true scope of his arrangements even he took pause. Jenny Lind made the agreement in early January 1850, and Barnum learned of it February 19, 1850. He raised the money he had to deposit in Baring Brothers' Bank only by converting everything he owned to cash, taking out mortgages on all his property, and finally relying on a personal loan from a friend. The fact that he could meet the demands indicates how profitable the museum had been, for this was the product of only an eight-year career. Everything he possessed rested on the venture's success, but Barnum was convinced that he could manage it.

In the beginning, however, Barnum met one memorable discouragement that has been repeated in every account of the Jenny Lind tour. On his way to meet Wilton in New York to learn the details of the agreement, Barnum discovered that the newspapers had somehow gotten hold of the story, so he mentioned to the train conductor that Jenny Lind would be visiting America in August. The conductor's response was devastating. "Jenny Lind! Is she a dancer?" His words, said Barnum, "were ice. Really, thought I, if this is all that a man in the capacity of a railroad conductor between Philadelphia and New York knows of the greatest songstress in the world, I am not sure that six months will be too long a time for me to occupy in enlightening the public in regard to her merits." Most studies of the Lind tour relate the anecdote, as Barnum did, to demonstrate American ignorance of the singer and to justify the great publicity efforts Barnum made to safeguard his investment.

Actually, Americans were probably not quite so ignorant. European managers had been able to make a sensation of Jenny Lind without recourse to the techniques Barnum employed. Max Maretzek, an opera manager whose Italian Opera House in New York underwent the difficult task of competing with the Swedish soprano, wrote bitterly that the anecdote revealed Barnum's lack of faith in American taste and discrimination. Jenny Lind's real artistry was not enough for Barnum. "Blind by nature to every consideration of this character, he took the knowledge of a rail-road conductor as his best authority in musical matters, and came to the conclusion that, as an artist, the fair Swede would be at the best a very uncertain speculation." Barnum, Maretzek went on, therefore determined to work upon the singer "*as a curiosity*," it being "a matter of the most perfect indifference to him" whether she produced enthusiasm for her music or excitement for her character. Reputation "was manufactured for her, by wholesale. It was not merely made by the inch, but was prepared by the cart-load."[5]

Maretzek's was the reaction of a rival impresario whose own efforts to improve American musical taste were overshadowed by Barnum's immense success, but it is undeniable that Barnum launched an unprecedented press campaign to acquaint the American public with the virtues of Jenny Lind. Her current concertizing in Europe, which was producing its usual quota of sensation, made excellent material for the letters published by New York newspapers and copied in every part of the country. Biographies were prepared and distributed, emphasizing Jenny's piety, her character, her interest in philanthropy and good works. In the last eight months, Barnum noted in his letter to the newspapers announcing the engagement (and including the details of the contract), Jenny Lind had been singing almost entirely for charity, and she was founding a benevolent institution in Stockholm at a cost of three hundred and fifty thousand dollars. "A visit from such a woman," he concluded, "who regards her high artistic powers as a gift from Heaven, for the amelioration of affliction and distress, and whose every thought and deed is philanthropy, I feel persuaded, will prove a blessing to America." Jenny's genius alone, ran a pamphlet distributed before her appearance, was not the basis of her superiority. "It is her intrinsic worth of heart and delicacy of mind; it is her pure and intense feelings that abide her potency. . . . A great and noble simplicity, combined with an ardent imagination."[6] There may have been a time when "actors and actresses, in the eye of the law, were mere vagrants." But Jenny Lind had changed all that.

Thus, Barnum was presenting not simply a great artist but a friend to humanity; he shrewdly surmised that Americans, with little popular knowledge of the kind of music Jenny usually performed, would be more attracted by her moral virtues than by her musicianship. The publicity campaign was topped off by Barnum's disclosure (made of his usual whole cloth) that Jenny had expressed a wish to give a welcome to America in a song written for the occasion. Her conductor and accompanist, Julius Benedict, offered to write the music (Benedict found this out after he had landed in New York). Barnum gathered a committee of judges that included several American editors and publishers, along with Benedict himself. By September 1, one week after the announcement, more than seven hundred poems had been submitted.

Jenny's departure from England had all the excitement of a royal tour, tinged with the sadness of leave-taking. Thousands gathered on the Liverpool docks to see her off, and as the S.S. *Atlantic* made her way from the harbor, salutes and cheers broke out from the crowds. Somewhat depressed and discouraged by the task that awaited her, Jenny had second thoughts during the voyage and for a time thought of returning home by the first ship. But her confidence returned, to be bolstered by one of the most tremendous welcomes in the history of New York, orchestrated carefully by Barnum himself. The *Atlantic* arrived in New York on a Sunday. Barnum met the ship at quarantine and presented Jenny with an enormous bouquet. Steaming through New York Harbor, the *Atlantic* docked at a Canal Street pier covered and surrounded by tens of thousands. "The wildest enthusiasm prevailed as the steamer approached the dock," Barnum remembered fondly, people falling overboard in their zeal to catch a glimpse of Jenny. Flags and triumphal arches awaited her on the wharf, and Jenny's carriage could barely make its way through the crowds that threw bouquets through the windows. Barnum estimated, or overestimated, that some twenty thousand people gathered around the Broadway entrance to the Irving House, the hotel he had engaged for Jenny. They stayed there for hours, the Musical Fund Society coming to serenade her during the night. Barnum led Jenny to a balcony to receive the cheers of the crowd below.

All of this extraordinary enthusiasm, of course, had developed before Jenny had sung a note in America. In a sense the musical performances, tumultuously received as they were, formed only an anticlimax. The outpouring of public sentiment was, under Barnum's gentle prodding, a tribute to an ideal, designed to reflect credit not only on the object of veneration but the venerators themselves. The spectacle of a proud republic voluntarily paying homage to a young woman (Jenny was already thirty but invariably described by Americans as a young girl) of great artistry demonstrated that the finer values, which Europeans had insisted were swamped by money-getting and chicanery, still ruled the New World. The popularity of Jenny Lind showed clearly, said a letter writer to the *New York Tribune*, that "this great people, so intent on acquisition, so bewildered at times by the rapidity of their own progress, have not forfeited the capacity of appreciating excellence in a new form, and on such a scale as the world has never before seen."[7]

The London *Times* also caught the note of self-congratulation. "There is always a certain relationship between the worshippers and the worshipped," it said, "and the most entranced homage will occasionally betray the contemplation of self."

New York's prostrate thousands "cannot help being proud of their city, of their visitor, of themselves, and of their singular good taste."[8] Barnum contrived to make the great soprano's success a test of Americanism itself, just as the tributes to Lafayette and Kossuth, on their earlier visits, testified to the grandeur of republican feeling. These audiences were not the petted aristocracies of petty European courts, but free men, proud of their independence.

Some reviewers, like Nathaniel Parker Willis, fancied that Jenny Lind herself appreciated these ecstatic tributes, however unbridled their energy. "Queens may have given her lapdogs," he wrote, "and Kings may have clasped bracelets on her plump arms, but she will prize more the admiration *for the whole of her*, felt here by a *whole people*."[9] In England, said Willis, who had seen Jenny perform there, "when the Queen was present, it seemed to me that Jenny wished to convey, in her manner of acknowledging the applause for her performance of La Sonnambula, that her profession was distasteful to her." She showed great reserve in her manner. In America, however, she was enthusiastic in her reception of mass adulation. She could tell the difference between the tributes of democrats and the fawnings of potentates. The sudden new passion for opera music in America revealed the national genius. Such a thing could never have happened in England: "The hardened crusts between the different strata of society, would never let a taste pass, with this marvelous facility, from one class to another. It is a proof of the slightness of separation between the upper and middle classes of our country — of the ease with which the privileges of a higher class pass to the use of the class nominally below — and marks how essentially, as well as in form and name, this is a land of equality."[10]

The identification of Jenny Lind with democratic sentiments was certainly clarified by the winner of Barnum's poem contest, a young poet named Bayard Taylor who later became a good friend of Barnum's. His piece, "Greeting to America," which formed a part of Jenny's opening concert, was declared the winner of the prize of two hundred dollars on September 5. It included the following verse:

> I greet, with full heart, the Land of the West,
>   Whose Banner of Stars o'er a world is unrolled;
> Whose empire o'ershadows Atlantic's wide breast,
>   And opes to the sunset its gateway of gold!
> The land of the mountain, the land of the lake
>   And rivers that roll in magnificent tide—
> Where the souls of the mighty from slumber awake,
>   And hallow the soil for whose freedom they died!

The poetry contest was too absurd to escape lampooning. William Allen Butler, a lawyer and the son of the attorney general in the cabinets of both Jackson and Van Buren, quickly rushed into print with *Barnum's Parnassus; being Confidential Disclosures of the Prize Committee on the Jenny Lind Song,* which went through three editions. In a series of parodies on the work of Longfellow, Bryant, Holmes and other well-known poets, Butler spoofed Barnum's moneymaking ambitions and publicity techniques. "The Manager and The Nightingale" had Barnum exclaiming:

> I've got the public sympathies; there's not another man
>   Can get up entertainment on my peculiar plan.
> Some folks pronounced it humbug, but that I reckon praise,
>   Because they have to add — how monstrously it pays.
> And the end is still the salvo, tho in the means you've skinned,
>   As sure as my name's Barnum and yours is Jenny Lind.[11]

Nothing daunted, Barnum had copies of the piece distributed and reprinted portions of it in his autobiography.

The first concert was scheduled for the evening of September 11 at Castle Garden, a huge auditorium in New York's Battery. Before the concert a formal contract between the singer and her manager was signed, Barnum making the terms more generous than originally contemplated. Jenny was to receive not only the thousand dollars for each concert but would divide the profits with Barnum after he took fifty-five hundred dollars each night for his charges and expenses. Jenny was also permitted to terminate the contract, at the end of the sixtieth or the one-hundredth concert, provided she paid certain penalties to Barnum.

Barnum, however, could well afford to be generous. It was becoming clear that he had, if anything, underestimated his potential profits. Remembering Fanny Elssler's techniques, Barnum determined to hold an auction for tickets to Jenny's first concert to increase public excitement. The sale, which was held several days before the performance, was later repeated with even greater success in other cities. Barnum also called on several acquaintances, including John N. Genin, a Broadway hatter, and a pill manufacturer, Dr. Brandreth, advising them to bid high for the first ticket since it would be the making of their fortunes. The auction developed its own personality and revealed Barnum to be, in Daniel Boorstin's phrase, the master of the pseudoevent, the planned happening that occurs primarily for the purpose of being reported.[12] Thousands paid a quarter apiece to jam into Castle Garden and watch the spirited bidding. John Genin received the first ticket for the princely sum of two hundred and twenty-five dollars and acquired overnight fame; his business swelled dramatically in the months that followed. Thousands of dollars more were raised at the auction, and the following Monday the rest of the tickets were sold. Barnum listed the receipts for the first concert at seventeen thousand eight hundred and sixty-four dollars, and Jenny's share of the profits for the first two concerts came to more than ten thousand dollars. These figures, which were more than ten times the great amounts that Fanny Elssler had taken in at her most successful appearances, forecast the huge profits that both manager and singer would receive.

The first concert surpassed all expectations. Preparing for the huge audience of five thousand, Barnum had divided the auditorium into four vast sections, each designated by a lamp of a certain color. The tickets were matched by color, and one hundred ushers, with colored rosettes and wands, helped customers find their seats easily. "Thus, tickets, checks, lamps, rosettes, wands, and even the seat numbers were all in the appropriate colors to designate the different departments," Barnum explained. The huge excitement that had been generated had to be channeled before and during the concert if Jenny was to enjoy a success, and Barnum was a master of these details, taking every precaution to ensure a peaceful, orderly evening. The five thousand people preserved, Barnum noted, "as much order and quiet as was ever witnessed in the assembling of a congregation at church," and indeed, the whole presentation took on something of the character of a sacred service. Beginning with a somewhat nervous rendition of the "Casta Diva" from *Norma*, Jenny moved on, interspersed with pieces by Benedict's orchestra and Belletti, to Meyerbeer's trio from *Camp in Silesia*, in which she was accompanied by two flutes, and then to some Scandinavian songs. The concert closed with Bayard Taylor's prize song, set to music by Benedict.

Many descriptions of the first concert have been reprinted from newspapers and periodicals, but one of the most moving can be found in a letter by Thatcher Taylor Payne to his wife Lizzie, describing the events.[13] Payne, like many others, arrived early to take his seat, supplied with plenty of reading material about Jenny to occupy his time. The unprecedented enthusiasm for Jenny, Payne wrote, was based mainly on her high character, and this was good for "it will extend and exalt the musical taste, and it will improve the character of the girls growing into women by showing them that simple graces, independent of beauty, men most widely and most heartily appreciate." Payne reported that the whole population was involved in the Lind tour. His house painter had offered a thousand dollars just to put his hand upon her shoulders "to tell whether the wings had begun to grow. She is an angel — sure." His butcher and market woman were similarly enthusiastic.

Jenny Lind's arrival: two views

THE SECOND DELUGE.
First appearance of Jenny Lind in America

Jenny Lind's admirers: two views

The romantic Jenny Lind

The camera's Jenny Lind

The end of the dream —
Jenny and Otto Goldschmidt, 1852

But the music itself was what most excited Payne. He found Jenny superior to any soprano he had heard, including the great singers Grisi and Alboni. In the *Camp in Silesia* aria, where she imitated the flutes playing with her, her voice was like "no flute blown by mortal breath — it had articulation, meaning, spirit, soul. Here where I expected mechanical tricks she was more than any where sublime." Call it "what you please," said Payne, "call it ventriloquism — give it any mountebank name — I defy the coarsest man or the finest and coldest artist to listen otherwise than with delighted and breathless suspense." By the concert's end, even Barnum was moved. When the audience called for him to appear, he said he wished "to sink into utter insignificance," and when people asked, "Where's Barnum," he added, to make his point more clear, "Henceforth you might say, Barnum's nowhere!"[14]

To top off the whole evening Barnum announced that Jenny had promised to give her share of the concert's profits to charity, and that the sum would amount to ten thousand dollars. The major portion of the gift went to two philanthropies, the Fire Department Fund and the Musical Fund Society, both of which had paraded in Jenny's honor on her first night in New York, with the remainder given to various asylums for orphans and the aged. Jenny followed the custom of donating part of her proceeds to charity in almost every American city she visited.

Public emotion increased rather than abated after her first concert. George Templeton Strong, a New York attorney and music lover whose diary is one of our great commentaries on nineteenth-century culture, followed the enthusiasm with ill-concealed irritation. He admitted the voice was fine and that Jenny was "a good, amiable, benevolent woman." But, he continued, "if the greatest man that had lived for the last ten centuries were here in her place, the uproar and excitement" would probably be less than she had caused. Jenny Lind was "like the good little girl in the fairy story who spat pearls and diamonds out of her mouth whenever she opened it to speak;

only Jane's expectorations are five-dollar bills each syllable." Strong speculated on how much each semiquaver realized for the management. But it was the excitement, the "Lindomania," that most provoked him. Instead "of an epidemic *lycanthropy* like that of the Middle Ages, it's a prevalent morbid passion for assuming the form of an ass and paying six dollars and so on for the privilege of drinking in her most sweet voice through the preternaturally prolonged ears of the deluded victims of this terrible new disorder."[15]

The British press had the most sport with the American mania, reporting every strange detail it could find or invent; Jenny's glove, for example, had been picked up in the street, and the finder was charging other Americans for the opportunity to kiss it; one shilling brought an outside kiss, but an inside went for two shillings.[16] On October 5, 1850, *Punch* ran a breathless article entitled, "Coronation of Jenny the First — Queen of the Americans." Beginning by noting that Jenny's description of the American flag, "the beautiful standard of freedom; the oppressed of all nations worship it," probably reflected her knowledge of the slave trade, the article reported that on the conclusion of her journey Jenny would "be crowned Queen of the United States, the actual President politely retiring. Jenny accepts office under contract always to sing, in so many airs, to the people of the smartest nation upon earth, what has been hitherto printed as President's speeches." Two stars and one stripe were added to the American flag, the stars to represent Jenny's eyes and the stripe, a lock of her hair.[17]

On the more serious side the *Athenaeum* noted that "the genius of hyperbole seems here to have exhausted itself on a negation. . . . We never remember child's play performed before by such a company. The whole thing looks like a vast 'make believe.' "[18] And the London *Times* brooded about future dangers such enthusiasm foretold. "That which can be done by a private adventurer, may with more ease be accomplished by the leader of a faction," it pointed out. Political safety itself was imperiled. "The same arts which make a singer's popularity, may create the political capital of a President or a Secretary. The deliberate substitution of prejudice for reason and experience, may be applied to measures as well as to music." The paper feared that "the same reckless system of exaggeration, the same intense vulgarity of means and littleness of ends," could be found in the United States Senate as well as in the concert hall.[19]

Criticism, however, had little effect on Jenny's progress. Her series of concerts in New York completed, she moved to Boston, Providence, and Philadelphia before returning to the metropolis. Then it was Philadelphia again, Baltimore, Washington, Richmond, Charleston, Havana, New Orleans, and a series of western cities before the return to the East Coast. Everywhere, she received mass adulation and enormous receipts, even hostile or prudent audiences transformed by her singing into energetic partisans. Competitors kept a respectful distance. "I must take care to keep beyond the magic reach of my potent townswoman, Jenny Lind," a Jewish rabbi and historian wrote from New York. "Alas for my poor lectures if they come into collision with her spells. Her notes are quite sure to absorb all the notes that are to be expended for amusement and instruction for one while to come. It will therefore not do to visit any city while she is there, or directly after she has been there."[20]

The soprano's triumphs penetrated even the West Coast. Josiah Flagg wrote from the mining camps of California that local papers were full of Jenny Lind (her portrait embellished his cabin), but the prices paid for first tickets made "even Californians stand back and indeed nobody believes that those who gave so much — *dug* their gold."[21] Flagg was referring to the auction scenes, wilder than the New York excitement, which preceded Jenny's performances. In Boston the auction produced almost twenty thousand dollars, and John Genin's great offer of two hundred and twenty-five dollars was almost tripled by Ossian F. Dodge, a singer, who purchased his seat for six hundred and twenty-five dollars. The price, wrote Charles

Rosenberg, a contemporary chronicler of Jenny's travels, "was but money placed out at interest. Indeed, it was destined to be the seed of a larger and more extensive crop of dollars, to which Dodge himself was to put in the sickle." His subsequent concerts showed Dodge's wisdom, and Rosenberg had little doubt "that he has already paid himself far more than cent per cent for his investment in the Lind ticket."[22] In Providence, on October 5, Colonel William Ross paid six hundred and fifty dollars for his ticket and did not bother even to attend the concert; in Philadelphia it was daguerreotypist Marcus Aurelius Root who parted with six hundred and twenty-five dollars.

Though subsequent auctions were more important for their publicity value than for the size of the bids, the extravagance of purchasers and of the general public, who were parting with hard-earned dollars to attend the concerts, bothered some Americans. In Boston, a rather bitter sequel to *Barnum's Parnassus* appeared, this one (titled *Jenny Lind Mania in Boston*) not mentioned by Barnum, castigating the local citizenry for their weakness and excitability. Asmodeus, the author's pseudonym, pleaded with his fellow Bostonians not to "rush madly to your coffers and scratch from thence your last dollar, and squander it upon Phineas and his ilk. Pause, ere you commit yourselves. Reason with yourself and wife. . . . See that the chalk marks of your milkman and butcher are not twelve feet long on your kitchen doors and walls. . . . Balance your accounts nicely. . . . shun Phineas, otherwise Peter the Humbug."[23] The portrait of Barnum in *Jenny Lind Mania in Boston* had him consorting with the devil, cheating Jenny Lind, and browbeating hotelkeepers to get free rooms. About the same time, an anonymous author in New York published "*Mahomet; or, The Unveiled Prophet of Inistan; A Boquet for Jenny Lind*, which placed the Lindomania in the context of the woolly horse and the mermaid. Barnum was "an insolent, shameless, reckless, ambitious reprobate, whose deeds so vividly, so truthfully attest the residence of his privy counsellor [the devil], and whose glory henceforth can be nought save the well merited scorn and execration of an outraged Christian public."[24]

Barnum's profits were so huge that resentments, hitherto kept under wraps, surfaced in angry diatribes. How could a musically ignorant public, unable to "tell the difference between a crochet and a grindstone, a grand cavatine from the dulcet strains of a barrel organ," as Asmodeus put it, flock in such numbers to a singer unless it had been victimized by a fancy-talking deluder? The whole experience must have been just another humbug.

Actually, of course, there was real admiration of Jenny Lind's artistry, as well as popular affection for her philanthropies. Both of these had operated in Europe to win her acclaim. But there were special reasons in addition to these why she excited so much affection in America (and England). Until Jenny's arrival the world of opera, and of what little concertizing existed in America, had been dominated by Italian singers. None denied the power and passion of these performers, but the floridity and intensity of their voices awakened fears of sensuality among Anglo-Saxons. That the Catholic Mediterranean world had produced these marvels came as no surprise, but the admiration was not unalloyed. "The sons and daughters of song had, until very recently," the *Home Journal* in New York wrote, "seemed, by a prescriptive and inalienable right, to spring from the soil of Italy. The rich and mellow climate of that delicious land had produced them so abundantly, that it was almost at length to be a right attached by nature to its warm and sunny shores."[25] Jenny Lind, however, demonstrated that musical gifts could exist anywhere, even in the "frozen" North. Her appearance was almost a paradigm of American contentions that artistic genius could not indefinitely be confined to the Old World, but must inevitably flower in the New, wherever Nature had planted it.

Indeed, it seemed that the Mediterranean had had its day. John Sullivan Dwight, America's foremost music critic, who came down from Boston to review Jenny's first concert, observed that it was too late "to await the advent of a Queen of Song from the warm South." The mission had been fulfilled and "the other end of the balance now comes up. The Northern Muse must sing her lesson to the world. Her fresher, chaster, more intellectual" strains would redeem men's souls "from the delicious languor of a music which has been so wholly of the feelings, that, for the want of some intellectual tonic, and some spiritual temper, feeling has generated into mere sensibility, and a very cheap kind of superficial, skin-deep excitability that usurps the name of passion."[26] However he reverenced Italy's "native gift of song," Italy had not the genius to produce such a "new revelation of song as this human nightingale or canary of Sweden." The *Musical World*, comparing Jenny's *Norma* with that of the great Italian star, Giulia Grisi, made similar judgments. Grisi was indeed great, but Jenny was "more truthful and touching." With "the fair Swede, we perceive the breaking up of the frozen lake, and its loosened waters; with the dark Italian, we tremble at the overflowing of the burning lava." We are "awe-stricken and oppressed by Grisi; we are softened into womanish tears by Lind."[27]

These observations were amplified by the comments of Henry T. Tuckerman, American essayist and biographer, in his sketch of Jenny Lind. He placed the soprano within the context of a cultural renaissance in "The Life of the North," a part of the flowering that produced Swedenborg, Linnaeus, Thorvaldsen, Ole Bull, Fredrika Bremer, Hans Christian Andersen, and Oehlenschläger's dramas. Through this creative surge "the simple, earnest, and poetic features of life in the North were brought within the range of our consciousness. It developed unimagined affinities with our own; and, as it were, to complete and consecrate the revelation, we heard the vocal genius of Northern Europe — the Swedish nightingale, Jenny Lind." Her success in England, Tuckerman went on, was based on her peculiar ability "to win Anglo-Saxon sympathies. She has the *morale* of the North; and does not awaken the prejudice so common in Great Britain [and by implication in

America] . . . against the passionate temperament and tendency to extravagance that mark the children of the South."[28]

Jenny Lind, then, was part of a Protestant Reformation in music, an antidote to the elegant but theatrical posturing that had so long ruled the vocal world. And like the religious movement itself, her approach was marked by simplicity, colloquialism, and an impatience with ceremony and artifice. Again and again American admirers praised the artlessness of the Nightingale, her ability to abandon or transcend the mechanical tricks that so many sopranos had practiced on their audiences, to display the exquisite absorption of the singer by the woman herself. *Harper's Monthly* compared her voice to natural splendors, "to the flood of melody from the nightingale's throat, to light, to water which flows from a pure and inexhaustible spring."[29] "One would imagine," wrote Tuckerman, "she had come with one bound from tending her flock on the hill-side, to warble behind the footlights; for, so directly from the heart of nature springs her melody, and so beyond the reach of art is the simple grace of her air and manners, that we associate her with the opera only through the consummate skill — the result of scientific training — manifested in her vocalism." Hers was "like the song of a bird, only more human. Nature in her seems to have taken Art to her bosom, and assimilated it, through love, with herself, until the identity of each is lost in the other."[30]

English critics had made similar observations. When she made her first appearance there in 1847, one of the newspapers commented that everything Jenny did seemed spontaneous, but without a fault. "Art, by her, has been only used to cultivate nature — not for a moment to disguise it."[31] And Nathaniel Parker Willis, the most voluble of her American admirers, agreed. Her very plainness was proof of divine inspiration. "How so shrinking, so almost repelling, so colorless and unsensuous looking a creature can *impassion* men of all kinds to the degree she does," he wrote, "is wonderful indeed." The soprano looked "as if sin or guile were an utter impossibility of her nature."[32]

But although the close relationship between Jenny's art and "divine nature" had been recognized elsewhere, the association held a special appeal in America. New England prophets like Emerson and Greenough, who reflected an operational aesthetic in their concern with popular verdicts and artistic literalism, also proclaimed another aesthetic that the versatile Barnum easily exploited: the religion of Nature. In his famous Divinity School Address of 1838 Emerson spoke for a generation of Americans reawakened to the natural magnificence of their continent. The rebellion against the constraints of Puritanism took, as one form, an outpouring of praise for Nature's perfection. In one sense a continuation of the ideals that animated Charles Willson Peale's museum, this new temper moved beyond the calm contemplation of Peale's generation into more mystical raptures. God revealed Himself not simply in the splendor of His plan (the Linnaean synthesis that captivated Enlightenment philosophers), but in the more specific pleasures and beauties of flowers, sunsets, mountaintops, and butterflies. Here lay true revelation, not in the books of scholars nor the codes of priests.[33]

What Emerson and his fellow philosophers elaborated in books and lectures, other Americans presented in art and literature. The Hudson River School of landscapists recorded on canvas their awe at Nature's sublimity; Fenimore Cooper emphasized the coarseness of civilization when placed beside the vast wilderness. In poetry, in song, in painting, and in drama Americans sought to identify themselves with the power and righteousness of Nature.

The raptures Jenny Lind excited, therefore, were part of this worship of the natural, admiration for her skill at subordinating artistry to goodness. Like Tom Thumb she displayed the benevolence of the Deity as well as His versatility. Praise for Jenny was praise for rational enjoyment; no man need feel shame for his expense of emotion. The dangerous passions that art could arouse were absent, subdued by the singer's noble soul and perfect technique. After hearing her sing the "Casta Diva" or "Herdsman's Song" a "man could hardly commit a disreputable action," argued one of Barnum's broadsides, "and we have no doubt that many an erring man might be reclaimed" could he be subjected to the sound of Jenny's voice. It would remind him of "his childhood's home, his mother's love, his sister's kiss, and the sinless pleasure of his early days."[34]

The good order of the concerts and the behavior of the spectators (with a few exceptions caused by poor planning) showed how wrong were the critics of Barnum and Lindomania. "No one who has beheld the perfect order of her vast and delighted audiences," wrote Willis, "the clockwork precision with which they are seated, and the quiet dignity of their egress, or contrasts it with great gatherings for similar purposes at Exeter Hall, the thunder of a congregated London police, and their shoutings to overrule confusion, and the collision of carriages," could help but be grateful for Barnum's management and the self-control of the American people.[35]

Emerson, the chief intellectual spokesman for the worshipers of Nature, agreed. "Jenny Lind need not go to California," he recorded in his journal in 1850. "California comes to her. Jenny Lind needs no police. Her voice is worth a hundred constables, and instantly silenced the uproar of the mob." Other sopranos, Alboni, for example, Emerson found "painful; mere surgical, or rather, functional" in their effects. But Jenny Lind had set the standard "which every artist and scholar think of as the measure of remuneration."[36]

The poets and poetesses of America joined in the acclamation. Hundreds of works saluted Jenny Lind on every possible occasion. "Fanny Crosby's Welcome to the 'Swedish Nightingale,'" the work of a blind educator, was delivered in Jenny's presence during a visit to the School of the Institute for the Blind in New York; Samuel H. Lloyd penned "To Jenny Lind (Written After Seeing Her from her Window Waving Her Handkerchief to the Multitude Below)"; Lydia Huntley Sigourney, "The Sweet Singer of Hartford," composed "The Swedish Songstress and Her Charities," while Mrs. L. G. Abell provided "The Women of America to Jenny Lind."[37] America's "scribbling women" were entranced by the spectacle of art, culture, and morality joined in the same person, and by Jenny's chaste, girlish demeanor. Heroine and male ideal that she was, Jenny posed no threat to the security of hearth and home; no men would drink champagne from her slipper in hidden dens of iniquity as they might toast Italian seductresses. Again and again poets likened her to an angel, a spirit carrying heavenly tones to the multitude below, her mission, "To warm this clod with fire from god/ By Harmony all divine!" The theme of discipline and restraint was sounded anew:

> High art is thus intact; and matchless skill
> Born of intelligence and self-control—
> The graduated tone and perfect trill
> Prove a restrained, but not a frigid soul;
> Thine finds expressions in such generous deeds,
> That music from thy lips human sorrows pleads![38]

So safe and secure was this artistic experience that the President, his cabinet, and most of official Washington found it possible to make their way to the concert hall and attend at least one of her performances. Henry Clay, Winfield Scott, Thomas Hart Benton and Lewis Cass, all powers and presidential contenders at one time or another, even visited Jenny in her Willard Hotel suite. But perhaps the most sublime display of the rational restraint of Jenny's appeal came in her encounter, described by Nathaniel Parker Willis, with America's most intellectual statesman. Attending one of the concerts in New York's Tripler Hall, Willis rose to the height of his most impassioned prose. As his eye moved over the audience before the performance, "we caught sight of a white object with a sparkling dark line underneath, around which a number of persons were just settling themselves in their seats. Motionless itself, and with the stir going on around it, it was like a calm half moon, seen over the tops of agitated trees, or like a massive magnolia blossom, too heavy for the breeze to stir, splendid and silent amid fluttering poplar-leaves." Lifting his opera glasses Willis suddenly realized he was viewing "*the dome over the temple of Webster* — the forehead of the great Daniel, with the two glorious lamps set in the dark shadow of its architrave."

Faced with this opportunity, Willis watched intently "to see signs of the susceptibility of such a mind to the spells of Jenny Lind." Courteously attentive to the overture that opened the concert, Webster asked Jenny to give one of the simple songs of her own land in place of the complicated music he was listening to. Such a desire was soon translated into action, as Jenny began a Scandinavian piece. Under the entrancing sound Webster pulled his left ear lobe, "his habitual first mark of interest in a new matter." Then as the sounds continued "Webster's broad chest grew erect and expanded," and with his head raised to its fullest he stared in rapture at the singer. During the applause that followed, Webster sat motionless, and after it died down "he rose to his feet and bowed to her, with the grace and stateliness of the monarch that he is." Willis congratulated Jenny Lind on her greatest triumph in the New World, "the sounding of America's deepest mind with her plummet of enchantment."[39] If the "Divine Daniel," the guardian of the Constitution, the symbol of the sublimity of the law, could be so moved by the genius of the Nightingale, any citizen could admit proudly to his own infatuation. The enchantress who held the Republic in sway posed no danger to its morals or stability.

And through all the triumphs, standing in the wings, tirelessly escorting Jenny from city to city, supervising the continuing publicity releases, checking the final arrangements, adopting various subterfuges to maintain her safety from the adoring crowds, stood the man who had organized it all. Obviously, Jenny Lind's attraction was not solely Barnum's creation; he had not given her the voice she sang with nor formed her character. But other great stars would tour America, some of them, said critics, greater musicians than Jenny Lind, without reaping a tithe of her glory. Henriette Sontag, Marietta Alboni, Teresa Parodi, the great Rachel herself would visit America in the 1850s, but none of them were managed by Barnum. They had no great crowds to see them off in Europe or welcome them in New York, no clamorous auctions, no adoring biographers or tellers of their good deeds. In desperation Max Maretzek spread the story that his import, Teresa Parodi, was about to become the Duchess of Devonshire. His houses overflowed, but even this paled beside Jenny's profits. "The monstrous sum of money drawn by Jenny Lind and her 'Mr. Merryman,'" moaned an English critic, "has led to the belief that America is paved with gold, and that an adventurer landing there may pick up any quantity."[40] The concert world had its fees and salaries inflated overnight. But there was only one fortune reaped, and that was shared by Jenny and Barnum.

Nor should one forget the prophecies of doom that greeted Barnum's first announcements about the coming tour. There "is not a public hall in the United States large enough to hold an audience, who, at a quarter of a dollar a ticket, would pay his expenses," argued one Bostonian, "and there is not enough —— fools left alive, since the great influx of heroes into Mexico, to fill Peter B. Brigham's far-famed Concert Hall, at $5 a ticket."[41] Barnum would have to rent churches, he concluded, to make any money at all.

In some respects, Jenny Lind's tour was Barnum's greatest feat. Every step of the way was prepared, every feature planned, every reception organized, every reaction nurtured. But his star was presented as the quintessence of spontaneity, lacking affectation or contrivance. Barnum labored long and well to bring together the various images — the modest girl, the benevolent philanthropist, the Nordic spellbinder, the shepherdess — but all were subordinated to the myth of simplicity, the image of innocence. It was The Spirit of Artlessness presided over by The Spirit of Artifice, and Americans loved it.

SIX

Disasters Encountered

THE JENNY LIND TOUR made Barnum rich. According to his published figures, the ninety-five concerts he managed took in more than seven hundred thousand dollars. Of this sum Jenny Lind received one hundred and seventy-six thousand dollars, while Barnum took more than five hundred thousand dollars before expenses. The average gross for each performance was seventy-five hundred dollars, unprecedented in the history of American entertainment. And these figures represented only two-thirds of Barnum's original plan, for Jenny annulled the contract with Barnum, paying him a penalty of thirty-two thousand dollars, and went on tour herself, under new management.

The split between the two took place in June 1851, after Jenny had been in America almost ten months. It was an amicable parting, although Barnum blamed her advisers for poisoning her mind against him by suggesting that she would have more dignity and greater profits if she selected new managers. Barnum's critics asserted that Jenny resented being treated like a circus act and made to perform in theaters that featured animal shows and unseemly farces.

Jenny remained in America for another year, but her profits were far less than they had been under Barnum's aegis. Some blamed the new management, others, the fact that the public was finally beginning to tire of the Swedish Nightingale. Her marriage in February 1852 to a young pianist, Otto Goldschmidt, also removed some of the romantic interest attached to the soprano. "Why is Madame Goldschmidt so much less than Jenny Lind?" asked *Harper's Monthly*. Because "she who has conquered the world by song and goodness, has herself been conquered," the magazine answered, and conquered by one "no better, no worthier, no stronger than the average of men."

Jenny had been reduced to the standard of "our dull every-day mortality."[1]

Whatever the cause, Jenny's departure from New York on May 29, 1852, attracted crowds far smaller than those that had greeted her twenty months before. She continued to sing for several years in Europe but her major activities centered on her English home and her children.

Among the factors that may have led to the end of the partnership was Barnum's irrepressible interest in doing many things at once. Managing the Lind concerts was not enough. One of the schemes he launched while Jenny was touring involved the creation of Barnum's Great Asiatic Caravan, Museum, and Menagerie. Chartering a ship, Barnum and his partners imported ten elephants who marched up Broadway pulling a chariot while Jenny Lind, at Barnum's request, reviewed the procession.[2] The troupe, featuring Tom Thumb (Sherwood Stratton was a heavy investor), toured for several years, with its lions, elephants, clowns, and curiosities, and according to Barnum made him a good deal of money. But in 1854 the show was disbanded and the managers, who included Seth B. Howes, a famous circus producer, went on to other things. Barnum, however, retained an elephant as a souvenir and "a capital advertisement for the American Museum." He used the beast for work on his Bridgeport farm, a portion of which lay conveniently near the railroad tracks. "The keeper was furnished with a time-table of the road," Barnum remembered, "with special instructions to be busily engaged in his work whenever passenger trains from either way were passing through." Pop-eyed commuters stared out in wonder at the Connecticut countryside, and farmers were fascinated by pachyderm power. Letters poured in seeking cost analyses and wondering whether agriculturists should imitate the practice. "I began to be alarmed lest some one should buy an elephant," Barnum confessed, and he printed a letter discouraging would-be owners, pointing out that the elephant's advertising value made him most useful to the proprietor of the American Museum.

There were other activities and investments. Barnum bought part of a steamship, one of his partners being Cornelius Vanderbilt; he sold a newly invented fire extinguisher (an "apparent miracle" that never quite worked); with two sons of the great newspaper editor, Moses Y. Beach, he began an illustrated weekly in New York modeled on the *London Illustrated News* for which he begged Bayard Taylor to get his artist friends to send their sketches from Admiral Perry's pioneering Japanese expedition. But the journal survived only one year.[3] In 1851 Barnum took the Bateman children, juvenile actors, on a successful British tour. He organized Barnum's Gallery of American Beauty, an early Miss Rheingold contest, in which the public voted from daguerreotypes for their favorites.[4] And he accepted, reluctantly, the presidency of the New York Crystal Palace, a rapidly failing exhibition hall that had opened in 1853 as a permanent world's fair. Although Barnum believed that its distance from the city's center made its future doubtful, he plunged in to revivify the enterprise, arranging huge concerts under French conductor Louis Antoine Jullien. George Templeton Strong, who was convinced the palace would fail unless Barnum took it over, attended the "Musical Congress," listening to the fifteen hundred performers. "It's a pleasure to see humbug so consistently, extensively, and cleverly applied," reported Strong. "The audacity of the imposition reconciled one to its grossness." But the building stock, which had once sold for one hundred and seventy-five dollars a share, fell to little more than twenty-one dollars. "The building seems all but gutted," Strong wrote. "Its character has changed. It is now merely an extension of Barnum's Museum.[5] Even Barnum's genius was insufficient to revive the dying institution.

But although Barnum soon severed his connection with the Crystal Palace, he never abandoned any enterprise entirely. Writing Moses Kimball in July 1854, he showed some fatigue. "Weary, fagged, tired, and almost sick, I have quit New York for the season and I trust *forever* as a nesting place." He thought of retiring on his income to the country. "I was an ass for having anything to do with the Crystal Palace," Barnum admitted ruefully; it was, after all, one of his few failures.

There remained hope however. Gathering his energies, Barnum outlined a new plan.[6] The building and fences, he told Kimball, had cost over seven hundred thousand dollars; the present owners were willing to sell and would be lucky to get two hundred and fifty thousand dollars. If purchased, the structure could be taken down and rebuilt somewhere else — perhaps in Boston — for one hundred thousand dollars. So, a total of three hundred and fifty thousand dollars was necessary for the undertaking. At six percent, a good income, such an investment might produce twenty-one thousand dollars annually. But if the Crystal Palace were reconstructed on the Boston Common and managed "by Boston businessmen," Barnum thought it might clear one hundred thousand dollars annually, or thirty percent. With great care he went over the daily expenses (under one hundred dollars in New York and possibly less in Boston). Refreshment saloons would pay the owners twenty percent of their gross receipts, which could be as high as fifty thousand dollars a year. A lecture room capable of seating five thousand could be opened in one portion of the palace, a site for musical performances and for "great statesmen" to comment on the issues of the day. One banker told Barnum he would take twenty-five thousand dollars worth of stock if Bostonians became interested, and Barnum added that he himself would purchase heavily. "Nor need I say how much it would help your Museum," Barnum added, indicating that the American Museum had cleared fifty thousand dollars the previous year, doubling the business it would have done without the presence of the Crystal Palace. Even New Yorkers would travel to New England to see it. You can "probably bring about the biggest thing you ever thought of touching and gain both gold and glory," Barnum prophesied.

However promising the speculation seemed to Barnum it bore no results; Kimball did not act on the suggestion and the Crystal Palace languished in New York until its destruction by fire four years later. In this scheme for a permanent exhibition and convention center Barnum was a generation or two ahead of his time.

Another speculation that Barnum entered into at this time was more disastrous in its consequences. Even while box-office receipts rolled in, he was searching for ways to increase his fortune; he was, above all, a businessman, constantly on the alert for new ways of making money. But troubles lay ahead, for his new interest was real estate.

The dramatic growth of the thirties, forties, and fifties was turning villages into towns and towns into cities. As the Northeast became more industrialized and its railroad networks created new markets, housing needs made land speculators rich. Municipal growth, in New York, Massachusetts, and Connecticut, seemed inevitable; vacant, undeveloped land accessible to factories or urban centers multiplied in value almost overnight. Spectacular fortunes were made in New York City, but there was opportunity in the hinterlands as well.

Bridgeport, at about the time Barnum decided to make his home there, had some eight thousand inhabitants and was only fifty-seven miles from New York City.[7] Some thirty trains went through the city each day, giving it good communication north and south. When Barnum determined to build Iranistan, he was attracted not only by beauty and convenience, but by the city's investment possibilities. In 1851 he purchased from William H. Noble a tract of fifty acres across the Pequonnock River from Bridgeport. Going into partnership with Noble, Barnum intended the area to be "the nucleus of a new city." They laid out treelined streets through their two hundred acres and began selling alternate lots for home-building. Sales were conditional on construction of a house, store, or factory within a year from the date of purchase and on purchasers keeping their property "clean and neat" and in an architectural style approved by the sellers. Barnum and Noble were developing a city within a city and wanted to keep the area desirable for prospective settlers. A footbridge to Bridgeport was built, and a toll bridge made toll-free. With the center of Bridgeport within easy reach, the two promoters encouraged growing companies to move their operations to East Bridgeport.

It was not enough, of course, for Barnum simply to admit he wanted more money. Benevolence had to be brought in as well. If "I could by the judicious investment of a portion of my capital," he explained in the autobiography, "open the way for new industries and new homes, I should be of service to my fellow men and find grateful employment for my energies and time." Moneymaking was secondary; Barnum had a passion "to build a city on the beautiful plateau across the river" and devoted his considerable energies to making the dream come true.

This dual role of urban planner and real estate investor got him into trouble. Profit and growth depended in part on the ability to attract industry. In 1852 Barnum helped move a clock company from Litchfield to East Bridgeport and brought in a manufacturer named Theodore Terry to go into partnership with him in the production of clocks. Three years later, in 1855, he learned that the Jerome Clock Company, an important New Haven enterprise, might be induced to move also and to merge with the Terry and Barnum Company. At this point stories diverge. Barnum insisted that Chauncey Jerome, the company's president, requested money to get the company through some hard times. In return for the loan the company would move. According to its official reports, its finances were healthy, and the loan would help the firm survive a bad season. Barnum knew Jerome to be personally wealthy, a benefactor of the Congregational Church; the company employed close to one thousand men. After some consideration Barnum lent the company fifty thousand dollars in notes and said he would accept drafts for another sixty thousand dollars. He specified that his total liability was to be limited to one hundred and ten thousand dollars.

Chauncey Jerome, in his 1860 autobiography, told a different story. He claimed that the transaction that merged the two firms had been concluded by his son while he was away. Jerome, naturally, trusted his son, who was secretary of the company. "I love truth, honesty and religion," said the clock manufacturer. "I do not mean, however, the religion that Barnum believes in," he went on, alluding to Barnum's Universalism. "I believe that the wicked are punished in another world."⁸ Jerome blamed the troubles on the heavy debts owed by Terry and Barnum, which the Jerome Company was obliged to assume because of the merger. "It is a positive fact that the stock of the Jerome Company was not worth half as much, three months after Barnum came into the concern," Jerome argued, "as it was before that time."

Whatever the details, and Barnum's account seems more reliable than Jerome's, the showman was duped. The Jerome Clock Company was in a dangerous position (Chauncey Jerome never alluded to that fact nor to Barnum's loan), and letters attesting to its financial soundness turned out to be from banks anxious for Barnum's loans because they held notes from the company. Barnum's notes were used again and again, and he discovered to his horror that his credit had been stretched to more than half a million dollars, his notes going to pay debts to the company's creditors. When he realized what had happened, Barnum paid all his personal claims at his own banks and stores and then he, and the company, failed. He was a ruined man.

Or so he put it, for he managed, before his bankruptcy, to sell the museum collection to his manager, John Greenwood, and another partner. They gave him notes for its purchase and hired the building from Barnum's wife, who owned the property lease, which provided an income of some nineteen thousand dollars a year. The notes from Greenwood, backed by a mortgage, were turned over to the assignee of Barnum's property.

There then commenced a series of court fights in which creditors sought full payment, unwilling to wait for the sale of Barnum's property, which would have brought them only partial returns on the debts. "My widespread reputation for shrewdness as a showman," Barnum wrote, "had induced the general belief that my means were still ample, and certain outside cred-itors," who had bought up his clock notes at a discount, on speculation, decided they should be paid at once. Barnum fought them successfully and managed at the same time to im-prove his future position. The clock factory that Jerome was supposed to occupy (the company never moved to East Bridge-port) was bought by the Wheeler and Wilson Sewing Machine Company, which also extended a loan to Barnum to be used for purchasing his Bridgeport property when it came up at public auction. Shrewdly he continued, with the help of some of his wife's property, to buy up land in East Bridgeport, knowing that in time its value would increase. "Growing trees, money at interest, and rapidly rising real estate, work for their owners all night as well as all day, Sundays included," Barnum com-mented happily.

The bankruptcy provided a theme for countless newspaper editorials. The irrepressible deceiver had been duped himself, and the opportunity was too good to miss. But many of Bar-num's friends rallied behind him, offering gifts or loans, while a meeting of Bridgeport businessmen expressed confidence in him and admiration for the "fortitude and composure with which he has met reverses into which he has been dragged through no fault of his own." *Frank Leslie's Illustrated News-paper* argued that "the spectacle of a man bravely breasting his misfortune is one that ought at all times to excite sympathy in generous minds." It condemned the "howl of exultation" which had greeted Barnum's ruin. "Had he, like some of our rich merchants, accumulated the basis of his wealth by early failures; had he robbed the widow and plundered the orphan like some of our Wall Street defaulters," then there would have been no such cries of triumph. Barnum had done nothing so serious; he had cheated the public only by seeking to amuse and instruct. His fraud had not impoverished anyone, and his "operations have not drawn tears save for laughter."[9]

These public expressions of friendship cheered Barnum im-mensely, although he refused offers of gifts because of their inadequacy to meet his immense obligations. He assumed the character of a Christian martyr who welcomed his trials as proof of his fortitude. "My poor sick wife," he wrote his Bridgeport supporters, "who needs the bracing air which her own dear home . . . would have afforded her, is driven by the orders of her physician to a secluded spot on Long Island where the sea-wind lends its healthful influence, and where I have also retired for the double purpose of consoling her and of recruiting my own constitution." But his faith had not failed: "I humbly hope and believe that I am being taught humility and reliance upon Providence, which will yet afford a thousand times more peace and true happiness than can be acquired in the din, strife and turmoil, excitements and struggles of this money-worshipping age. The man who coins his brain and blood into gold, who wastes all of his time and thought upon the almighty dollar, who looks no higher than blocks of houses, and tracts of land," such a man, Barnum moralized, may try to console himself with safe investments, "but he misses a pleasure which I firmly believe this lesson was intended to secure to me."

There were many ironies about these statements. Barnum's wife, as he himself admitted, remained a wealthy woman, and his own troubles had come from a desire to convert his "blocks of houses and tracts of land" into profit. But moralizing came easily to Barnum. The habit — implanted through years of fighting clerical opponents of his amusements — of forcing didactic messages from the most neutral material was not easily discarded. It was hard to know when Barnum was talking about one of his exhibits or about himself and his family; the sentimentality, the hyperbole, the refuge in stock phrases and platitudes embellished both his advertisements and his personal recollections. Even in moments of crisis he retained his capacity for developing a role and playing it to full effect.

But the dreary position of a bankrupt, so different from his recent prosperity, depressed Barnum. He decided early in 1857 to abandon his problems temporarily and take some exhibits, notably General Tom Thumb and Cordelia Howard, a juvenile actress, to Europe. "With these attractions," Barnum wrote, "I determined to make as much money as I could." He sent the profits home, not merely to redeem some of the clock notes "at reasonable rates," but to repurchase parts of his estate at the auctions. Barnum refused to give up hope in real estate.

In later years these actions drew different interpretations. Barnum was enraged in the 1880s when several of his enemies in Bridgeport sold stories to New York and New Haven newspapers (in a clumsy attempt at blackmail) claiming that his European trip astonished friendly creditors who still believed he would pay in full.[10] His absence, these critics went on, was used by agents to spread rumors that he was totally broken and forced to lecture for money. They then bought up his notes at ten cents on the dollar from the confused and frightened creditors.

Barnum presented Tom Thumb and Cordelia Howard to crowded houses in England. There also, he looked up old friends who remembered the triumphs of the 1840s and made new friends. Albert Smith, a literary companion and hack writer at the time of Barnum's previous visit, had become a successful entertainment manager and was of some use. W. M. Thackeray, who had met Barnum in New York, offered financial help until he discovered that the showman (or literally, Mrs. Barnum, because of property arrangements) was worth more than the novelist, even after the clock fiasco. Barnum called on Julius Benedict and Giovanni Belletti, both of the Jenny Lind tour, and saw Jenny's husband, Otto Goldschmidt. Managers, actors, critics, and bankers dined with him, some of them offering help or employment. His English travels helped restore not only Barnum's finances but some of the self-confidence that might have been a bit deflated by the bankruptcy procedures.

From England Barnum moved his attractions to the Continent, touring France, Germany, and Holland. The trip allowed him to expound on the value of self-control, which continued to hold an almost supreme position on his list of approved virtues. The gaming tables of Baden-Baden fascinated him, and the addicted players, who "have been known to sit at the table, without once rising, even to eat or to drink, through the entire day and night session," seemed objects of pity. Several suicides occurred each year at such spas, Barnum reported, because of the ruin that compulsive gambling and surrender to appetite inevitably produced. The Dutch, on the other hand, less faithful patrons of Barnum's amusements than the pleasure-seekers at Baden-Baden, were more admirable as human types. The country itself, recaptured from the sea by the industry of "whole generations of human beavers," testified to the rewards of discipline and control. "It is rare, indeed, to meet a ragged, dirty or drunken person" in Holland, Barnum wrote admiringly. Frugal, neat, and temperate, the Dutch possessed ideal qualities, as well as a few sharpsters who tried to part him from some money.

In the late summer of 1857, Barnum returned to take care of some business and personal matters. He attended the marriage of one of his daughters in Bridgeport and was staying at a New York hotel when, on the evening of December 17, Iranistan burned to the ground, a total loss, the first of a series of disastrous fires that would plague Barnum's enterprises for the next decades. The house, unoccupied, was being repaired by workmen, and Barnum speculated that a lighted pipe left by one of them had caused the blaze. He estimated the house was worth one hundred and fifty thousand dollars, and he had only twenty-eight thousand dollars in insurance on the property. The grounds were eventually purchased by Elias Howe, who died before he could build on the site. The purchase money, like the insurance, went to satisfy creditors.

Returning to England in 1858, Barnum helped manage Tom Thumb's successful tours, and at the suggestion of friends prepared a lecture called "The Art of Money-Getting." "I told my friends that, considering my clock complications, I thought I was more competent to speak on 'The Art of Money-Losing,'" he wrote in the autobiography, "but they encouraged me by reminding me that I could not have lost money if I had not previously possessed the faculty of making it." He made his English debut as lecturer December 29, 1858, to enthusiastic reviews, and the following year repeated his lecture almost one hundred times, in various parts of England. The text itself must have benefited considerably from Barnum's delivery, for the printed version reads like a collection of platitudes, pleasantly supported, of course, by anecdotes, apt quotations, and personal experiences. Barnum was fond of quoting other masters of exhortation, like Benjamin Franklin and Henry Ward Beecher, and also of repeating the prudent adages that the conventional wisdom of his era claimed were infallible. Live economically, he urged, dispense with luxuries in order to achieve a surplus rather than a deficit, don't mistake your vocation, avoid debt, persevere against difficulties, concentrate your energies, avoid being overly visionary but let hope predominate, read the newspapers, be charitable, treat customers politely, and advertise, advertise, advertise your business. Certainly, much of the advice enshrined principles that he himself had acted upon, but his own success could not be systematized: it rested on originality, audaciousness, and imagination, qualities which could not be created by the maxims of a visiting lecturer. But there were some, like English millowner John Fish, who insisted that their business success was based upon Barnum's advice and principles of procedure.

Barnum himself always respected money-makers, particularly self-made men. As a general rule, he argued at the conclusion of his lecture, "money getters are the benefactors of our race. To them, in a great measure, we are indebted for our institutions of learning and of art, our academies, colleges, and churches." Misers were no argument against wealth, just as hypocrites were no argument against piety. And in America, the absence of primogeniture meant that at some point the hoarded wealth of the miser would be scattered to the benefit of all.

In private Barnum took much the same line. To employees

he was fond of repeating free the advice for which he charged on the lecture platform and quick to commend efforts toward personal independence. Some years later he was so impressed with one success story, the *Vagabond Adventures of Ralph Keeler*, that he wrote the publisher asking to meet the author. Keeler, who had started out as a minstrel dancer, had become a contributor to the *Atlantic Monthly* while still in his twenties. He was a friend of Mark Twain and Bret Harte and was memorialized by William Dean Howells as Fulkerson in *A Hazard of New Fortunes*.[11] Many showmen, said Barnum in his letter, have grown wealthy and retired with honor, but none ever started so low as Keeler. "How a poor forsaken orphan boy could manage to rise above such degrading surroundings, secure a liberal education, visit the principal cities of the old world, and become a gentleman of culture, and this too, all accomplished by the outlay of a sum barely exceeding $200, is to me utterly incomprehensible." Barnum urged the publishers, Fields, Osgood and Company, to transmit his invitation to Keeler. "I would like exceedingly to compare notes with him."[12] An actual meeting would have been amusing. Keeler himself had read Barnum's autobiography when he was still a dancer, but one of his teachers, Francis Lynch, had been managed by Barnum in his early days and was so outraged by Barnum's inaccuracies that he forbade Keeler to mention the book.[13]

Whatever its deficiencies as a literary document, "The Art of Money-Getting" admirably illustrated its own theme, for it brought Barnum thousands of dollars, which he applied toward redeeming his debts and increasing his property. The European trips also proved helpful in locating more curiosities for the American Museum. Although Barnum had temporarily abandoned his ownership, he knew he would be back, in time, and continued to ship home attractions that would benefit the collection.

Tom Thumb, the lectures, commissions on museum purchases, his wife's income, and an austere living style combined to lift the burden of the remaining clock notes. By the spring of

1860, almost five years after his ruin, Barnum was financially independent once again and able to repurchase the museum collection from its interim owners. On March 31 the building reopened under its original ownership, advertising "Barnum on his feet again." That night, Barnum stepped on the stage of the lecture room, expressed his hopes for the future, and described his experiences during the previous five years. He explained how his wife's property had been used to purchase his notes and buy back portions of his own estate. He thanked some of his more generous creditors and detailed his European ventures. "Many people have wondered," Barnum went on, "that a man considered so acute as myself should have been deluded into embarrassments like mine. . . . I can only reply that I never made pretensions to the sharpness of a pawn-broker, and I hope I shall never so entirely lose confidence in human nature as to consider every man a scamp by instinct, or a rogue by necessity." "The fact is," he had written in a letter a few years before, "I am not, nor never was half so cute, nor cunning, nor *deep* as many persons suppose." He was just a hard worker, and it seemed better to suffer from too much faith than from too little.

And then, following encomia on East Bridgeport and the moral qualities of the museum ("The dramas introduced in the Lecture Room will never contain a profane expression or a vulgar allusion"), Barnum stepped aside and the entertainments began. The five-year hiatus had cost him time and money but had not dulled his instinct for entertainment or his genius for advertising.

The Barnum of these later years, a man of increasing wealth and public position, had other interests besides his show business. In the sixties and seventies his energies would expand into politics and urban management and continue strong in temperance and religion, where he had already demonstrated some concern. The first needs, of course, were to reestablish his family and expand the collections. His wife, Charity, had been living in rented houses or boarding during the previous few years to save money. His children had grown up. Caroline, born in 1833, had been married in 1852 to David W. Thompson, a Bridgeport businessman; Helen, born in 1840, married Samuel H. Hurd, another businessman, in 1857. Hurd eventually went to work for Barnum, becoming treasurer of the American Museum, and later, of the circus. Pauline, his youngest daughter, was only fourteen in 1860 and still at school.

With Iranistan burned and the grounds sold, Barnum built a new home for his wife, Lindencroft, a comfortable, genteel house, but lacking the exotic trappings of the first residence. Barnum was sufficiently famous now; he did not require that the architecture of his home contribute to his advertising. Solid, middle-class respectability was sufficient.

To sell his real estate Barnum advertised that he would lend money, at six percent interest, to purchasers who could then build their homes on the lots. He estimated that something between fifteen and eighteen hundred dollars would purchase the land and the materials necessary for adequate housing. He also built homes to rent, but this he found unpleasant. Taxes, repairs, interest, and insurance wore down his profits, while "the landlord is often looked upon by the tenants as an overbearing, grasping man." Men "are more independent and feel happier who live in their own houses; they keep the premises in neater order, and they make better citizens. Hence I always encourage poor people to become householders if possible." Like many another American, Barnum continued to view property ownership as a guarantee of civic responsibility. It indicated determination and self-discipline, the qualities he valued so highly, and he gave special advantages to purchasers who neither smoked nor drank.

His philosophy of ownership did, to be sure, change somewhat. By 1881 he was advising his secretaries to lease lots for ninety-nine years rather than sell them. The lease would be renewed and revalued every five years. This would permit men of moderate means to have homes, Barnum argued, and the buildings would belong to his estate at the end of the ninety-nine years. As he grew older, Barnum thought more and more of the importance of leaving a memorable legacy, and leasing was more profitable than selling.

The streets of East Bridgeport were named after members of the Barnum and Noble families, and the two partners presented the public with acreage for parks and churches. They also owned much land across the river, and by the eighties Barnum believed that Bridgeport would soon become the largest city in the state. He devoted a great deal of energy to promoting the place as a paradise for prospective residents or businesses, and saw his own real estate holdings increase more than ten times in value during his lifetime.

But the museum still claimed his fullest energies. The lecture room celebrated its reopening under Barnum's aegis with all-star casts, including Emily Mestayer, J. Delmon Grace, and T. H. Hadaway, who appeared in various melodramas. In the summers drama languished and giants and dwarfs took over the lecture room, but from fall through spring Barnum had one of the best repertory companies in the city, performing the latest popular plays with elaborate costumes and stage props. In 1861, keeping up with the times, the museum presented *Anderson, the Patriot Heart of Sumter*. The enthusiasm of audiences for the Stars and Stripes, Barnum advertised, "would strike terror to the heart of every traitor, and convince him that the Union must and will be preserved." Later that same year a steward on a captured Union schooner who killed his captors and brought the rebel brig into New York "will receive visitors at all times and relate his experience with Southern chivalry."[14]

The ever-popular Tom Thumb was now joined by a series of other midgets, who added romantic interest as well as novelty. In 1862 Barnum exhibited George Washington Morrison Nutt, a New Hampshire midget who reminded him of the Tom Thumb of the first years. Christening him Commodore Nutt, Barnum repeated many of the procedures that had worked a decade earlier. With his own carriage, footmen, and Shetland ponies,

Tom Thumb grows up:
Barnum with Mr. and Mrs. Tom Thumb and Commodore Nutt

The wedding party

Nutt proved a valuable attraction. Barnum brought the two midgets together in the summer of 1862 to play before the public, some of whom insisted, much to Barnum's amusement, that Commodore Nutt was actually General Tom Thumb, and Tom Thumb himself was an imposter whom Barnum was trying to pass off in his place. "It is very amusing to see how people will sometimes deceive themselves by being too incredulous," Barnum noted, in this demonstration of one of his favorite themes.

Commodore Nutt (known popularly as "The $30,000 Nutt" because of his cost to Barnum) possessed the same wit and audacity that Tom Thumb had used to charm European royalty, only Nutt employed his on President Lincoln, who invited him to the White House and traded puns. It went harder with Nutt when he matched himself against Tom Thumb. The two became rivals when Barnum brought an attractive and refined midget to his employ named Mercy Lavinia Warren Bumpus. Lavinia Warren, as she was known, met Commodore Nutt first, but Tom Thumb was the more established of the two — wealthy, the owner of horses and yachts, sophisticated and worldly. It quickly became apparent to both men that they had fallen in love with Lavinia, and Tom Thumb took every opportunity to impress her with his financial standing. Barnum described the wooing in the pages of the autobiography with questionable taste but in fascinating detail. After announcement of their engagement, both Lavinia and her general exhibited at the museum to enormous crowds. Barnum was accused of having arranged the romance for purely business purposes; this he denied, but he happily pocketed the profits that came his way and helped arrange the wedding. It was "suggested to me that a small fortune in itself could be easily made out of the excitement," Barnum wrote, by arranging the ceremony for the Academy of Music and charging for admission. "But I had no such thought," he insisted piously. "I had promised to give the couple a genteel and graceful wedding, and I kept my word."

The wedding took place in fashionable Grace Church, February 10, 1863.[15] Admission to the ceremony was by invitation only, and the guests included General Ambrose Burnside, Mrs. John Jacob Astor, and Mrs. William H. Vanderbilt. Members of the church protested against this "marriage of mountebanks" and were angered by their inability to sit in their own pews during the ceremony, but the rector pronounced the rites "as touchingly solemn as a wedding can possibly be rendered." Much of the notoriety the marriage attracted was founded on sexual curiosity, and Barnum was blamed for encouraging a rather crude level of speculation. But aside from exhibiting the two midgets and arranging both a fashionable service and the wedding reception, he did nothing to nourish the idle gossip.

President Lincoln received the married couple at the White House during the wedding tour. This gave Barnum's critics still another opening. A pseudonymous poet, "Cymon," published a seven-page pamphlet in 1863, *The Pigmies and the Priests*, charging that the Tom Thumb wedding was a plot between Barnum (Bamboozleem) and Lincoln (Foo-Foo) to ease the melancholia caused by the disasters of the Civil War.

> *But blood and tears deface the records of his reign —*
> *His armies were defeated, his kingdom rent in twain;*
> *A second-rate Magician was this feeble old Foo-Foo,*
> *For half his realm seceded to his rival, Bully-boo.*
>
> *Then came the great Bamboozleem, with his familiar spirit,*
> *(his familiar was a demon, a terrible 'What Is It?')*
> *Astride upon his magic steed, (the woolly one,) he spoke:*
> *'When mortals take to snivelling, then Necromancers joke.*
>
> *You fret because you haven't got one mighty man to show,*
> *What matter for the giants, then when pigmies are the go;*
> *There's but one great* Invisible, *we always have been told,*
> *And now it's fully proved the great invisible is —* Gold.
>
> *Then cast your cares away, and laugh at melancholy,*
> *This is the very time of times to come out strong and jolly;*
> *The biggest firms burst up, the fondest couples die,*
> *But then there's no philosophy in sitting down to cry.'*[16]

The charges of "Cymon" were undoubtedly the most bizarre ever made against Barnum, but he had, after all, been likened to the devil by earlier critics. What was new was his juxtaposition with the President of the United States and national policy. Barnum never mentioned the poem, which couldn't have achieved too large a circulation but which indicated the furor his name could still arouse. The Tom Thumbs, of course, were not affected. They returned from their wedding trip and retired for a time. But in later years they resumed public appearances, both in America and Europe, under Barnum's experienced management.

By the 1860s the museum building, enlarged and refurbished several times, bore evidence of Barnum's unceasing efforts to lay his hands on any piece of exotica that could be found.[17] The basement of the five-story building housed tanks for fish and large animals, cages, machinery employed in the building's maintenance, and a gas works. The ground floor was devoted to the offices of the ticket sellers and the spaces for panoramas and dioramas, which had long been popular among Barnum's patrons. The second floor contained exhibits of the greatest variety: a fortune-teller, a one-armed Civil War veteran who guessed weight, an enormous tank in which at various times swam two whales from Labrador that had cost Barnum thousands of dollars to transport. Present also was a fat girl, the lightning calculator, giantesses and dwarfs, and other popular curiosities. In an adjoining room was an exhibit of glassmaking, wax figures of Napoleon, Victoria, Tom Thumb, Christ and his disciples, and many historical celebrities. On this floor Barnum's office was stationed, as well as those of the other officers of the museum. There were also dozens of marble and glass cases filled with fish, and Ned, the learned seal, who entertained guests with his antics. The walls were hung with pictures of eminent men, mainly by Rembrandt Peale, and contortionary mirrors. The third floor contained the entrance to the parquet of the lecture room, used by most of the country visitors; the more fashionable set occupied boxes above. On this floor also was case after case full of butterflies, insects, sharks' teeth, stuffed animals, Revolutionary War mementos, and other assortments. A catalog printed in the 1860s listed, for example, among the contents of Case No. 794: "Ball of Hair found in the stomach of a sow; Indian collar, composed of grizzly bear claws; the sword of a sword fish penetrating through the side of a ship; an Algerine boarding pike; African pocket-book; Chinese pillow; a petrified piece of pork, which was recovered from the water after being immersed for sixty years; fragment of the first canal-boat which reached New York City through the canals; wrought metal Mexican stirrup; Turkish shoes; African sandals," and a host of other items. The cases nearby contained coach lace from Washington's carriage, a box made from the wood of the tree under which Penn ratified his treaty with the Indians, a portion of the throne of Louis XVIII, a buckle belonging to Peter Stuyvesant, a key to the Paris Bastille, antiquities from Herculaneum, Indian peace pipes, South Seas masks, and Buddhist images from the Far East.

The catalog sought to teach a little cultural relativism along with its information. "However uncouth these unsightly and miserable attempts at sculpture appear to the inhabitants of civilized nations," it declared, speaking of Asian idols, "they are highly revered and valued at home, where they receive the worship and adoration of millions of ignorant Heathen." Visitors could spend days wandering through the cases. "Who can forget, be he man or boy," recalled the *New York Times* after one of Barnum's fires, "the startling effect produced upon him when first he came upon the Three Men of Egypt, whose blackened skulls and grinning, ghastly faces stuck offensively out from the top of the funeral wrappings?"[18]

There were yet two more floors to the museum. Fourth-floor cases were filled with mineral and geological specimens, Indian curiosities, and more mementos, such as the club that purportedly killed Captain Cook. There were figures dressed in historic costumes and demonstrations of a sewing machine. Finally, on the fifth floor, there was Barnum's famous Happy Family, a collection of monkeys, dogs, rats, cats, pigeons, owls, porcupines, guinea pigs, cocks, and hounds, all of whom lived in amicable peace together. And nearby, for the less squeamish, was a case of boa constrictors, and a few more oddities which could not be fitted in below.

Many of the curiosities posed problems of credibility to the onlookers. There were painted pigeons, in a color no naturalist had ever found. On one wall was a famous petrifaction representing a horse about whose body wound a boa constrictor in the act of striking at the arm of the rider. Some felt the design was the product of a clever stonecutter, but others insisted it had to be a genuine slice of the hazards of prehistoric life. And then there was the "What Is It?" believed by some to be a "missing link" between the human and animal creation, in reality William Henry Johnson, a deformed black dwarf called "Zip" who would exhibit for decades after the museum shut, in the circus that Barnum helped to found. Barnum spread a story that the "What Is It?" had been captured in Africa by a party in pursuit of gorillas, but he did not fool too many visitors.

Stopping in to see the place one summer day in 1860, George Templeton Strong found the "ancient and seedy museum . . . instinct with new life. The old wax figures are propped and brushed up and some of the more conspicuously mangy of the stuffed monkeys and toucans have disappeared. There is a colossal fat boy on exhibition (a real prodigy of hideousness), in addition to the miraculous calculator."[19] Strong was particularly impressed with the aquarium, and the tropical fish Barnum had imported for it. Barnum's marine interests were not confined to New York. Later in the sixties he became owner of Barnum's Aquarial Gardens on Washington Street in Boston ("Performances of a chaste, interesting, and wholly moral nature will take place on the stage every afternoon and evening"). In 1862 Barnum dropped Oliver Wendell Holmes a note and complimentary ticket. "I am anxious that the Boston public shall know how much I am trying to do for them at the low figure of a quarter," he told Holmes, hoping the physician would pass on the information.[20]

As New York's great curiosity, the museum was naturally on the itinerary of the famous 1860 visit of the Prince of Wales. The royal party visited the giants and dwarfs, the living skeleton and Albino Family, and seemed pleased; Barnum called on the prince in Boston and the two reminisced about their first encounter, fifteen years earlier, with Tom Thumb. "The only place of amusement in America honored with a visit from the Prince of Wales," Barnum's guidebooks read after the royal favor had been shown. No opportunity was too sacred to exploit.

Thus, Barnum's advertisements may not have exaggerated too much when they stated, "Perhaps there never was before in the world such an instance of extraordinary success as this museum presents." "Mr. Barnum devotes his constant energies and attends personally to the minutest details of the Museum," one advertisement continued. With "an almost reckless disregard of expenditure," this "Napoleon of his profession" pursued curiosities through the world and claimed there were some eight hundred and fifty thousand items on display. "The genius of Barnum is truly American. He has not rested content, as many other men would have done, after . . . great efforts," but remains "the same active spirit as ever." And citizens who still doubted the propriety of a visit were assured by the owner that he used "the same precaution to protect any visitors while in the Museum that I would my own family, so that any lady or child shall be as safe here as in their own house."[21]

Barnum tried to be up to the minute in everything. In 1849 he asked E. D. Gilman, a New Englander just returned from California, to give a short lecture on gold mining — wages paid, equipment necessary, living conditions, and other subjects of interest. While doing this, he was to pass his hand over a twenty-five-pound lump of gold, implying it was from California. Gilman replied that this would be humbug, for seven ounces was the largest lump he ever heard of. "My dear sir," replied the impresario, "the bigger the humbug, the better the people will like it."[22]

In the Civil War years Barnum continued to seek topicality. His lecture room presented melodramas with war themes and a Miss Cushman, who had been a spy for the Union Army, appeared with brief lectures on her duties and descriptions of her adventures. She was "prettily dressed," according to one reminiscence, and did a series of quick changes to show the power of military disguise.[23] After Appomattox Barnum sent a telegram to Secretary of War Stanton offering five hundred dollars for the petticoats in which Jefferson Davis supposedly was captured. "Barnum is a shrewd business man," noted George Templeton Strong in his diary. "He could make money out of those petticoats if he paid ten thousand dollars for the privilege of exhibiting them."[24] But Barnum had to content himself with a life-size figure of Davis in female dress resisting the Union soldiers who had come to arrest him. A dramatic scene, but without the authentic relics Barnum would have preferred.

The American Museum was not destined to outlive these latest pranks very long, however. Shortly after noon on July 13, 1865, a fire, originating in the museum's engine room, spread through the building. In a short while the entire establishment was in flames, and tens of thousands of New Yorkers crowded the streets nearby to watch the spectacle. Desperate efforts were made to save animals, costumes, and some of the more valuable relics, but almost nothing was salvaged except the day's receipts, placed hurriedly in an iron safe by the treasurer, Samuel Hurd. As the animals, including snakes and a tiger, tried to flee the inferno, spectators panicked and some were injured in the crush. The whale tank was broken in an effort to douse the flames in the floors below, and the whales themselves were burned alive. When the statue of Jefferson Davis in petticoats, so recently installed by Barnum, was thrown through the window, spectators caught it and hanged it to a lamppost in Fulton Street. A few rare coins, the fat woman, the learned seal, and some wax figures and small animals were saved, but a collection valued by Barnum at more than four hundred thousand dollars (and insured for only forty thousand dollars) was totally destroyed.

The fire also engulfed other buildings on Broadway, Ann, and Fulton streets. Knox's Hat Store; P. L. Rogers, a clothier; a restaurant; some publishers; and a cigar dealer were among the unfortunate victims, but Barnum's was all people could talk about. Newspapers had a glorious time describing the antics of the animals and the crowd (thieves and pickpockets were arrested during the conflagration, normal procedure in the frequent fires that plagued New York) and spent an inordinate amount of space detailing the dying agonies of the animals in a jocular and unfeeling fashion. "After the fire," wrote the *Tribune*, "several high-art epicures groping among the ruins found choice morsels of boiled whale, roasted kangaroo and fricasseed crocodile, which, it is said, they relished. . . . Probably, the recherché epicures will declare the only true way to prepare those meats is to cook them in a museum wrapped in flames."[25] After the day's sensation was over, however, the papers, like most of the citizenry, mourned the loss of an irreplaceable institution. Granted "its humbugs and exaggerations," wrote the *New York Times*, the museum "still deserved an honorable place in the front rank of the rare and curious collections of the world." Its geological, conchological, and ornithological collections were among the best in the country. The museum was "a landmark of the city; has afforded us in childhood fullest vision of the wonderful and miraculous; has opened to us the secrets of the earth, and revealed to us the mysteries of the past; has preserved intact relics of days and ages long since gone, and carefully saved from the ravages of time and the gnawing tooth of decay the garments and utensils of men of note long since mouldered."[26] Barnum's ad writers could not have done any better.

George Templeton Strong was a bit more ambiguous. The museum, he noted in a diary entry, "has long been an eyesore, with its huge pictures" and "the horrible little brass band that was always tooting in its balcony" and tormenting passers-by at one of the city's busiest corners. But even Strong admitted the building's historic and sentimental associations.[27]

Barnum, who had rushed down from Bridgeport when he heard the news (although he maintained a stoical calm on the floor of the Connecticut legislature when he first found out), thought briefly of retiring. He could afford it, and the task of rebuilding the collection would be enormous. But he decided to start again, moved, he wrote in the autobiography, by two considerations: his hundreds of employees and New York's continuing need for a good museum. Renting some quarters on Broadway near Spring Street, in buildings known as the Chinese Museum, Barnum sent his agents scurrying to bring back new animal, vegetable, and mineral curiosities; calling the repertory company back, he opened Barnum's New American Museum on November 13, 1865, and thousands began flocking back to his attractions.

The task of stocking the new building was made easier by one of Barnum's tangles with the publisher of the *New York Herald*, James Gordon Bennett, an antagonist of three decades' standing. Despite occasional losses to dishonest businessmen, and with the one great Jerome Clock exception, Barnum was a shrewd judge of property values and a hard bargainer. After the museum building burned down, he still held an eleven-year lease on the lot. Because of the rise in real estate values, the lease was priced at more than two hundred thousand dollars. Bennett, wanting a new building for the *Herald*, was interested, and gave Barnum two hundred thousand dollars for his lease. Bennett also agreed to purchase the land, for which he promised five hundred thousand dollars. He thought he had obtained a bargain, but then discovered that his advisers, in valuing the land at half a million dollars, had not known of the lease on the property or they would have deducted the two hundred thousand dollars from their estimates. Bennett woke up to find that he had paid more for the piece of land than any lot its size had ever gone for, and he asked Barnum for his money back. Barnum, of course, refused, and the owner of the land demanded his payment. In retaliation Bennett refused to accept any advertisements for the New American Museum.

An infuriated Barnum called together the association of theater managers. According to his account he persuaded them to boycott the *Herald* as a body and place no advertisements for entertainments in that newspaper. Barnum may have been a bit too eager to take full credit. According to some theater historians Max Maretzek, now directing the Academy of Music, was even more influential in leading the protest. Bennett had refused to accept his advertisements also, and his dictatorial practices — which included browbeating managers who refused to have their printing work done at the *Herald*'s printing plant — and high advertisement rates had caused general irritation. Bennett thought the boycott would be temporary, and even printed some advertisements free. Those receiving this favor, however, headed their notices in other newspapers with the line, "This Establishment does not advertise in the *New York Herald*." Bennett lost considerably from the decline in advertising and in job printing; circulation suffered and in the end he was forced by the courts to pay the money he owed for the property. In 1868 theatrical advertising resumed in the *Herald*.

Thus, on the site of the American Museum, a great white marble building appeared, to house the *New York Herald*. George Templeton Strong, once again, was not impressed by the transformation. Terming the newspaper "a national curse," he argued that its structure was "even worse, as an example to the public, than its predecessor. That represented the triumph of claptrap and humbug. . . . This is the fruit of a systematic immorality, equally dishonest and infinitely more maleficent. I suppose that no man can be named who has done as much to blunt the moral sense of the people on public questions." Presumably Barnum was still in the running for this unenviable honor when it came to "private questions."[28]

Barnum did not have too long to relish his victory over Bennett. In March 1868, on one of the coldest nights of the year, the New American Museum burned to the ground, destroying the collection and the hundreds of animals inside. Once again Barnum was underinsured, and he took this fire as notice to get out of the museum business. He lent his name and advice to other museums, but by the end of the sixties this phase of his career had closed.

Ironically enough, it ended just as Barnum was returning to the older scholarly ideals that had animated Charles Willson Peale's museum some eighty years earlier. Twenty years of collecting, writing, and lecturing had given Barnum great familiarity with the world of natural science. Although not an expert himself, he frequently corresponded with biologists, zoologists, taxidermists, and university curators. No one else maintained so large a force of agents throughout the world, searching for rare species. When fires destroyed his collections, Barnum frequently sent the remains to institutions like the Smithsonian or the Museum of Comparative Zoology at Harvard, and he would become increasingly generous in the seventies and eighties, when the circus expanded his interest in rare animals. In 1865 he proposed to help start a national museum and managed to interest various members of the government in his scheme, and later still he aided the establishment of a major natural history museum at Tufts University in Medford, Massachusetts.

In this, as in so many other activities, Barnum followed the taste of his day. The years following the Civil War witnessed the founding of many museums in major cities, supported by new wealth and the growing professional self-consciousness of American academics. Although these new museums did not manifest the religious vision held by Peale, they retained some of the earlier rhetoric.[29] Barnum marched in step. With fortune and reputation securely established, he could afford to sound a note of enlightenment. The days of the "Fejee Mermaid," when he had poked fun at expert scientists, were only memories by the 1860s. The road to respectability led through association with prestigious institutions and their leaders, and Barnum exulted in his friendships with Joseph Henry of the Smithsonian and Louis Agassiz of Harvard. The new museums of the late nineteenth century were more selective and less sensational than Barnum's enterprises had been, specializing in either the fine arts or certain aspects of natural history, but he had popularized the museum idea to generations of Americans, and the new breed of curators acknowledged their debt to him.

Of course, even in this more scholarly atmosphere, Barnum still kept his eye on the main chance. In the summer of 1865,

The American Museum in flames, 1865

Barnum's rebuilt . . .

. . . and burned again

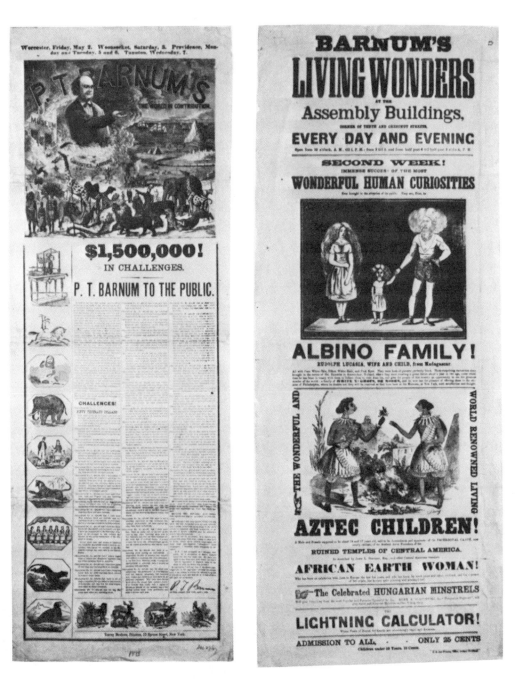

More wonders

P. T. and Charity

after his first museum had burned, Barnum wrote his friend, the poet Bayard Taylor, proposing a novel scheme.[30] He desperately needed new exhibits and hoped that by timely articles in newspapers (some perhaps written by Taylor), thousands would send in relics. But more important still was the objective of getting "presents for my new Museum from all the Public Governmental Museums and Europe." Barnum envisaged exhibits from the Louvre "labelled Presented by Louis Napoleon" and mummies from the viceroy of Egypt, items from Queen Victoria, the pope, and Jenny Lind. No matter how slight the value of the items "the names of the donors would render them *very* attractive," and a beginning might be made by having the President and his cabinet issue a signed document labeling the fire a national loss and asking for international contributions.

Naturally, Barnum needed an agent to stimulate European generosity. Horace Greeley was working on his Civil War book, and Harriet Beecher Stowe probably wouldn't go. That left Bayard Taylor, and Barnum, in "*strictly confidential* terms," asked Taylor to make the trip, promising appropriate remuneration. "You can scarcely imagine how intense and general the sympathy and regret are for the loss of the museum," he added.

But one week later, even these ideas had expanded. Barnum was enthused by the support shown by newspapers, historical societies, clergymen, and statesmen for establishing a new museum. And having sold his 11-year-old lease for two hundred thousand dollars to Bennett, "a fabulous, incredible" sum "he dared not speak aloud," Barnum was now a millionaire. Astor had given the public a library, Cooper an institute. "Why should not Barnum (who in fact was always more of a philanthropist than a humbug) establish a *free museum* for the instruction and edification of the *Youth of America*. In fact erect a five story building and open in it a well stocked collection of the works of Nature and Art."

Unfortunately, said Barnum, one million dollars wouldn't begin to give America a British Museum, and he still had to support his family. So he would erect the building but house gifts presented by governments and private collectors. The War Department, the Patent Office, foreign potentates, all could contribute.

But, as Barnum put it, there was a catch. The British Museum was open three or four days each week for six or seven hours. And it was closed for a few weeks each year. Those wanting longer hours and more viewing days for the "American British Museum" had an option. For alongside Barnum's free national collection, this great philanthropic enterprise, would stand a more familiar sight, "Barnum's American Museum — with its Giants, Dwarfs, Fat Woman, Bearded Ladies, Baby Shows. . . . To this Museum I charge an admission fee of 25 or 30 cents, children Half Price. Museum open from sunrise till 10 P.M." Visitors to Barnum's would be admitted also to the national collection, free, at all hours from sunrise till ten P.M. Those not wishing to pay for Barnum's would be admitted to the national concern free also, but "at *fixed hours — same* as in Europe and fixed *days* same as in Europe." I suppose, Barnum admitted modestly, "that 9/10s of the National visitors will conclude to visit the Museum, but if they don't, there's no harm done."

Barnum was aware, of course, that he could not publicize his full scheme. "I have herein shown you the interior — the skeleton — the internal machinery" he told Taylor, "but to the public it will *look* a little different for it will simply be announced that for such and such reasons Mr. P. T. B. will do etc., etc., free National etc., in which everything will be placed that is contributed," and also that P. T. B. "intends to rebuild and reestablish his American Museum wherein he will centralize his P. Lecture Room and all living curiosities and sensational attractions."

Bayard Taylor's response to all this is unknown, and perhaps discouraged by a lack of enthusiasm (and free contributions) Barnum never went ahead with it. But the audaciousness and scope of the plan revealed him once again to be a master at coupling public and private interest, a speculator who managed to present an enormously profitable enterprise as a giant philanthropy.

But of this artful maneuvering, the public knew nothing. In the late 1860s Barnum's reputation was benefiting from his energetic pursuit of exotica. The museum had begun as a means of acquiring wealth, its forms and exhibits dictated by public taste. As the collection grew, Barnum emphasized its comprehensiveness and scientific value. He now appeared as a benefactor of youth and scholarship, as well as recreation. But the successive fires had finally gotten too much, even for him. Distinction could be won in other fields besides showmanship. It was time to turn more attention to Bridgeport and play with political ambitions that were destined to disappointment.

SEVEN

Business and Politics

THE CIVIL WAR brought many changes to Barnum's life, among them an increasing preoccupation with politics. A religious dissenter in Federalist Connecticut, Barnum had been a Democrat and remained loyal to the party right up to the Kansas-Nebraska debates. In 1850, whether impelled by principles or profit, he was still suspicious of political reformers. That year he assured Thomas Ritchie, editor of the *Washington Union*, that rumors about Jenny Lind donating money to abolitionists were untrue. Her "oft expressed admiration for our noble system of government, convinces me that she prizes too dearly the glorious institutions of our country, to lend the slightest sanction to any attack upon the union of these states."[1] A stand against slavery still appeared dangerous and seditious.

By 1860, however, Barnum had converted to Republicanism. He illuminated Lindencroft in honor of Lincoln during the campaign, and after the war began, purchased three substitutes at one hundred dollars each to serve in the army, although he was overage and needed none.[2] He was also active in fighting Copperhead sentiment in Fairfield County, and on one occasion came close to participating in the destruction of a Democratic newspaper. In August 1861, Barnum and several dozen Bridgeport citizens got into their carriages and drove to a peace meeting in nearby Stepney Depot. "I am quite confident," Barnum wrote in the autobiography, "that not one of us had any other intention in going to this meeting, than to quietly listen to the harangues, and if they were found to be in opposition to the government, and calculated to create disturbance or disaffection in the community, and deter enlistments," do nothing more than report the matter to Washington.

But events turned out otherwise. The Bridgeport carriages

were joined by some omnibuses filled with soldiers. When the Bridgeport men arrived, they moved quietly into the crowd to listen to the speeches. But on their heels came the soldiers who, seeing the peace banner flying above the American flag, tore it down. There was some confusion and the peace advocates produced a few guns, but no one was hurt. The soldiers then carried Barnum to the platform, and although some of the speakers tried to keep him off, Barnum pushed to the front and made a speech "full of patriotism and spiced with the humor of the occasion." Some loyal resolutions were passed and the "Star-Spangled Banner" was sung. Then the party returned the ten miles to Bridgeport "with the white flag trailing in the mud behind an omnibus." Back in Bridgeport the soldiers began to threaten the office of the *Farmer*, a local newspaper with peace sympathies. Barnum urged them to stop and felt no harm would come. But after he left, a crowd rushed into the newspaper office, wrecked it, and threw its type into the street. "I did not approve of this summary suppression of the paper," Barnum wrote, "and offered the proprietors a handsome subscription to assist in enabling them to renew the publication of the *Farmer*." In fact, it was reissued, but no more peace meetings were held in the area.[3]

Despite his regret at the newspaper's destruction, Barnum exhibited no remorse at the breakup of the peace gathering. A strain of absolutism ran through Barnum on a few critical issues, and his zeal for civil liberties declined somewhat when his moral sensibilities were challenged. His outspoken patriotism and Republican loyalties demonstrated to others that the showman was not without ideals or moral commitments. After the 1863 draft riots, in fact, rumors grew that Lindencroft would be destroyed because of Barnum's energy in serving on various vigilance committees. Elaborate precautions were taken, but the only result was to foil some would-be burglars.

In 1865 Barnum was elected to the Connecticut legislature from the town of Fairfield, accepting the office because he felt "it would be an honor to the Constitution of the United States to abolish slavery forever from the land." He voted for the Fourteenth Amendment and also made an impassioned speech for amending the Connecticut constitution by eliminating the word "white" from the qualifications for suffrage. Arguing that the freedmen had not created the disadvantages under which they suffered, Barnum insisted that "ignorance is incompatible with the genius of our free institutions. In the very nature of things it jeopardizes their stability, and it is always unsafe to transgress the laws of nature." He confided that some years previously he had been frightened that foreign voters would reduce America to anarchy, but he was now convinced that foreign elements could be assimilated "to a truly democratic form of government."

"Knock off your manacles and let the man go free," he pleaded. "Take down the blinds from his intellect, and let in the light of education and Christian culture. When this is done, you have developed a man. . . . Let universal education and the universal franchise be the motto of free America, and the toiling millions of Europe who are watching you with such intense interest, will hail us as their saviors."[4] Despite his impassioned rhetoric, however, Connecticut retained suffrage for white men only.

Barnum was proud of his speech. He spoke for an hour and a half, receiving many compliments from the statesmen who were present. The Connecticut state senate adjourned and came in a body to listen. Writing a few days later to Theodore Tilton, managing editor of the *Independent*, a highly influential Congregationalist journal, Barnum requested more coverage. He emphasized his own wit and determination. "Those who undertook to interrupt me hauled off for repairs some time before I finished." Barnum begged Tilton to put him right before the readers, showing a rare moment of remorse and concern for his public reputation: "For thirty years I have *striven* to *do good* but (foolishly) stuck my worst side outside — until half the Christian Community got to believe that I have horns and hoofs — and now as I have got old, I begin to feel a desire that the present and future generations shall 'nothing extenuate or set down aught in malice.' Let them show me *as I am* — and God knows that is bad enough."[5] The war, and politics generally, opened the door to redemption, and Barnum marched in expectantly.

Barnum's legislative career made another claim on public gratitude by virtue of his assault on the railroads. As an old Jacksonian he had a natural hatred for monopolies, those "engines of political corruption" and "enemies to public welfare." At the very start of the session Barnum observed the railroad interests combining to try to elect the Speaker of the House. "A great railroad company," he said, "like fire, is a good servant, but a bad master."

Barnum set about to defeat the railroad "ring" in caucus, and did so; their candidate for speaker was not nominated by the Republicans. Barnum then began a long, tangled struggle with the railroads on the issue of passenger rates. As a land speculator he was quick to sense what would happen if commutation costs increased. Many living near New York's rail routes "had built fine residences in the country, on the strength of cheap transit to and from the city," and they were already groaning under the enormous increases posted on Vanderbilt's Hudson River and Harlem Railroads. Now Vanderbilt seemed about to influence the New Haven to do the same, supported by his flunkies in the legislature.

But the interests met their match in Barnum. " 'Yankee stick-to-it-iveness' was always a noted feature in my character," he wrote, giving details of the battle. "Every inch of the ground was fought over, day after day, before the legislative railroad committee. Examinations and cross-examinations of railroad commissioners and lobbyists were kept up."

When Barnum introduced a bill forbidding companies to modify fares paid by the month or year unless they changed all their other fares proportionately, the railroads fought back bitterly. The new law would have forced them to increase the fares of single-trip passengers, thus throwing prospective customers to the steamboats; commuters, however, were totally dependent on the railroad. As a climax to his speech urging passage, Barnum read the legislature some telegrams describing a secret meeting held by the New York and New Haven Railroad in which they conspired to raise commuting fares by twenty percent immediately, in case the Connecticut bill became law. Barnum proposed an amendment making the fares of two weeks earlier the approved rate. "The opposition were astounded at the revelation," and the bill passed. In 1866 Barnum was re-elected to the legislature and was instrumental in getting the gubernatorial nomination for a citizen of Fairfield County, his own bailiwick.

In February 1867, the Republican convention of the Fourth Congressional District in Connecticut nominated Barnum — on the fourteenth ballot — for Congress. Politics had always been "distasteful to me," he insisted. "I possess naturally too much independence of mind, and too strong a determination to do what I believe to be right, regardless of party expediency." To do the dirty work, "to shake hands with those whom I despised, and to kiss the dirty babies of those whose votes were courted" — all this, he felt, was impossible. But he accepted the nomination and began a spirited campaign against the Democratic candidate, a distant relative (his great-great-great-grandfather was a son of Thomas Barnum, founder of the line), William H. Barnum, who eventually became a powerful Democratic party chieftain and congressional figure.[6]

The campaign was bitter. The *Bridgeport Evening Standard*, supporting P. T., claimed he was being victimized by "the most malignant and libelous vituperation ever showered upon the head of a candidate for office in Connecticut."[7] Charges surfaced that William Barnum was spending money too freely, and the candidates received an unusual amount of attention from the metropolitan press. Greeley's *Tribune* supported P. T., but on March 7 the *Nation* published a biting editorial, "The Two Hundred Thousand and First Curiosity," urging Republican voters to scratch the showman's name.

Deprecating what it termed an increasing indifference to the character of America's public men, the *Nation* argued that moral decline had caused nations to die in the past, and America was doomed unless the process was arrested. New York Democrats were not helping matters, electing pugilists and gamblers like John Morrissey to high office. If Republicans nominated men like Barnum, they deserved defeat. Barnum had been antislavery and was a friend in good order, admitted the *Nation*. But he personified humbug, a Yankee smartness that "eats out the heart of religion and morality even more effectually than the display of great crimes or great vices, and which, if it were to spread, might easily end in presenting us with a community regular in its praying and singing, and decent in external crust, but in which all below was rottenness and uncleanness."[8] Indulging what would become its Mugwump sentiments, the *Nation* pontificated that Connecticut was too refined, educated, and patriotic to be represented by the owner of the woolly horse and the bearded lady. Letter writers protested that P. T.'s opponent was openly corrupt and argued that the showman was filled with "benevolence and public spirit," but the *Nation* held fast.[9]

More ridicule came from quite a different quarter. On March 5, 1867, the *New York Evening Express* published a piece entitled "Barnum's First Speech in Congress," a prediction "by spiritual telegraph" of what floods of rhetoric might be expected if indeed he was successful in the election. The article was written by the young Mark Twain and he caught, as other parodists had caught before him, Barnum's incessant self-advertisement, this time coupled with traditional political warnings about the future of America: "Because the Wonderful Spotted Human Phenomenon, the Leopard Child from the wilds of Africa, is mine, shall I exult in my happiness and be silent when my country's life is threatened? No! Because the Double Hump-backed Bactrian Camel takes his oats in my menagerie, shall I surfeit with bliss and lift not up my voice to save the people? No! — Because among my possessions are dead loads of Royal Bengal Tigers, White Himalaya Mountain Bears, so interesting to Christian families from being mentioned in the Sacred Scriptures, Silver striped Hyenas, Lions, Tigers, Leopards, Wolves, Sacred Cattle from the sacred hills of New Jersey . . . and so forth, and so forth, and so forth, shall I gloat over my blessings in silence, and leave Columbia to perish? No! . . . Rouse ye, my people," Twain had Barnum conclude, shake off the torpor, impeach "the dread boss monkey [and] reconstruct the Happy Family!"[10]

In the April election the Republicans suffered losses throughout the state. The first Democrat in more than a decade was elected governor of Connecticut. Some blamed voter identification of Republicanism with the radicalism of Ben Butler and Charles Sumner, while others pointed to the successful campaign of the Democrats to keep blacks from getting the suffrage. Moreover, workingmen were upset by the failure of the Republican-dominated Connecticut legislature to pass a law limiting the workday to eight hours. In fact, one reformer charged that the bill was defeated "by a dodge engineered by P. T. Barnum (the humbug)."[11] Whether it was the editorials in the *Nation*, the Twain burlesque, the hostility of workers, or his show business associations, Barnum was defeated, running well behind his ticket. Joseph Hawley lost the governorship by a statewide margin of almost one thousand votes, but Barnum lost his seat by five hundred of the fifteen thousand cast in his district. Hawley, the Republican, carried Bridgeport by fifty-seven votes, but P. T. lost it by one hundred. Barnum was also unable to carry Danbury, his early neighborhood, and was badly defeated in Greenwich.

George Templeton Strong pronounced his satisfaction in the privacy of his diary. This "prince of professional humbugs" was one burden Republicans could not carry into Congress. "I do not at all regret the result. If the Republicans will adopt charlatans as their candidates, I am thankful for their defeat. Would that the voters of this city [New York] had a like sense of decency."[12] And the *Nation* hoped that party professionals would not miss the lesson. Scratching unsuitable candidates was the only remedy left to independent voters, except on the rare occasions when issues overshadowed the qualifications of individual men.

Barnum took his defeat philosophically. He noted in the autobiography that his opponent's seating was contested on the grounds of alleged bribery and corruption, but he added piously that he had nothing to do with the charges. If "I had been defeated by fraud, mine was the real success," he concluded. The next few years, however, did see Barnum move a bit out of the spotlight for the first time in more than two decades. The fire of 1868 ended his museum business, and as his wife's health worsened he sold Lindencroft. In 1869 he moved into another home, Waldemere, right on Long Island Sound. He had already purchased a New York town house on Fifth Avenue, for he was frequently in the city on one sort of business or another.

Although these years brought him somewhat less publicity than he was accustomed to, Barnum was not idle. For one thing, there was his temperance activity. He had first become interested in the subject in 1847. Touring with Tom Thumb, he observed a great deal of intoxication "among men of wealth and intellect" and began to brood about what might happen if he became a drunkard himself. Barnum had never been in any danger of that; his drinking had been moderate, mainly at dinners and social occasions. But fear of losing self-control had always plagued him. Describing his reactions to the museum fires of 1865 and 1868 in the autobiography, Barnum recounted with some pride the fact that he was able to continue with his activities on both occasions — once giving a speech in the legislature, the other time having breakfast — without betraying by so much as a grimace that a calamity had overtaken him. It was not so much his optimism that explains his steadiness as his belief that giving way to excess emotion was unseemly and inefficient. It is hard to find much private passion in any of Barnum's relationships; his energy was devoted to his enterprises and his life style; there was little left for grief, pity, love, or hate.

When he worried, Barnum took no chances. The best way to defeat temptation was to avoid it. After hearing a friend, the Reverend E. H. Chapin, lecture on the social perils caused by the moderate drinker (the drunkard might ask, "What harm can there be in drinking, when such men as respectable Mr. A and moral Mr. B drink wine under their own roof?"), Barnum returned home and poured his champagne on the ground. From that day on he tasted no liquor.

But having saved himself, Barnum felt the need to save others. "I talked temperance to all whom I met, and very soon commenced lecturing upon the subject in the adjacent towns and villages." His lecturing technique, spiced with anecdotes and pert rejoinders to occasional hecklers, made him an effective proselytizer. Moreover, the showman's reputation for shrewdness and his frequent, publicized combats with moralizers deflected the usual objection to temperance advocates that they were sincere if arrogant bluenoses who mixed heavy doses of self-righteousness with their prescription for social happiness and economy. Barnum had so publicly divested himself of the cloak of Puritanism that his crusading took on a psychologically disinterested flavor. His concern lay with efficiency, and he happily displayed statistics proving the financial rewards of temperance to the family and to the taxpayers of the community. In all of his temperance lectures after 1869 he read a report by some New Jersey Overseers of the Poor that told how Prohibition had shrunk the expenses paid for poor relief and police protection to almost nothing. "In the course of my life I have written much for newspapers, on various subjects, and always with earnestness, but in none of these have I felt so deep an interest as in that of the temperance reform," Barnum insisted.

His temperance lectures sometimes coincided with his business enterprises: booking Jenny Lind into her theater, Barnum would seize the opportunity to spread his liquor views (only on nights, of course, when the Swedish Nightingale was not singing), and sometimes the same theater that presented a concert to one audience displayed Barnum himself the following day. In the 1850s he visited states where Prohibition had become an electoral issue and campaigned for the Maine Law. He was one of the podium stars for the antiliquor interests and invariably drew a full house.

His lecturing, of course, was not confined to temperance or nonprofit appearances. In the sixties and seventies Barnum joined the throng of celebrities who toured the country's institutes, lyceums, athenaeums, and literary societies, giving set pieces like "Success in Life." His normal fee was one hundred dollars a lecture, plus expenses. In 1866 he gave sixty lectures throughout the country for the Associated Western Literary Societies, one of the several centralized lecture bureaus that acted as agents for popular speakers. He was also hired by Redpath's Lyceum Bureau in Boston, perhaps the most successful lecture management firm in the country. Besides Barnum, it handled Mark Twain, Petroleum V. Nasby, Josh Billings, James Whitcomb Riley, James B. Gough, Henry Ward Beecher, and Ralph Waldo Emerson. Some of Redpath's lecturers made more than forty thousand dollars a season, and a few, like Beecher, received fees of one thousand dollars for single appearances. Because of Barnum's many other interests he never reached this class, but there were years when his lecture income approached ten thousand dollars.[13]

Major J. B. Pond, who worked for Redpath and then went on to manage his own celebrity tours, first met Barnum in 1853 in Wisconsin, when Barnum was campaigning for the Maine Law. Later on, Pond engaged Barnum to give twenty lectures on temperance in New England, paying him his expenses and two thousand dollars. Pond remembered Barnum as "the most prudently economical man" he had ever known, always concerned with saving money, whether it was his own or someone else's. Pond also concluded he had never met "a more heartless" individual than Barnum, however "plausible" and "pleasant-speaking" he appeared. Every portion of his appearances, as well as his entertainments, was reduced to a system that cut costs to their minimum. Extravagance, or its appearance, was useful only as an advertising technique. Barnum told Pond that "there was only one liquid a man could use in excessive quantities without being swallowed up by it, and that was printer's ink."[14]

Despite his lecturing activities, after the museum conflagration of 1868 Barnum felt at something of a loss. "Sometimes like the truant schoolboy I found all my friends engaged, and I had no playmate. . . . Without really perceiving what the matter was, time hung on my hand, and I was ready to lecture gratuitously for every charitable cause that I could benefit." Privacy and retirement seemed better in theory than in practice; he began to travel widely and to arrange more tours of curiosities. When John Fish, his old admirer, came over from England with his daughter Nancy, Barnum journeyed with them around the country, visiting California, meeting Brigham Young (and inviting him to appear in the East, under Barnum management), purchasing sea lions in San Francisco to show in New York, and discovering a new midget, smaller than Tom Thumb, whom he named Admiral Dot. In 1869 Barnum traveled with an entourage of midgets headed by Tom Thumb and Lavinia and also sent a group of attractions, including Chang and Eng, the Siamese twins, to England. Up to his old tricks again, Barnum spread the rumor that Chang and Eng were consulting surgeons concerning the possibility of separation; the peculiar perils attending such an operation, as well as the thought that once separated the twins would no longer constitute a sight worth seeing, helped draw enormous crowds to their showings.

Barnum devoted these few years of semiretirement to providing improved facilities for Bridgeport citizens. A large property owner in both Bridgeport and East Bridgeport, he made many civic improvements. He helped purchase the land to make Seaside Park, a plot bordering on Long Island Sound, "the most delightful public pleasure-ground between New

York and Boston." With the help of some friends Barnum donated the acreage after ensuring that the city treasury would improve the land for park purposes. He served on a variety of Bridgeport institutions — as president of the Bridgeport Hospital, a director of the Pequonnock Bank, vice-president of the Bridgeport Board of Trade, moderator and trustee of the First Universalist Church, and in 1875, as mayor.

He was elected to office in the largely Democratic city on April 5, 1875, in a period which brought him new opportunities for action. Barnum's first wife, Charity, who had been ailing for some years, died in November 1873, while he was in Hamburg purchasing wild animals. It was impossible for him to attend the funeral, but he went to London to spend several weeks in seclusion. While there he was comforted by his old friend John Fish and got reacquainted with Fish's daughter, whom he had seen on their recent tour of the United States. Ten months after his wife's death, in September 1874, Barnum married Nancy Fish in New York. She was forty years his junior, but it proved to be a remarkably successful marriage. Barnum remained in reasonably good health until shortly before his death seventeen years later; he was a wealthy and entertaining man with an entourage of interesting friends, and his wife's youth, good looks, and energy brought him the kind of companionship he had been missing for years. Like his New England ancestors Barnum felt bereavement and the life of a widower to be unnatural; comfort meant more than condolences, and activity meant more than rest.

Thus, when Barnum received the Republican nomination for mayor on March 30, 1875, he accepted; his popularity in Bridgeport had evidently risen, for although the Democrats now normally carried the town (in the race for the governorship that same year, Charles R. Ingersoll, a Democrat, carried Bridgeport by twenty-four hundred and eighty-seven votes to his Republican opponent's eighteen hundred and sixty-six), Barnum received more than twenty-one hundred votes to his Democratic opponent's nineteen hundred and seventy-six. His council was almost evenly split, thirteen Republicans to eleven Democrats. The *Bridgeport Daily Standard* described Barnum's election as a compliment "due to the man who, more than any other one perhaps, has aided and assisted the material growth and prosperity of our city."[15]

Certainly Bridgeport seemed to be prospering in 1875. More industries were being attracted there, and its population of about twenty-five thousand represented a doubling in fifteen years. Close to one-third of the population now lived on the formerly deserted east side of the river, a tribute to the success of Barnum and Noble's urban planning techniques. The Bridgeport press happily printed newspaper comments on the election from across the country. Barnum brought the city continual publicity. Fall River, Philadelphia, Albany, and Brooklyn papers congratulated Bridgeport on the election. The lord mayor of London could not rival Barnum's resources, noted the *Buffalo Express.* Captives from Fiji and Borneo could follow in his state procession, "and all the beasts of the forest and jungle will roar in chorus. . . . His civic guests may ride to inspect the public schools of Bridgeport on camels, ostriches, elephants." Ordinary mayors might have cats about their premises but "Barnum may have sleek tigers; bald-headed eagles will keep off mosquitoes in hot weather."[16] The menagerie and museum associations, so costly to Barnum's congressional ambitions, paid off dividends when running for local office; all Bridgeport could share in the spectacle.

Barnum, however, was not content to be a merely ceremonial figure. His desires for economy, law enforcement, and limitations on liquor consumption evoked controversy right from the start. Even his inaugural speech provoked comment. Much of the address was unexceptionable. He spoke of the need for prudent management, justice, and impartiality in the administration of municipal government. He called for enforcement of the liquor laws, attention to drainage, pure water, and the sale of adulterated food. He recommended constructing municipal baths and putting treasury surpluses out at interest, rather than allowing them to lie idle for months at a time.

And then he concluded with a paean to hard work and discipline. It was painful, said Barnum, to see so many idling their time away at baseball. Speaking like the Jacksonian Democrat he still insisted he remained, Barnum argued that "no person needs to be unemployed who is not over-fastidious about the kinds of occupation. There are too many hands (and heads) waiting for light work and heavy pay. Better work for half a loaf than beg or steal a whole one." It was the soil that was the "foundation of American prosperity." Too many people had become consumers rather than producers and thought "more of fashion than economy." Ironically enough for a master of entertainment, he urged that the poor restrict their purchases to necessities and leave the luxuries alone. "While we should by no means unreasonably restrict healthy recreation, we should remember that 'time is money,' that idleness leads to immoral habits, and that the peace, prosperity, and character of a city depend on the intelligence, integrity, industry, and frugality of its inhabitants."[17]

This, of course, was the Barnum of the lecture podium, retailing his moral maxims in an unchanging way for decades, oblivious to the transformations overtaking the American economy and apparently forgetful of the need for exotica and extravagance that had given him his own fortune and celebrity. The *New York Times* wondered just a bit about Barnum's criticism of idle youth. The *Times* was prepared to blame parents a little more. Country fathers and mothers, it wrote, "are led astray by ambition to see their boys mount to a higher sphere than they themselves have attained. They compete to give their children better educations than they need." It would be better for more farmers' sons to stay on the farm instead of filling the ranks of idlers at street corners. And in the city, labor unions frequently did not permit boys to be apprenticed to useful trades; their restrictions made it impossible for many parents to teach children the value of hard work.[18]

The *Times*'s position was, in some ways, even more conservative and anachronistic than Barnum's, but at least the newspaper recognized systematic causes besides personal inadequacy for poverty and unemployment. Barnum always individualized social problems, and like many self-made men, insisted that solutions required only self-control, industry, and ambition. To make the choice easier, Barnum was prepared to remove temptation from the paths of others, just as he had from his own.

To a large extent the Sunday liquor laws had fallen into disuse in Bridgeport, along with many other sabbath regulations. In his youth, of course, Barnum had been an energetic opponent of Connecticut sabbatarianism, but in his old age it was a different story. "Laws are made to be obeyed," he declared at his common council meeting, "and should be rigidly upheld by those whose sworn duty it is to enforce them."[19] The police tolerated a certain level of illegal liquor-selling as a necessity, and they were reprimanded. Two special policemen testified that they had attended a picnic while on duty, on a Sunday, and drank lager beer in a saloon with their stars on. They were suspended for sixty days. The owners of taverns appeared before the council to protest Barnum's strict enforcement. One accused the mayor of showing disrespect for Germans by his actions; another declared that if he could not sell liquor on Sundays, he wished all Sunday laws equally enforced.[20] The police commissioners admitted that Sunday laws were not enforced; livery keepers, for example, let teams of horses on Sunday without finding out whether the loan was for business or pleasure. Barnum countered that all he wished was to promote happiness. So far as the Germans were concerned, he was unsympathetic. "Can my Fiji cannibals slay and eat ladies here because they can in the Fiji islands?" he asked in a letter to the *Daily Standard*. "Can circuses perform in Bridgeport Sundays because they can in Paris?"[21]

Besides the Germans, tavern keepers, and the police, Barnum came close to alienating Jewish citizens. He was accused of having used the expression "miserable Jews" in referring to those buying whiskey on Sunday. In a rather strange fashion, a committee of Jewish citizens exonerated the mayor from having said it. They argued that Barnum might have used the expression but he was referring "not to Jews as a race, but to persons of all creeds disobeying the law." Barnum categorically denied the whole incident, said he was referring to "miserable whiskey," and had Jewish friends from Bridgeport and New York write in to testify to his lack of prejudice.[22]

Other Barnum crusades took after houses of prostitution (which the police insisted did not operate) and governmental extravagance. He appointed a retrenchment committee to investigate various departments of municipal government, much to the anger of some longtime incumbents. "Give any man or any set of men, or indeed any political party continual power to be exercised without supervision," Barnum insisted, "and the chances are that such power will be abused."[23] These also were old Jacksonian tenets, but they bore passage to another era with greater ease than did Barnum's individualism and emphasis on personal discipline.

There were other feuds between Barnum and his common council. In October 1875, Barnum vetoed a three-year gas company contract that he claimed was wasteful, forcing those who did not use gas to underwrite those who did. The council, however, overrode his veto. By the end of his term of office Barnum, as well as his opponents, was tired of the bickering; it had been too short a time for him to effect any major reforms, and he had his mind on many other business interests. When he presided over his last common council meeting on March 29, 1876, Barnum decorated the desks with flowers, perhaps a symbol of his gratitude at reaching the end of his tenure. Local newspapers praised his administration, the council itself unanimously passed a vote of congratulation, and Mayor Barnum turned back to amusements, although he would serve again in the Connecticut legislature, and he continued to play an active role in various Bridgeport philanthropies and improvement projects. Seaside Park was expanded, and his legacy helped found the Barnum Institute of Science and History in the city; there would be bequests for the hospital, the Universalist Church, the public library, and an orphan asylum. (Not all gifts to Bridgeport were so happily accepted. Taking Barnum's economy ideal quite literally, the town refused his gift of a bronze fountain, cast in Germany, because of the expense of keeping it in operation. Barnum thereupon presented it to his birthplace, Bethel, which welcomed it with two brass bands.)[24]

In the late seventies another Barnum scheme embroiled him in controversy and found him once again arguing for a loose interpretation of the law. No longer in municipal office, his strict constructionism, useful on the liquor issue, had disappeared. The subject of this dispute was Mountain Grove Cemetery, a garden cemetery that Barnum had helped to found some years before. Much to the opposition of local citizens, he had moved the old city burial grounds from the Division Street graveyard, thus disinterring the bones of the dead. "Let us hope Dear Mr. Barnum," an angry correspondent wrote him years later, "that you will not have the difficulty of gathering together your arms, legs and ribs, as will those of our Uncles, Aunts and grandfathers, who were transported in such dire confusion by you to the cemetary [sic] which will ere long receive your ashes."[25]

Barnum and others hoped to raise money for landscaping the new cemetery through a fair. They planned to stimulate attendance by distributing some of the gifts they had received according to lots. But some of the local clergymen refused to support the fair unless all plans for a lottery scheme were abandoned. When letters of protest began to appear in newspapers, citing Connecticut laws prohibiting lotteries and raffles, Barnum wrote in defense of the plan. He insisted the promoters did not expect to hold "lotteries or gaming in the common acceptance of these words. Property is *presented*" to the fair, and it was not in a spirit of speculation but of help. "Clergymen bred in colleges and devoted to their professions are not generally the most competent *business men*. Is it not wiser for them to look after the living and let business laymen look after the dead?"[26]

The local clergy could not, of course, let this pass. The Reverend H. N. Powers wrote to the *Bridgeport Daily Standard* that Barnum, a state legislator, was advocating "the violation of a law plainly set forth on statute books of this commonwealth." Somewhat disingenuously Powers added that he had voted for Barnum in the election and wanted to know if he was now teaching "that it is right for any man to deliberately break any law of the land at his discretion?"[27]

The next day Barnum returned to the attack. At his best in these polemics, his letter was four times the length of Powers's and involved a sharp personal attack as well as a defense of his position. Barnum argued that there were laws against transacting business on Sunday: a check dated on Sunday, or received on one, was not collectible; moreover, said Barnum, citizens have no right to visit neighbors to ask for or receive money. Yet Powers himself had been part of a church group urging people to write and sign checks in church on Sunday for a religious cause. "You raked in money enough in a few hours one Sunday to satisfy the Sunday segar-sellers and stable-keepers of Bridgeport for a year." Moreover, Barnum added, there are laws against giving theatrical exhibitions without a license; yet "in your church parlors" charades and tableaux were presented and money was received for admission. By their "suicidal policy" ministers "are losing a hold on the public conscience which all lovers of true religion cannot but deplore." If, concluded Barnum, Powers insisted that the crucial thing was the spirit of the law and the motive of the apparent transgressor, then he agreed, but this was precisely the justification he himself was using.[28]

Another clergyman, George A. Hubbell, attacked Barnum from his pulpit and received punishment as severe as Powers's. "This George A. Hubbell," wrote Barnum to the newspaper, "came to my home a few weeks ago, fawning and begging for the use of pictures, which he obtained, and then exhibited them contrary to the technicalities of the law, which demand a payment of license for all such shows." This George A. Hubbell, "who probably years ago denounced railroads for running a mail or milk train on Sunday, now rides in the cars every Sabbath from Westport to Bridgeport and back." Quoting Scripture, Barnum labeled him a hypocrite and a whited sepulchre. Hubbell wrote back rather feebly, quoting more Scripture: "All liars shall have their part in the lake which burneth with fire and brimstone," and Barnum responded still again, ending, "Profane man! The argument is closed." Interest in the fair seemed to increase during the controversy. After the fair closed, a huge success, the *Bridgeport Daily Standard* observed that "the latest rumor is that P. T. Barnum induced the clergymen to issue the Memorial so the fair might be advertised by the discussion."

Induced or not, this was Barnum at his best, battling on the side of libertarianism against an entrenched ministry, happily getting free advertising through the letter columns of newspapers, employing polemical exaggeration and biting sarcasm to make his point, and in the end asserting that having made "a lifelong study of the science of advertising, and discovering on this occasion an opportunity of working it to advantage, what I have written for the papers has been chiefly for that end. That it has been effectual none will deny!"[29] In politics, Barnum's natural position was as a member of the opposition, a gadfly and critic. In office, the same conscience that prompted him to challenge authoritarian paternalism produced an authoritarianism of his own.

Thus, his political career revealed the tensions between Barnum as moral absolutist and as moral relativist. Despite opponents' charges that a show business career had dulled his ethical sensitivities, Barnum was actually too much the moralist for political survival. In entertainment he equated morality with success. But government was something else, demanding different objectives, and Barnum did not hesitate to regulate the lives of his fellow citizens to achieve his version of a good society. His older creed of noninterference involved mainly state and national governments. Local communities, he felt, had the right to self-regulation.

Serious matters Barnum took seriously. His religion was a case in point. Despite his high-spirited anticlericalism Barnum remained a faithful Universalist to the last. He didn't merely acquiesce in Universalist principles, he defended them against all comers on the platform and in print. His pamphlet, *Why I Am a Universalist*, was an effective defense of his religion which, Barnum believed, growing numbers of Americans were adopting. Charges that his career demonstrated the moral deterioration caused by a creed that denied the existence of eternal punishment stung Barnum. According to local rumors, because Barnum's Universalism prevented his acceptance by the YMCA in Bridgeport, he went ahead and left money to build the secular and competing Barnum Institute of Science and History.[30] Some slights the showman could not forget.

But the moral dilemmas raised by Barnum's career were most systematically explored in his own writings. Never one to leave a good issue to another's charge, he confronted directly the ambiguities of the showman's function in his famous autobiography. Mingling the hardheaded businessman, the good-natured philanthropist, the lover of high culture, and the free-thinking democrat, Barnum made his self-portrait both a best seller and an essay on confidence in a democratic society.

EIGHT

The Man of Confidence

O N OCTOBER 17, 1854, Barnum wrote a letter to a newspaper friend, A. B. Norton. Only forty-four years old, he was just finishing his autobiography, entitled *The Life of P. T. Barnum.* "I am literally besieged by the New York, Boston, and Philadelphia publishers for the privilege of publishing the work," Barnum modestly confided, but he added that any newspaper publicity would be welcome.[1] His final decision came within two weeks, and on October 27 he signed a contract with J. S. Redfield of New York. Promising to advertise "in a most liberal manner" and produce a book of "good paper and in good muslin covers," Redfield agreed to pay Barnum thirty percent of the book's retail price of one dollar and twenty-five cents.[2]

So began the career of a book as complicated as Barnum's own life. The 1855 autobiography was printed again and again, and caused a sensation on both sides of the Atlantic. In 1869 a new autobiography, *Struggles and Triumphs*, was brought out in subscription form by J. B. Burr and Company of Hartford. Almost annual additions were made by the author, who bought out the publisher's plates and in 1883 produced still a third version, more concise (and in smaller type), with annual appendages made through 1889. By the late 1880s Barnum was boasting that over a million copies of his autobiography had been sold, and special cars carried it by the crate when his circus traveled through the country.[3] It was one of the three or four best-known autobiographies in nineteenth-century America and outdid all others in the promotional techniques that were used to sell it. As with everything else Barnum produced, the book promised much and delivered a great deal. It was controversial and unexceptionable, candid and contrived, repetitious and arresting, all at the same time. And it offered an elaborately worked out justification for its author's life and achievements.

As "the most democratic province in the republic of letters," autobiography was a popular literary form in mid-century America.[4] Ministers, reformers, statesmen, and generals rushed into print with their recollections. One student of the genre has concluded that most writers tried to create "character-types, rather than highly individualized personalities," because of their "psychological and aesthetic ineptness." Before 1870 Americans did not "look inward to trace the development of the mind or to question the process by which their psychic and emotional natures had been formed."[5] Thus, autobiographers concentrated on the public and not the private figure, emphasizing ideals of manhood rather than their individual peculiarities.

To some extent Barnum's autobiography fits this description. He did employ traditional archetypes to gain easy recognition, and he avoided probing the private depths of his nature. So external and casual did the book appear that contemporaries charged it had been ghostwritten. Charles Godfrey Leland, the poet, suggested that Rufus Griswold, a journalist associate of Barnum, might have done the job.[6] But the autobiography so accurately mirrors Barnum's personality, and so subtly presents his philosophy, that the charge seems misplaced. Apparently unrelated or irrelevant, the endless series of anecdotes actually develop a carefully controlled picture of life in America, and Barnum's contribution to it.

The book's early chapters form, in their own way, Barnum's apologia. His reminiscences show how youthful associations and values shaped his temperament. "I feel myself entitled to record the sayings and doings of the wags and eccentricities of Bethel," he wrote, "because they partly explained the causes which have made me what I am." And what he was did not always correspond with what others thought of him. For Barnum spoke of being "born and reared in an atmosphere of merriment," but his reminiscences of village life are hard and unsentimental. The fraudulent battles between peddlers and shopkeepers, the elaborate (and sometimes nasty) practical jokes, the teasing of children and abuse of dumb animals — these rather than quilting bees or barn raisings dominate Barnum's account. In later life he would remember that "the public whipping post and imprisonment for debt both flourished in Bethel" and record his gratitude at living "in a more charitable and enlightened age."

The "merriment," then, was an ironical label. Compassion, affection, idealism, and relaxation rarely punctuated the stream of old memories that described his boyhood. The death of his bankrupt father Barnum wedged between a joke played on a local hatter and the bottle lottery, which first exposed the boy's entrepreneurial gifts. His father's death appears to the reader as it may have to Barnum, an unpleasant incident sandwiched decisively between the materials of daily life. He felt little gratitude for traditional social institutions. They had given him only minimal protection. Recalling their weakness, at least the inadequacies of church and school, Barnum mixed bitterness with contempt.

Self-education was vital. Each man had somehow to acquire the skills to master his environment. Experience, Barnum emphasized, was his most valuable instructor. There is hardly an anecdote in the seemingly casual array he assembled that is not freighted with some important lesson: beware of appearance, shun the abstract, exploit every opportunity, and discipline the will. Barnum's boyhood had been an outdoors school, and he was passing on his discoveries as a legacy to others.

The first lengthy story in the book underlines Barnum's passion for realism. It portrays a boyhood hero, John Haight, whose escapades and youthful tricks, while they displayed boyish wit and energy, led Haight to eventual ignominy and obscurity. Why did Barnum recall the episode? In order to point out a moral. If only John Haight had been "carefully trained," he might have turned out to be a "blessing to his race." Without discipline the most charming personalities lose their chance for success and fall into the abyss that Haight entered. Barnum valued self-control as a major virtue; it lay behind his idolization of certain politicians and his well-publicized self-denial, at various points in life, to pay off his debts or expand his investments.

Realism, moreover, meant more than self-control; it meant getting behind certain social myths and public slogans. The pastoral ideal was fine for some, but bucolic pleasures could be abandoned if they violated one's taste. Piety was admirable, but many clergymen were hypocrites, and their congregations were often little better. One long anecdote described a group of orthodox Congregationalists who fought the installation of a stove in their church. But after it was purchased, they wanted it nearest to themselves. The deacon, who contended "in a whining tone of voice" that the stove made his section of the church "three times as cold" as it had been earlier, was a wonderful symbol of religious bigotry: his ignorance of thermodynamics was matched by his suspicions of his fellow communicants.

What was true of the religious was also true of the secular. In a Sunday school Barnum, answering a question on the Bible, defined the selfishness of every member of society: merchants, farmers, physicians, and clergymen. Expounding the meaning of the "one thing needful," he arrived at a pious conclusion: the one thing needful, he told his teacher, was "to believe on the Lord Jesus Christ, follow in his footsteps, love God and obey his commandments," but before he arrived at this point he had noted that for the merchant it was "plenty of customers, who buy liberally," for the farmer, "large harvests and high prices," for the physician, "plenty of patients," and for the clergyman, "a fat salary, with multitudes of sinners seeking salvation and paying large pew-rents." Despite the "tittering among the audience," his teacher admitted this was "a well-written and correct answer to the question." To be praised by the target of criticism was reward indeed. Barnum cherished the memory and repeated the maneuver many times.

These early pages of the autobiography seem to enshrine the

value of exposure. Surface appearances invariably misled, and Barnum attacked any group claiming special privileges or professional confidences: judges, ministers, lawyers. Most of the anecdotes of boyhood center on planned illusion. Always the real and the apparent diverged, and the apparent was often more convincing. After a tale involving a friend and a pair of misplaced stockings, Barnum argued that "scores, perhaps hundreds of innocent men have been executed on circumstantial evidence less probable than that which went to prove Amos Wheeler to be the owner of the old stockings bearing his initials." The fortuitous, the accidental, and the ascribed all merited investigation, and Amos Wheeler achieved his immortality because Barnum wished to drive the moral home.

Barnum had another reason for emphasizing the hard character of his New England youth. Like other autobiographers he sought a frame on which to exhibit his own life with some recognizability. To gain public sympathy and foreign comprehension he selected a model of Americanism and then represented himself as the finest flower of that new species.

The choice of an archetype was not difficult. Barnum dedicated his work to "The Universal Yankee Nation, of which I am proud to be one." Since the 1820s artists, statesmen, travelers, and novelists had searched for a type to represent the ordinary American. They had created several stereotypes — wild river boatmen, backwoodsmen, cavalier plantation owners. But the figure that exerted the most fascination, particularly for Europeans, was the Yankee. Clever, energetic, and flexible, always eager for a hard bargain, the Yankee fixed his eye on the main chance, was proud but taciturn, aloof from subtle moral distinctions, and armed with a dry wit and a keen eye. Though Europeans tended to define the whole country as the Yankee's domain, Americans narrowed his operations more closely to New England and the areas of her colonization.[7]

Yankees were invariably traders of one kind or another. "Outwitted in one bargain," wrote an English visitor, the Yankee "overcharges his next customer or client." Because it was rarely worthwhile to complain about tricks that might eventually be turned to one's advantage, nonresistance was the foundation of the Yankee's social compact, just as resistance was the basis of his political creed.[8]

The Yankee was not universally popular. Southerners, entangled in debt, resented the mercenary selfishness of northern merchants; country folk feared being outwitted by slick peddlers of wooden nutmegs or sanded sugar; westerners deplored pettifoggers of narrow vision; Englishmen complained that Yankees lacked souls and were indifferent to the charms of leisure that gave civilized life its value. But whether the larger portrait was pleasing or not, few denied the advantages of Yankee energy or the ubiquity of the Yankee presence wherever opportunity awaited exploitation. The Yankee strode across America "with spanking quickness," clearing vast forests, bridging rivers, the "advanced guard of the human race."[9]

Barnum's book appeared decades after the first efforts to sketch the type; Captain Marryat, Harriet Martineau, Charles Dickens, and other travelers had already made the outlines of the Yankee personality familiar, while actors like Dan Marble and James Hackett had explored the Yankee's comic possibilities on the stage.[10] Barnum was aware of the recognition to be reaped from his resemblance to the model. And of all Yankees, the Connecticut variety was considered the most enterprising. "It is said," wrote Lady Emmeline Stuart-Wortley on her American tour in the 1840s, that "if you ask a Connecticut Yankee in any part of the world how he is, he will, if not 'sick,' answer 'moving, Sir,' equivalent to saying 'well;' for, if well, he is sure to be on the move."[11]

Thus, Barnum took pride in his continually changing occupations. They illuminated the checkered, fast-moving route that self-made men took as their road to fortune. Nothing was too arduous or too strange for the hungry Yankee. Newspaper editor, lottery operator, merchant, carnival manager, Barnum was strong enough to survive disappointment and temporary defeat, resilient enough to retain the optimism that nourished the ambition of the true Yankee. And like other Yankees, he experienced not only a variety of functions but a spectrum of ranks. "I have been in jails and in palaces; have known poverty and abundance, have travelled over a large portion of two Continents," occasionally in "imminent personal peril." Here was the instability and adventurousness that had come to be identified with Yankeedom in the first sixty years of independence. Life had been good, Barnum testified, and despite some setbacks he had always expected it to be so. Despair was a foreign, un-American quality.

So the book proceeds, moving from boyhood to the early years on the road, the Joice Heth affair, the false starts in New York, the take-over of the American Museum, and on to Tom Thumb, the Hoboken buffalo hunt, the Fejee Mermaid, and Jenny Lind. Recognizing, as some critics did not, that his audience relished detail even when the details concerned imposture, Barnum told as much as possible about his escapades, giving names, dates, figures, and descriptions. There are details omitted and episodes distorted, but in general, the autobiography is unusually comprehensive. Every clause in the contract with Jenny Lind was reprinted, every concert's receipts set down and averaged. The operational aesthetic applied to the book as well as to the events described. In large enough quantities, information covered a multitude of sins.

To remain in character throughout, Barnum found it necessary to refer his actions to self-interest. His neighbors and ancestors had worshiped "sharpness," not integrity; by admitting his own cunning motives Barnum appeared an honest author, however much he had been a deceitful entrepreneur. One reviewer pointed out that even when recounting an act open to charitable interpretation, Barnum insisted that he was governed by neither generosity nor justice; it was invariably selfish calculation. "He seems to fear," wrote the reviewer, "that he shall be suspected of having sometimes acted without an eye to the main chance."[12] This would have betrayed both his education and his philosophy.

Alexis de Tocqueville, analyzing the American temperament twenty years before Barnum published his *Life*, made a similar point about Americans in general. Fond "of explaining almost all the actions of their lives by the principle of self-interest," Americans insisted that "an enlightened regard for themselves" inspired all gestures of goodwill. But such explanations frequently failed to do justice to the facts. In the United States people often did "give way to those disinterested and spontaneous impulses that are natural to man; but the Americans seldom admit that they yield to emotions of this kind; they are more anxious to do honor to their philosophy than to themselves."[13]

But there are signs that Barnum was not entirely content to honor his philosophy rather than himself. He did assert that self-interest had motivated his career and implied it was a sufficient ground for action. But he also admitted to being "a public benefactor to an extent seldom paralleled in the histories of professed and professional philanthropists." This hardworking businessman, who deserved emulation by the industrious and ambitious, was asking for admiration not because he was successful but because he had benefited humanity. Part of the reason for this request was vanity, but part was philosophical. Barnum was grateful for the realism that had brought him wealth, but he was occasionally uncertain about its benevolence. His Connecticut youth had taught him to avoid gullibility, but at some cost: Connecticut was not an ideal society. Dispersed widely enough, the qualities that had made Barnum rich might make humanity unhappy. Democratic individualism served private ambition better than it promoted social sympathy. And Barnum wanted to be known as public-spirited.

There were several routes that bridged this gap between his celebration of himself as a hardheaded materialist and as a generous benefactor to the race. As usual, Barnum took them all.

First, he announced that for moral and practical reasons he had always limited his misrepresentations. Financial swindles or deceptions that sought to steal large sums he would not tolerate, and he warned his readers against such temptations. "Know whom you deal with. Do not try to get money without giving fair value for it." His own bombast maintained certain proportions. He discussed, for example, his reduction of Tom Thumb's age. Announcing the youngster as only five, his true age, "it would have been impossible to excite the interest or awaken the curiosity of the public. The thing I aimed at was, to assure them that he was *really a dwarf* — [Barnum did not distinguish between dwarf and midget] and in *this*, at least, they were not deceived." Thus, if Barnum condemned certain kinds of imposture he was not being hypocritical, for the scale of some deceits was beyond his own desire or experience. The public, in short, might be grateful that Barnum had not taken more advantage of them than he had.

Indeed, Barnum spent a good deal of time exposing roguery. He campaigned against mediums, animal magnetists, religious maniacs, and greedy financiers. The exposés are detailed in his 1865 volume, *The Humbugs of the World*, which amplified and extended some of the sentiments he expressed in the auto-biography. Various chapters, "Trade and Business Imposi-tions," "Money Manias," "Medicine and Quacks," describe famous deceptions practiced on credulous believers. "It would be a wonderful thing for mankind," Barnum wrote piously, "if some philosophic Yankee would contrive some kind of 'meter' that would measure the infusion of humbug in anything. A 'Humbugometer' he might call it. I would warrant him a good sale."[14] He warned against lottery sharks and phony auction-eers and against the desire to get something for nothing that lay at the root of so many swindles.

But condemning deceit and disclosing his own limits formed only one portion of Barnum's self-justification; taken alone it would have meant an endorsement of cynicism and a disen-chanted realism, and his temperament would not permit so jaundiced a view of reality. The issue of illusions and ideals was more complicated than that. Barnum's catalog of humbugs, therefore, differs significantly from the list in David M. Reese's

1838 volume, *Humbugs of New York: A Remonstrance Against Popular Delusion, Whether in Philosophy, Science, or Religion*. Reese, a vitriolic New York physician, declared that "humbuggery" was "the talisman of wealth and fame" and that gulling was the prerogative of the age. Reese condemned many things, like ultraism and phrenology, along with the standard swindles. He singled out for ridicule temperance reformers, peace crusaders, and abolitionists. These zealots had distorted judgments; they magnified solitary evils to gigantic proportions and spent their energy gulling portions of the public into supporting their efforts at reform. Some believed the era's chief evil was slavery, others were convinced it was Catholicism; both were wrong, argued Reese. It was personal melancholia that magnified slavery or Catholicism into problems, not general experience. Extremists were to be feared as much as swindlers, because both exploited human weakness.[15]

Barnum, however, did not treat reform as a humbug. Near the time his autobiography was published he was writing reformer Thomas Wentworth Higginson about the evils of slavery, the importance of women's rights, and the dangers of bibliolatry. "Much in the Bible we should burn if it was printed in an almanac or any other book."[16] Barnum was, of course, a temperance crusader and highly committed to certain freedoms. He would never exhibit the kind of pessimism David Reese expressed about reform.

But more significantly, he entertained an entirely different notion of the function of exaggeration. Certain levels of idealism required it, and a little humbug in addition. More Americans were imposed on from believing too little, insisted Barnum, than from believing too much. "Many persons have such a horror of being taken in," he wrote, "that they believe themselves to be a sham, and in this way are continually humbugging themselves." Hundreds who believed implicitly in his (fake) angel fish refused to admit the reality of a whale exhibited in the American Museum, although Barnum had gone to great expense in obtaining it. His comment was a reflection on the bitter, hard-bitten life he had known as a Connecticut youngster: a good school for personal success, but a bad school for social values.

Barnum's claim to public gratitude was to present himself as a healer, a lubricant for the continual pressures engendered by the money-getting and competition of American life. National practicality, self-discipline, and industry, the qualities that had made Barnum rich, had crowded out "those needful and proper relaxations and enjoyments" that despotic governments distributed so generously. Americans worked too hard. "The consequence is, that with the most universal diffusion of the means of happiness ever known among any people," Americans were miserable. There was too little harmony and content- ment. Every society, including America, needed recreation and mutual confidence. Without them the anxieties of daily exis- tence would outweigh the benefits of total freedom and trans- form life into a series of unpleasant trials.

So, Barnum told his public that the greatest humbug of all was the man who believed everything and everyone to be hum- bugs. "Honor he thinks is a sham. Honesty he considers a plau- sible word to flourish in the eyes of the greener portion of our race." Without confidence a man virtually "slanders his father and dishonors his mother and defiles the sanctities of home and the glory of patriotism and the merchant's honor and the mar- tyr's grave and the saint's crown." The man without confidence does not realize "that every sham shows that there is a reality, and that hypocrisy is the homage that vice pays to virtue."[17]

This burst of lyricism contrasted dramatically with the hard- boiled cynicism usually associated with Barnum. But it was well for him to grow impassioned: his notion of humbug as social therapy was essential to the process of legitimizing enter- tainment in a myth-breaking society. From the eighteenth century onward, many Americans who sought to ally their na- tion with historical progress and the triumph of democracy had emphasized the rational clarity of the new republic. In their first burst of Revolutionary enthusiasm patriots declared war on the arts of illusion that had blinded humanity for so long, hampering efforts to strike the shackles confining human liberty. Artists, costumers, and pageant masters would have to abandon their cosmetic enterprises. Self-government would be open and unadorned, conducted without the trappings of ceremony and deceit so common in Europe.[18]

The attack on disguise operated on many levels. Americans debated whether to permit their diplomats abroad court uniforms and swords and wondered if judges should wear wigs and robes in court. Thomas Hamilton, a British visitor in the 1830s, protested the national opposition to rituals and insignia. "If man were a being of pure reason," Hamilton argued, "forms would be unnecessary. But he who should legislate on such an assumption, would afford ample evidences of his own unfitness for the task. Man is a creature of senses and imagination, and even in religion, the whole experience of the world has borne testimony to the necessity of some external rite, or solemnity of observance, to stimulate his devotion and enable him to concentrate his faculties." If Americans meant to be consistent, Hamilton went on, they should never address their judges by a title of honor. Homage and ceremony in British courts, he reminded Americans, was tribute not to the judge but to the law: "We regard ceremonies of all sorts, not as things important in themselves, but simply as means conducing to an end. It matters not by what particular process; by what routine of observance; by what visible attributes the dignity of justice is asserted, and its sanctity impressed on the memory and imagination."[19]

Americans, however, were not generally impressed by such arguments. The new urban police forces and railroad conductors joined in their opposition to uniforms, associating them with the livery of European monarchies. The Age of the Common Man had little tolerance for badges of distinction. Since credentials no longer guaranteed competence, adornment was unnecessary.

Social conservatives and defenders of the arts slowly but successfully counterattacked these prejudices with arguments of their own, and Barnum participated with his "moral lecture room." Didacticism was central to these justifications. Americans were as susceptible to temptation as any other people, it was argued, and their political system required special wisdom and virtue. Despotic and "arbitrary governments," wrote Horace Mann, "have dwarfed and crippled the powers of doing evil as much as the powers of doing good; but a republican government, from the very fact of its freedom, unreins their speed, and lets loose their strength."[20] But institutions and amusements that preached and molded offered relief from the pursuit of gain and at the same time encouraged virtue. Democratic artists and Christian educators could attack vice; with community encouragement the same arts that repressed in Europe could liberate in America.[21]

Didacticism, however, was not enough for Barnum, who wrote about the liberating effects of amusements. Nor was it enough for some of his contemporaries, who worried about the nature of social confidence in a country so compulsively competitive and suspicious of pleasure. "The impulses that incline to pleasure, if opposed, tend to vice," warned newspaper editorialists. The outlawry of innate tastes violated natural rules, destroyed intimacy and confidence between children and parents, and numbed a sense of moral excellence. "Our moral sense operates only in one direction," the *American Whig Review* complained. "Our virtues are the virtues of merchants, and not of men. We run all to honesty, and mercantile honesty. We do not cultivate the graces of humanity. We have more conscience than heart, and more propriety than either. The fear of evil consequences is more influential than the love of goodness. There is nothing hearty, gushing, eloquent, in the national virtue." Scrupulousness of a high order could coexist with great selfishness, the journal pointed out, and thus our "social condition makes us wary, suspicious, slow to commit ourselves too far in interest for others."[22]

The problem of social confidence engrossed many in the mid-nineteenth century, appearing in the works of political philosophers, reformers, pedagogues, and novelists. Not only does "democracy make every man forget his ancestors," wrote Tocqueville, it "separates his contemporaries from him; it throws him back forever upon himself alone and threatens in the end to confine him entirely within the solitude of his own heart."[23]

The theme of confidence invaded discussions of private conflict as well as public virtue. Some artists, like Hawthorne, understood the social texture surrounding individual actions and feared the effects of rampant individualism and competition. Hawthorne knew, notes Quentin Anderson, "that life is rootedly reciprocal, that people are known through their relationships to other people, and that the fantasies we try to enact, the aspirations we express, the religious convictions we uphold, are to be praised or dispraised on the ground that they foster or impoverish our relationships with those around us."[24]

Hawthorne makes clear his concern with social sympathy in many places. In *The House of the Seven Gables* Phoebe suspects Judge Pyncheon of evil within minutes of her first encounter. Indeed, the judge is dangerous. But "a doubt of this nature," suspicion of a respected official, "has a most disturbing influence," wrote Hawthorne, "and, if shown to be a fact, comes with fearful and startling effects on minds of the trim, orderly and limit-loving class, in which we find our little country girl." Bolder dispositions might enjoy discovering that a distinguished man shared the vices of a common humanity. "A wider scope of view, and a deeper insight, may see rank, dignity, and station all proved illusory, so far as regards their claim to human reverence" without feeling that the world was coming apart. But Phoebe had to "smother" her own intuitions to "keep the universe in its old place."[25]

Hawthorne did not imply that Phoebe was wrong to suspect the judge. But alongside this revelation of evil he was arguing that most men need a sense of order to nourish their social confidence. It was dangerous (even if sometimes necessary) to penetrate disguise and learn of hidden secrets, to seek truth ruthlessly and compulsively. The myth-breaker had to take care. Artists and scientists who sought to divest themselves of all illusions became, inevitably, moral cripples, threatening the peace and happiness of those around them. The quest for truth could be self-consuming. If there is any single "message" in Hawthorne's work, writes A. N. Kaul, "it is the one which pleads for the wisdom of recognizing the limitation of man's reach and capability, and for a relaxed attitude of brotherly tolerance, love, and compassion."[26] Hawthorne's "true world is revealed as dependent on the moral communion of men," concludes another critic. Without sympathy the community cannot survive.[27]

The pervasiveness of social suspicion is also a theme in many of James Fenimore Cooper's novels.[28] Cooper's obsession with manners and his attempt to show their close interaction with morals argues a view of social forms that Thomas Hamilton could have seconded: ceremonies and titles were not necessarily bad in themselves; deference to face values, acceptance of social hierarchy, concern for honor, and anticipation of good intentions were all antidotes to the commercial ambitions and competition threatening to destroy the fabric of community in America. This threat, apparently as inevitable as it was dangerous, provided the personal tension that impelled Cooper to sketch his tales of confrontation between westward migration and a golden age of noble savagery.

The writer who most explicitly confronted the issue of social confidence was Herman Melville. In 1857, almost three years after Barnum's autobiography appeared, Melville published *The Confidence-Man.* Wandering through a maze of allegory and horror on a Mississippi *Narrenschiff,* a mysterious stranger, wearing many disguises, rings the changes on human deception. A deceiver himself, he mouths a dangerous philosophy of confidence and optimism and exploits human greed and hypocrisy. The book, argues Richard Chase, "exposes all that was wrong with the liberalism of Melville's day: its commercialism, its superficiality, its philistinism, its spurious optimism, its glad-handed self-congratulation, its wishful vagueness, its fondness for uplifting rhetoric, its betrayal of all tragic or exalted human and natural values, its easy belief in automatic progress."[29] It was an attack on a social philosophy that had to be saved from itself and divested of false hopes and simplistic moral distinctions.

Melville's book, and some of his other works, have interesting connections with Barnum. Chase points to the links between Barnum's enthusiastic hoaxing and various passages in *Moby Dick*.[30] Melville himself, in some unsigned articles for *Yankee Doodle*, a short-lived humor magazine of the 1840s, parodied Barnum's aggressiveness in gathering exhibits and his ingenuity in publicizing them. The subject of Melville's parody was General Zachary Taylor's trousers, symbolic of the topical exotica Barnum featured in the American Museum. Several incidents within *The Confidence-Man* pertain directly to Barnum: Calvin Edson, the museum's thin man, is referred to in one chapter; the Siamese twins are mentioned in another; and the Confidence Man plays a trick on the ship's barber exactly like one Barnum recalls in his autobiography.

The Confidence Man, however, is not modeled on Barnum. It is the problem Melville explores that connects him to the showman; his greater artistry highlights the dilemma Barnum confronted. Although the Confidence Man, be he God or devil, practices many deceits, he also denounces suspicion and skepticism. He urges again and again the virtues of faith and truth and deplores the despair produced when cynicism replaces confidence. The novel examines just the problem Barnum's career posed: that of maintaining confidence in a world of sham, of crediting benevolence when its advocate symbolized fraud.

The Confidence Man does not stay on one side of the issue. To "doubt, to suspect, to prove — to have all this wasting work to do continually," cries one of his victims, "it is evil." "From evil comes good," answers the herb doctor, one of the Confidence Man's many disguises. "Distrust is a stage to confidence."

"True knowledge comes but by suspicion or revelation," he says on another occasion. "That's my maxim." If the Confidence Man is lying, then one need not believe his espousal of skepticism. Perhaps confidence is the answer after all. Melville seems to indicate as much in his portrait of the man who almost defeats the devilish disguiser, a Missourian named Pitch. To maintain himself and become eternally vigilant Pitch abandons normal feelings; he sacrifices his humanity and grows misanthropic. He survives the devil's wiles but at great personal cost. The choice is a hard one. To be human is to be cheated, to be victorious is to become inhumane. The alternative to false confidence is a "society without faith or charity," a world of "solitary, dehumanized" men, disillusioned, isolated, and unhappy.

Seated in a barbershop, speaking to a man who hands out hair dyes and wigs, the Confidence Man debates the issue of disguise. When the barber, with his insight into human vanity, suggests that most men are deceiving asses, the Confidence Man opposes him eloquently. Man's desire to look better merely attests "a proper respect for himself and his fellows." Decoration, embellishment, and concealment of deformity are not attempts to present a false face but efforts to improve others by improving oneself. The use of cosmetics and attacks on ugliness enhance the quality of social discourse. Painted faces help create handsomer interiors. Because illusion influences reality it should not be scorned as a weapon of morality.

Once again it is difficult to make a stand. So nice a philosophy comes from the mouth of a scoundrel; it fails to comfort us. Illusion may be a social need or the devil's business. In *The Confidence-Man*, Harold Kaplan concludes, "the simplemindedness of trust and the universality of deception seem to play themselves out to an impasse. They become equally unattractive and dangerous," leading to a stalemate "in a book which reads as if it baffled Melville's resources of judgment."[31]

Barnum's treatment of illusion was less subtle than Melville's, but he was able to resolve the issue to his own satisfaction. The hard realism that marks the early pages of the autobiography thaws eventually into a defense of healthy illusion. Humbug is "exhibiting a fly through a microscope and passing it off as an elephant to one who pays," wrote an angry Max Maretzek. But Barnum argued that humbug was not fraudulent if it yielded pleasure, and pleasure eventually produced benevolence and even morality. Distrust and skepticism alone would not guarantee ethical behavior: his Connecticut years proved that. Exaggeration was not the worst sin in the catalog. If we are all gulled in one way or another perhaps the only thing to do is to admit our humanity, accept illusion as a need, and develop the therapeutic possibilities of humbug. In a good society it could do little harm.

Readers of Barnum's books, in the nineteenth century at least, did not recognize the dilemma he posed, and Melville's novel was ignored for decades. To Barnum's admirers his autobiography was simply a road map of the route to success. English industrialist John Fish, his future father-in-law, wrote Barnum, "I am sure I should have worked as a mill-hand all my life if it had not been for you."[32] An American lecturer declared he knew "of no book which is better adapted to become a thoroughly instructive and agreeable guide through life." The *Knickerbocker Magazine* wished only that there "were more just such 'humbugs' in the world" and praised the volume as a true and reliable history, adding that Barnum's self-denial, frugality, industry, and temperance formed a model for his readers to emulate.[33]

There were a few Americans who examined the issue of social confidence from Barnum's point of view. In 1849, police arrested a Thomas McDonald in New York on charges of swindling a citizen out of his gold watch. Newspapers, in perhaps the first use of the term, called McDonald a "Confidence Man," because he duped strangers out of possessions by presuming on their confidence in his honesty. After some genteel conversation McDonald would ask strangers if they had enough confidence in him to lend him their watch until the next day. And many did so.

This confidence man may well have been a model for Herman Melville, but more interesting is the reaction he produced at the time. The New York press applauded his arrest, but several newspapers had some additional thoughts. The *Merchants' Ledger*, in a piece reprinted by the *Literary World*, argued that there were many confidence men in society, and their success was not altogether a dangerous sign. That swindlers could trade on the "confidence of man in man, shows that all virtue and humanity of nature is not entirely extinct in the 19th century. It is a good thing, and speaks well for human nature, that, at this late day, in spite of all the hardening of civilization, and all the warning of newspapers, men *can be swindled.*" Anticipating both Melville and Barnum, the *Ledger* continued that the costs of skepticism were high. "The man who is *always* on his guard, *always* proof against appeal," may be himself "a hardened villain." Not necessarily a thief, "he lives coldly among his people — he walks an iceberg in the marts of trade and social life," and his fellows cannot put any confidence in *him*. In Melville's terms, such a skeptic was Pitch, the Missourian; in Barnum's words, he was a "humbug himself."[34]

But to other Americans, and even more emphatically to many Europeans, the justification of exaggeration that the autobiography made signaled a dangerous decline in public taste and even a threat to a social safety. Severn Wallis's ferocious attack in the *Southern Literary Messenger* on Barnum's *Life* and Harriet Beecher Stowe's book, *Sunny Memories of Foreign Lands*, typified southern rejection of the Yankee character. Barnum was simply another imposter revealing his tricks, an insignificant mountebank forcing his twaddle on the public. He had done nothing worth reading about. "There was a time," Wallis wrote, "when people must have lived lives before they could sell them. It was necessary for them to have been something, or to have done something." Barnum fitted neither category. Instead of "dropping the trifles of their trifling lives into the wallet where time puts alms for oblivion, both men and women deposit them in a sort of charity-box or savings-institution." Wallis could not understand why Americans read the book, "the shameless confession of a common imposter, who has taken the money of the public by downright falsehood," a man with "a narrow and heated mind," whose success was based on "fanaticism" and "greed." American affection for Barnum rested on sympathy with trickery; "success may render almost any thing tolerable to us."[35]

The *Christian Examiner*, equally out of sympathy with Barnum, refused to admit that the Yankee type was at fault. William H. Hurlburt reviewed Barnum's book along with another Yankee biography, James Parton's *Life of Horace Greeley*. America, said Hurlburt, was "the chosen land of quackery." There was a fatal confusion between the words "popular" and "excellent." Exaggeration and hyperbole threatened to damage our literature and art. Taking up the gauntlet that Barnum threw down to experts, and recognizing Barnum's philosophy as an aesthetic argument, Hurlburt insisted that any true work of art "can only be fully comprehended and deeply felt by those whose fortunate natures or whose felicitous training may have fitted them to receive its lesson." Great works reached "the less gifted many" entirely through the "refining, the elevating, the ennobling influences" that they exerted upon the "gifted few." Americans accepted scientific expertise: they must do the same for the arts. Barnum was aiding the vulgarization of taste, just the "type of low-minded, money-making, vulgar, and shallow 'Yankee'" that Europeans and the "chivalry of the South" loved to lampoon. Both his aims and his mind were vulgar, like his fantastic house and its furnishings. He seemed "to have regarded his conscience as a kind of magic-lantern, and his lies as analogous to optical illusions." This was no model for New Englanders to take. Let them turn to Horace Greeley, a man too often dogmatic, arrogant, and prejudiced, but one who has "lived for ideals," who is "honorable," and who has defended the independence of the mind.[36] Ironically, Greeley and Barnum were close friends.

A parody of the *Life*, the *Autobiography of Petite Bunkum, the Showman*, published in New York in 1855, caught Barnum's exaggerated confessionalism, his egotism and money mania, and his reduction of the exotic to the commonplace. The author seized on Barnum's delight in typifying his experiences and laboring platitudes. Bunkum was born "at an early period of my life, in the 'Wooden Nutmeg State,' and was reared in the agricultural pursuit of a farmer's boy." Barnum's insatiable attempts to puff his enterprises at every point were also caught. "Even at that early age," noted Petite Bunkum, "my genius shone forth resplendently, even now as the brilliant lights illuminate the front of my Museum, with its ten millions of curiosities and its 'Happy Family,' consisting of a tame rat and a small kitten living together in domestic harmony — admission twenty-five cents."[37]

But the bitterest abuse, the angriest denunciations, and the most articulate attacks came from across the water. *Blackwood's*, *Fraser's Magazine*, and *Punch* flayed the showman. *Blackwood's* declared that if Barnum was a representative figure, America must be worse than Dickens had said it was. The reviewer had rarely seen "a more trashy or offensive book than this." Missing entirely Barnum's implicit defense of illusion, *Blackwood's* argued for its maintenance. Tom Thumb it considered a "deformity," and the giants, fat ladies, and other curiosities "loathsome." "When Providence, in its inscrutable ways, sends such an addition to a household, it is as carefully kept out of sight, as if it were a fairy changeling." This was good, said *Blackwood's*, for Nature's errors did not deserve publicity. The illusion of benevolence had to be served. The Joice Heth affair was "hideously repulsive," and Barnum's confessions prompted only disgust. The book itself was Barnum's most daring hoax, stimulating "amazement at its audacity, loathing for its hypocrisy, abhorrence for the moral obliquity which it betrays, and sincere pity for the wretched man who compiled it. He has left nothing for his worst enemy to do."[38] *Fraser's* contended that in Britain the author of such an account would be tarred and feathered, and no respectable publisher would dare to put out this story "of a man who has traded throughout on the credulity of mankind by a system of organized deception." Barnum's was "a Propaganda of Imposture."

Mingled with the disgust, in *Fraser's*, was anger at the British public's support of such Barnum enterprises as Tom Thumb. Barnum, admitted the journal, "attacked us in our weak point — our reverence for respectability. Snobs as we are, we fell the easiest of preys. A house in Grafton Street, invitations of the nobility to private views, dinners with the American ambassador . . . a command from the Palace," these were Barnum's lures. And the British bit. The tragedy was that as a result of his labors true art would suffer. "Ashamed of a false enthusiasm," people won't be tempted into a real one. Barnumism "will drive all true artists from the profession. . . . Our drama and amusements may degenerate."[39] The whole business was dangerous as well as sickening.

Punch contented itself with proposing Barnum for President, because he was a complete and noble representative of the nation, a man who had honored the sacred name of Washington by exhibiting his nurse; who had given northern farmers an invaluable animal to contend with the icy winds, the woolly horse; who had humbled the crowned heads of Europe by showing them "slavering over a loathsome dwarf, and enriching him with a colossal fortune." Such was the genius who deserved the highest gift the American people could bestow. He was the very "type and symbol of the glorious Republic."[40]

The virulence of the British reaction deserves explanation. Barnum was obviously being viewed as the vanguard of an invasion, a step toward the Americanization of culture. Just as Gresham's Law posited that bad money would drive out good, British reviewers were convinced that Barnum's success meant an era of self-proclaimed tricksters who would push honest showmen out of business and substitute exaggeration and deceit for modesty and accuracy. There were also recriminations for some of the specific effects of Barnumizing in England. The Tom Thumb exhibition took place at just the time that Benjamin Robert Haydon, the English painter, set up a display of his own historical canvasses.[41] Enraged and humiliated by the midget's success and his own failure to draw customers, Haydon committed suicide. The incident seemed to typify the fate of high culture in a world dominated by entrepreneurs like Barnum.

But most infuriating of all was Barnum's call for public approbation. Swindlers had existed for a long time, but none had the effrontery to call themselves philanthropists or to make money from revelations of their own cunning and deceit. This was intolerable. He does not realize, complained *Blackwood's*, that "all his professions of piety and religion are utterly negatived by his conduct." He thinks that by professing teetotalism, paying his debts, and treating his family well "he is entitled to claim *carte blanche* as to anything else."[42] It was clear that the British press took a different view of the audience than Barnum did. Showmen were supposed to present honest entertainments that diverted; they supplied a service that their patrons consumed. Barnum, on the other hand, relied on his audience for his taste; he made their reactions a part of the entertainment process itself. It took a true democrat to argue that a moral audience made a moral art, that standards were fixed by the entertained, not the entertainer. No such confidence in popular tastes or popular morals supported the British reviewers; morality was indivisible and independent of support, not selective and majoritarian.

Barnum, however, insisted that his ethics be practical as well as inspirational. A strain of philosophical pragmatism runs through his published confessions. When ideals interfered with appropriate conduct or hampered the believer, they should be abandoned. The temperance campaign attracted his energies not because drink imperiled human souls but because it interfered with efficiency, family stability, and the process of moneymaking itself. Formal statements of principle Barnum considered breakable, and inconsistency between conduct and commitment was not necessarily alarming. The autobiography contains many portraits of men who made life miserable for others by acting on principle. Ideals did not make the man; accomplishment counted for more. Barnum's exaggerations did not destroy the reality of the American Museum's attractions and that was what separated humbug from outright swindling. Much to the fury of orthodox moralizers, Barnum compartmentalized ethics and achievements. When act and ideal clashed he refused to make a categorical choice. Circumstances often made it necessary to review the ideals that improved the conduct of life.

Thus, the autobiography raised complicated and diverse issues. Credulity and deceit, disguise and sincerity, hypocrisy and idealism, art and artifice were subjects of critical importance in a society that had abandoned traditional rituals of accreditation. Antebellum Americans worshiped both equality and achievement. Their great men had to perform special services and fulfill popular myths. Barnum served both needs. He functioned partly as a Trickster, a figure who appears in many cultures, sometimes as a clown, sometimes as a jokester, sometimes as an ogre, but always as the spirit of disorder and the enemy of boundaries. The Trickster's actions, suggests Roger Abrahams, "are extremely aggressive, destructive, and forbidden. Therefore, his acts must be countenanced because of some aspect of our dream world; his actions must represent a way of getting around taboos and other restrictions without actually upsetting the order of society." The Trickster behaves as others would behave were they not constrained by fear of consequences. "Vicariously, sympathetically, through the acts of this egocentric sensualist, man expunges the pleasures that might otherwise destroy both his ordered world and himself."[43]

Barnum's exaggerations and confessions, his humbugs and deceits, were the dreams of many Americans who could not try them. His audacity in donning the mantle of morality appealed to Americans convinced that the older boundaries of human behavior were no longer quite valid, but who dared not overstep these limits themselves. Barnum was not merely a Trickster, however, because he continued to clothe his amorality in moral garments. Even American fantasies had to be constrained. Nonetheless, he had become one of the lightning rods of the American imagination, drawing off the anger of the gods from the community's sins to himself. And his wealth and success suggested that divine wrath did not always punish outrageous indulgence.

In this context the autobiography is not simply the chronicle of a life, but a text on the social functions of illusion and the role of the deceiver in an egalitarian society.

NINE

The Circus

LIKE A GOOD TROUPER, Barnum had saved his best act for last. Or at any rate, his most enduring one. Viewed from 1810, the year of his birth, Barnum's circus forms only one of his many show business achievements, a satisfying but by no means unexpected triumph. Viewed from the middle of the twentieth century, however, the circus stands as Barnum's one enduring monument to fame, the legacy his name left for the future. The American Museum, Tom Thumb, Jenny Lind, the Fejee Mermaid, and Iranistan are dusty relics brushed off by each generation's biographers. But "The Greatest Show On Earth," now approaching its second century, has accomplished through sheer survival what none of Barnum's other feats could manage: guarantee him immortality. In this sense the climax of his career, the circus represents a different, and some might feel, a less creative phase as well. The expectations and experiences of Americans in the 1870s and 1880s contrasted with those of their parents and grandparents. These new audiences venerated Barnum as a walking legend, but they didn't duel or match wits with him. Bonhomie and ornament took over where competition and coyness had once reigned. It was a tribute to the showman that he managed to thrive on the tastes of antebellum and postbellum Americans. But then, he had always been adaptable.

Barnum's entry into the circus business in 1870 did not lack preparation. In the 1830s he had traveled with one of the pioneers of the American circus, Aaron Turner, and later formed his own troupe, although Barnum's Grand Scientific and Musical Theater toured only a short time and consisted of a juggler, a magician, a clown, and some musical performers. Barnum's Great Asiatic Caravan, Museum and Menagerie, organized in

1851, exhibited until 1854, displaying the first herd of elephants in the United States, along with lions, some freaks, Tom Thumb, and a brass band. Taken along with the American Museum, these two groups gave Barnum experience with each of the three elements that made up the late-nineteenth-century circus: the menagerie, the exhibition of freaks and acrobats, and the variety show.

The menagerie was the oldest of these American entertainment forms.[1] Importation of wild or exotic animals went back to the early eighteenth century; well before the Revolution, colonials had seen their first lions, camels, polar bears, and leopards. By the 1780s small collections of animals were being shown in the eastern cities, and in the early nineteenth century larger animals, like elephants, became more common (and more profitable).

The circus itself, comprising exhibitions of horsemanship, acrobatics, and clowning, also antedated the Revolution in America. Almost all the performers and producers were European. The most permanent eighteenth-century circus was established in Philadelphia by an Englishman, John Bill Ricketts, in 1793, and witnessed by several American Presidents. Ricketts' show, like others through the Jacksonian era, was small in scale, featuring a few performers: a clown who could perform on horseback, some jugglers and tightrope walkers. It could not compare in size or splendor with the great shows of horsemanship and acrobatics that Philip Astley was presenting at just this time in his Royal Amphitheatre of Arts in London.[2] Playhouse as well as circus, Astley's had begun as a riding school shortly after mid-century, and the equestrian emphasis remained strong in all its shows.

Although the splendor of Astley's establishment still lay beyond American experience, there were signs of growth by the 1820s and 1830s. Nathan Howes and his brother Seth, Isaac A. Van Amburgh, Aaron Turner, Edmund and Jeremiah Mabie, and John Robinson began to organize circuses and tour in wagons on the improved roads connecting American cities. By the 1830s there were dozens of wagon shows, some with no more than six or eight performers, touring the East. Unlike Ricketts' these shows featured wild and exotic animals, with less emphasis on the brilliant horsemanship that dominated European circuses. The distinction between circuses and menageries gradually disappeared in this period, as equestrians, clowns, and beasts mingled under the same tents. Animal trainers like Isaac A. Van Amburgh not only placed their charges on display, but made them obey commands and give performances.

Animal importation was controlled by a group of dealers in Putnam and Westchester counties, New York, who formed a syndicate in the 1830s that came to be known as the "Flatfoots." The Flatfoots included in their ranks John J. Nathans, a circus rider; Lewis B. Lent; and George F. Bailey, and sold stock in their enterprise. The Flatfoot syndicate had rivals, but it indicated the great advantages of centralization and control, even in the first years of the American circus.

No American town was large enough to support a permanent circus, the way Paris or London could, so the American companies concentrated on travel. The great distances and intensive competition brought dividends to shows that innovated and experimented with travel arrangements. In the 1850s some circuses playing the western states employed riverboats in place of tents and wagons, floating from one town to the next without needing to reconstruct facilities in each place they visited. The Floating Circus Palace of Spaulding and Rogers, a giant two-hundred-foot boat, housed an arena seating twenty-four hundred, along with a concert saloon and a museum boasting "over 100,000 curiosities."[3] A few circuses exploited the railroads, but none of them did this systematically before the Civil War.

Many of the early circuses acquired an unsavory reputation. To attract respectable folk, some shows featured their menageries during the day and limited circus performances to evening hours. Other showmen advertised that they had no circus at all, and Barnum himself did not use the word in his own entertainments until the 1870s. Confidence men and local toughs inevitably infiltrated the crowds; there was heavy drinking, some prostitution, and frequent violence. Exhibits sometimes pandered to sexual curiosity. W. C. Coup, one of the circus pioneers, recalled that both showmen and patrons were belligerent: "The sturdy sons of toil came to the show eager to resent any imagined insult; and failing to fight with the showmen, would often fight among themselves. . . . It was no infrequent occurrence to be set upon by a party of roughs, who were determined to show their prowess and skill as marksmen with fists and clubs if required. As a consequence showmen were armed. . . . Almost daily would these fights occur, and so desperately were they entered into that they resembled pitched battles more than anything else."[4] Well into the twentieth century old circus employees remembered riots involving death or serious injury, and clerical opposition to the circus as a dangerous and immoral amusement was widespread.

By the time Barnum got seriously involved in 1870, the institution had achieved some stability. A former clown, Dan Castello; Adam Forepaugh, a Philadelphian; the Sells brothers; W. W. Cole; and James A. Bailey were making their presence felt, and the railroad had become a major element in successful management. But although these circus owners were talented and even inspired, no one had yet fully exploited the growing American taste for the spectacular and the exotic. Large menageries and talented performers were expensive, and so was the staff necessary to move hundreds of animals and humans about quickly. Moral suspicions lingered. To realize the possibilities of the market, capital, expert management, and extensive publicity were necessary. These needs were met by the circus Barnum helped form in 1870.

The original partners were two old circus men, W. C. Coup and Dan Castello. Coup had gained experience as a circus roustabout before becoming assistant manager of the Yankee Robinson Show. With Castello he had organized Dan Castello's Circus and toured the Midwest, but Coup had larger ambitions. He needed more money and a greater name for his circus to achieve the size and splendor he wished for it. Writing to Barnum and flattering the showman, he persuaded him to join in organizing P. T. Barnum's Museum, Menagerie, and Circus. They signed their contract in the fall of 1870.

Barnum had become steadily more interested in animal exhibitions in the 1860s, and before the second fire he had formed a company with the Van Amburgh menagerie that traveled in the summer and exhibited the animals in the museum in the winter. The menagerie included the only giraffe then in America, lions, tigers, and many other valuable animals. As part of his more scholarly concern with natural science, he planned to construct buildings and cages in Bridgeport to acclimate rare animals and birds and thought of establishing a zoo in New York. He interested President Andrew Johnson and various cabinet members in the scheme,[5] but then came the 1868 fire and his brief retirement. Barnum, therefore, was receptive to Coup's inquiries, the more so because the enterprise he joined was the largest traveling circus in the country. It opened officially in Brooklyn in the spring of 1871 and went on to make several hundred thousand dollars in its first season.

As usual, Barnum claimed that success rested on his own energy, but Coup was the aggressive and innovative partner, pioneering, in 1872, a more systematic utilization of the railroads than any circus manager had dared attempt and also persuading the railroads to run excursion trains (at reduced rates) for circus customers. Coup planned to bypass smaller towns, where daily receipts were limited, and make the audience rather than the circus troupe do the traveling.

The strategy worked. Covering ground quickly, circuses could play large towns without stopovers on the road; but the details of coordinating more than sixty cars filled with men, animals, and equipment, keeping them on time, and supervising their loading and unloading as well as the construction of the great tents, required great logistical adroitness. Coup was expert, and also inventive. He designed his own flatcars so that circus wagons could be placed easily aboard them, made the wagons themselves more adaptable, and probably developed a system of inclined planes for loading and unloading.[6]

So complex was circus management that in the next two decades it was often likened to military mobilization, and the circus became a symbol of administrative coordination in an age that venerated and developed executive skills. "Routing a big circus is like maneuvering an army in time of war," commented one of Barnum's press agents.[7] A more neutral observer argued that "man's intelligence has devised nothing more compact, more orderly, more admirably adapted to its purpose, than the train of a great modern circus," this "kingdom on wheels, a city that folds itself up like an umbrella. No army knows such severe discipline," and "every 24 hours it solves a military problem that would have staggered Napoleon himself."[8] Circus movements were watched by army officers in various countries, including the United States, who were eager to imitate their precision and efficiency.

In keeping with the new requirements of organization, late-nineteenth-century circus managers sought a better reputation for their employees. "Most people," wrote one journalist, "have an idea that the circus is a free and easy place, and that those who travel with it are a Bohemian crowd, whose leisure hours are spent in more or less riotous pleasures." But this was a misconception. For "sobriety, industry, and general virtue and morality," no other community could compare with the circus.[9] "The very nature of the business," wrote another, "with its claims on brain and body, forbids immoral or vicious excesses." Most circus women "spend a few hours each Sunday in church."[10]

Besides his contributions to circus management, W. C. Coup was also instrumental in making another major circus reform: the addition of a second ring. This meant, as he admitted, giving a double performance, but it solved the problem of crowd disruption by keeping the audience in its seats. In the one-ring shows it was "impossible to prevent the people who were farthest from the ring from standing up. They would rush to the front and thus interfere with many other people."[11] Given two rings, audiences stayed where they were, just as well off in one part of the tent as in any other. Rival circuses imitated the arrangement, and the Barnum and Bailey circus eventually expanded it into the familiar three-ring setting, adding two stages in addition.

Besides quieting the crowds, the additional rings also required changes in circus performances. The old talking clowns, masters of witty invective (and sometimes of vulgar jokes), found it impossible to talk to audiences amidst the noise and distraction of a three-ring circus; slapstick and pantomime replaced verbal sallies.[12] Intimacy was lost, along with certain kinds of interactions between performers and spectators. The circus was becoming too big to permit audiences to do more than stay in their seats and watch the show, passive prisoners of their own excitement and bewilderment. The sparring, jostling, articulate masses who swarmed through Barnum's museum in the fifties and sixties were different from the quieter crowds of the seventies who sat enraptured by the trapeze artists and animal acts.

Railroads, of course, permitted thousands to attend who lived far from the touring sites, and in six months the show did almost a million dollars' worth of business for Barnum and Coup. So large did the outfit become that its managers dispatched one portion to tour the southern states as an independent show.

But an old nemesis still pursued Barnum. In August 1872, he purchased the Hippotheatron buildings on Fourteenth Street in New York, which had housed the Lent Circus. Barnum intended to open there a "Museum, Menagerie, Hippodrome, and Circus that would furnish employment for two hundred of my people who would otherwise be idle during the winter." The show opened in November, before several thousand customers and to enthusiastic newspaper reviews. But just before Christmas the buildings burned to the ground within half an hour, destroying the whole collection. "It is somewhat singular that fire is constantly seeking out Mr. Barnum's 'great shows'" the *New York Times* observed, wondering out loud if the fires were the result of carelessness "or causes still less creditable."[13] As usual, Barnum was underinsured, estimating his loss at more than two hundred thousand dollars. Arson was ruled out, but there was no doubt that the arrangements had been handled in a cavalier manner: the month before, the New York fire marshal had declared the museum and menagerie unsafe to the public and to surrounding buildings but his warning had been ignored. The fire, which occurred at four in the morning, luckily did not cause the horror of a mass panic, but threatened the Academy of Music and Tammany Hall across the street and set fire to Grace Chapel. The animals lost included four giraffes, two polar bears, tigers, lions, sea lions, camels, pelicans, apes, gorillas, along with costumes and equipment. The fire marshal's office assigned the cause to the steam pipes: placed too close to the wooden boards, they ignited the whole structure. A controversy about the fire's cause erupted in the pages of New York newspapers, and in the future Barnum would find the city more concerned with the precautions he took when his building plans required approval.

Barnum turned immediately to refurbishing his collections. Mobilizing his agents around the world, he gathered a new show by the spring of 1873. Addressing a benefit performance for his equestrians in New York, Barnum announced he was prepared to invest another half million dollars, if necessary, to start again: "The public will have amusements, and they ought to be those of an elevating and an unobjectionable character. For many years it has been my pleasure to provide a class of instructive and amusing entertainments to which a refined Christian mother can take her children with satisfaction." Just as he had done with the museum, Barnum smothered his enterprise with moral adjectives, and it was as "The Great Moral Show" that newspapers began to refer to it.

The 1873 Barnum's Travelling World's Fair opened at the American Institute Building in the spring, before leaving on a tour of New England, Canada, and the Midwest. It included an

Indian rhinoceros, elaborate chariots, banners, tableaux and costumes, hundreds of horses and elephants, automata, stuffed birds, statuary. Its splendor could "compete with state journeys of oriental potentates." Beginning a long-lived tradition, the show paraded through the streets of New York the night before opening, stunning the thousands who gathered to watch. Acknowledging its brilliance, the *New York Times* reported that Barnum considered this effort, "succeeding the burning of his late museum on 14th Street, to be the crowning triumph of his life."[14] Although Barnum estimated the expenses at more than five thousand dollars a day, the show made money. "I suppose there is a limit beyond which it would be fatal to go, in catering for public amusement," he wrote, "but I have never yet found that limit."

While Barnum was abroad on a purchasing trip in the fall and winter of 1873, Coup and Barnum's son-in-law, Samuel H. Hurd, the show's treasurer, obtained a lease of some land owned by the Harlem Railroad between Twenty-sixth and Twenty-seventh streets and Fourth and Madison avenues. They intended to build a hippodrome on it to exhibit the circus and other spectacles in a permanent building. When Barnum returned to America in April 1874, the giant building, four hundred and twenty-five feet long and two hundred feet wide, was already completed.

The superintendent of buildings did his best to make the structure a bit safer than originally intended. The seats were cased underneath with tin or sheet iron to prevent the wood from being easily ignited. The two grand entrances, fifteen feet wide, could admit two fire engines abreast, newspapers announced, and there were twenty exit doors. Coup spent a good deal of time detailing the safety precautions, with good reason. Under pressure from the Board of Underwriters' Association and property-owners near the hippodrome, the Board of Aldermen had appointed a committee to examine the structure.[15] Property-holders complained that Barnum's record did not inspire confidence in the building's longevity, and the aldermen feared a panic in the event of fire: the building was designed to accommodate eight thousand spectators, and the seventies and eighties were decades of disastrous theater fires, both in the United States and Europe. Citizens charged that few insurance companies would touch the building, and some spoke of petitioning the Board of Health for action. Coup argued that elaborate precautions were being taken: six hydrants, with hoses, were to be placed across the length of the building, a fire apparatus attached to each of the forty pillars surrounding the ring, and extinguishers distributed through the arena. The largest audience could be evacuated within five minutes. Something Coup said must have convinced the municipal authorities, for the hippodrome opened in April with one of Barnum's most elaborate spectaculars.

Barnum had purchased an entire pageant, called the "Congress of Monarchs," from the Sanger Circus in London for one hundred and fifty thousand dollars. The purchase included chariots, harness, costumes, armor, flags, and banners. The sight of heralds, knights, guards, and soldiers in their various national costumes, encircling thrones on which sat Queen Victoria, Napoleon and his marshals, the Pope (surrounded by cardinals and bishops), the Pasha of Egypt, the Czar of Russia, the Emperor of China, all climaxed by the appearance of the Stars and Stripes, Revolutionary soldiers, and Indians, drove the New York audiences wild.[16] Nothing like this concentrated pomp and splendor had ever been shown before in America, and its appearance marked the transformation of the traditional circus into something of a nineteenth-century light show, a pageant dazzling spectators with bombardments of color, light, music, and thrills. Barnum's circus employed dozens of skilled craftsmen to design, paint, gild, and carve the accessories these pageants demanded. Each circus opened with a procession that seemed more elaborate than the last.

If Barnum's early entertainments had focused on problem-solving and competition between showman and audience, his later productions permitted more passive spectatorship. This was artifice caught up in its own splendor and profusion; on-lookers had nothing more to do than sit back and enjoy it. The stationary observers gaped and rubbernecked while the complicated show mingled peril with magnificence. The circus tent was a dream world, a setting for fantasy, not an arena of competition the way the museum had been. In the eighties and nineties specialists in pageantry appeared, like Imre and Bolossy Kiralfy, who produced "Nero and the Destruction of Rome" and "The Fall of Babylon," and John Rettig of Cincinnati, whose productions included "Montezuma and the Conquest of Mexico" and "Moses, or the Bondage in Egypt."[17] As their titles indicate, these presentations were de Mille–type extravaganzas with casts of hundreds (some circus pageants involved twelve hundred people), supported by almost as many animals, along with exotic music, dancing, and scenes of violence. After the "Congress of Monarchs" had sated audiences at Barnum's hippodrome, there came "A Fete at Pekin," which supposedly surpassed the "Congress" "in the richness of the costumes and other paraphernalia." The Empress Haamti, seated in a royal palanquin borne by mandarins, followed by Tartar cavalrymen, imperial soldiers, court ladies, lantern-bearers, and warriors of the Yangtze, ascended a flag-bedecked throne and watched military maneuvers, a Chinese ballet, flamethrowers, and whatever other curiosities the Barnum troupe could offer. One month later, Barnum had switched to "Blue Beard," a "Grand Dramatic and Equestrian Spectacular Pantomime."

In these presentations horses (and elephants) played a major role. But unlike the great days of hippodrama in nineteenth-century Europe, emphasis was not placed on the feats animals performed, nor on the plays written especially for them, but on vast pantomimes that replaced dramatic action with scale, variety, and sheer splendor.[18] A thirst for pageantry, induced, perhaps, by growing dreams of imperial glory, gripped these American shows. They set the pattern for the twentieth-century circus as well.

Barnum's hippodrome, however, offered more than merely static entertainment. The great circular track around the arena was the setting for a variety of dangerous races by men and women drivers. There were races by ladies riding English thoroughbreds, a Roman chariot race for two-horse and four-horse chariots, a scene in which Texas cattle were lassoed, hurdle races, elephant and camel running matches, a buffalo hunt, and as a climax, a stag hunt in which all the riders and a pack of hounds participated. The risks were real, and rumors grew about deaths and injuries. One of Barnum's agents sought to deny a newspaper statement in 1874 that "many persons" had been killed. But, said the *New York Times*, "we only know that several people have been killed there. Considering the popular thirst for excitement, it is possible that several may not be reckoned too many. But, considering the claims of humanity, even one death is too many."[19]

Further developing his special combination of pageantry and danger, Barnum announced plans to send a balloonist across the Atlantic. He had been playing with the idea for some years and had consulted European experts. Some of them advised against the attempt; others, like Professors Hodsman and Nadir, assured him that it could be done. Barnum employed a series of aeronauts, but in the end he featured Washington H. Donaldson.[20] Daily lift-offs were planned as part of the hippodrome show, and in May 1874, Barnum announced that at some point in the future the balloon would lift off for the trip. Should it burst, he added, "the people will have had their money's worth in having witnessed the rest of the show."[21] By exhibiting the aeronauts in England Barnum expected to get back the fifty thousand dollars or more that the experiment would cost. Further profits would come from auctioning off journalistic coverage of the aeronauts' reports. What had been one of Poe's hoaxes thirty years earlier now seemed about to become a reality. But in the end, after a number of ascensions, Barnum abandoned the project. He claimed he did not want to endanger the lives of the balloonists, but he had already received the necessary free publicity, and the expense, along with the risks, may have discouraged him.

Despite these attractions the seasons of 1874 and 1875 were not very successful, and Barnum's attention was diverted by other matters including his political career in Bridgeport. Coup decided to leave the partnership, angered by Barnum's selling the use of his name to other circuses. In December 1875, the animals and costumes owned by the show were auctioned off in Bridgeport. The wild-beast market was not good, noted the *Times*. "In the language of those sprightly sheets, the Prices Current, monkeys are dull and heavy, elephants are flat, and rose cockatoos are quiet." A large elephant went for forty-five hundred dollars, and the infant hippopotamus brought twenty-five thousand dollars, but tigers, lions, and leopards were averaging only six hundred dollars each, monkeys could be had for eight dollars apiece, and the tapirs, hyenas, and kangaroos had to be withdrawn from the sale entirely.[22]

But with the end of his mayoral term in sight, and spurred by the excitement of the centennial year, Barnum announced early in 1876 his intention to organize a new show, more colossal than any ever before assembled, and purchased various European shows and menageries. From this time until his death he was never without a circus. Barnum's centennial show toured the country, giving the people "a Fourth of July celebration every day." A Goddess of Liberty, a live eagle, Revolutionary uniforms, and fireworks added to the patriotic effect. To intensify his publicity efforts Barnum ordered a ten-thousand-dollar railway car to serve as an "advertising coach." The outside was covered with representations of his animals and processions (along with his own portraits), and the interior, in black walnut with an Axminster carpet, housed those in charge of distributing bills, photographs, and information to the surrounding countryside.

All his enterprises, of course, fully exploited the Barnum legend. His autobiography was distributed by the bushel, and circus programs emphasized the benevolence, intrepidity, and morality of the presiding genius. "P. T. Barnum was born to be a showman," ran one program, "but not a charlatan nor a mountebank. . . . Look at the conformation of that massive head," it went on, referring to an accompanying portrait, "how evenly and admirably balanced! Behold the kindness and beneficence of the face; the tenderness of those eyes; the cheerfulness and exuberance of that mild, expressive countenance. Who could dream of shrinking or turning away from such a look — from such a face?" Those "quick, piercing eyes which take in at a single *coup d'oeil* the ever-recurring demands of the race for diversion and amusements" were among the "craniological elements" that helped Barnum blend into his entertainments "a very large preponderance [of] wholesome and moral instruction." It was, as usual, an unruffled and benevolent exterior that Barnum wished to present to the world, purifier "of so many of the abuses which have crept into its public amusements."[23]

Thus, at every opportunity Barnum introduced favorable comments by ministers, educators, presidents, and crowned heads testifying to the educational and uplifting effects of his enterprise. The old battle was still on. As late as 1890 he was dueling with clergymen. The Reverend Mr. Thompson, a Bridgeport Episcopalian, attacked him from the pulpit for bringing over ballet girls from England to travel with the circus. Barnum was equal to the occasion. Calling Thompson the "reverend rascal," he pointed out that money for the church over which Thompson presided had come from his pockets (and by implication, from the circus itself).[24]

Thompson was an exception, however. On the whole, Barnum's campaign to sell the giant show as a moral exhibition that might be attended by Sunday schools (children would learn of the natural history of the Bible through his animal exhibits) was successful. Henry Ward Beecher and E. H. Chapin gave him testimonials, as did General William T. Sherman, Presidents Garfield and Arthur, Roscoe Conkling, and Robert Todd Lincoln. By 1876 Barnum was using "The Greatest Show On Earth" to describe his circus, and the sobriquet stuck.

There were strong challengers, however. Smaller circus owners kept Barnum busy by suing for libel and damages, claiming he was using their names and ruining their profits (W. C. Coup explained in his recollections that this was a favorite technique for harassing circus rivals), but more serious were the larger outfits, such as Adam Forepaugh's circus, the Sells Brothers' Great European Seven Elephant Show, and most prominent of all, a combined circus known familiarly as the London Circus, presided over by the greatest circus man of his generation, James A. Bailey.

By 1879 Barnum's activities had become complex and dangerously strenuous for a man of his age. The circus, his vast real estate holdings in Bridgeport and elsewhere, the lectures he continued to give, required able subordinates. In late 1879 he was fortunate enough to hire Henry Eugene Bowser, a Bridgeport resident originally from Canada, to serve as his confidential secretary. Bowser was primarily in charge of managing the Bridgeport properties, but he inevitably became involved in all of Barnum's other enterprises as well.[25] Barnum, Bowser, and another employee, Charles R. Brothwell, were known around Bridgeport as the "Busy B's," and their offices at 269 Main Street hummed with activity. Bowser collected rents, paid Barnum's domestic staff their monthly salaries (by 1881 five servants were employed at Waldemere), took care of Mrs. Barnum's allowance, and recorded the circus receipts. Bowser's meticulousness, in fact, preserved the only detailed financial records of these years and affords some insight into the scope of American circus management.

In the late 1870s, according to Bowser's diary, Barnum's circus was taking close to half a million dollars in receipts annually, fluctuating from $445,266 in 1877 to $461,208 the following year, and going down to $429,765 in 1879. The profits decreased steadily. Despite the more than twenty-five hundred customers who attended an average Barnum circus show in

1879, his profits dipped from $81,016 in 1877 to $78,941 in 1878, to just $60,357 in 1879. Bowser had no figures for 1880, and the circus may well have been losing money. By the late seventies, Barnum had in effect leased the circus to a number of experienced managers, including George F. Bailey and John J. Nathans. Bailey and Nathans were part of the Flatfoot syndicate, and they ran the show until 1880.

By that year it was clear that Barnum had run into a formidable competitor. James A. Bailey's London Circus was successfully competing with Barnum in his own territory, and taking away the larger share of the market. On May 11, 1880, the loyal Bowser confided to his diary that apparently everyone in Bridgeport had gone to see the London Circus, and there was no one in the office to collect the rents due that day. After Bailey turned a congratulatory telegram from Barnum on the birth of a baby elephant into a spectacular advertising coup, Barnum decided he had had enough.

Meeting in Bridgeport several times in 1880, the two men and Bailey's friend, James L. Hutchinson, signed a contract on August 26 for a new traveling show, the direct ancestor of the fabled Ringling Brothers Barnum and Bailey Circus, which still dominates the amusement world. Barnum agreed to contribute half the capital (and take half the profits), Hutchinson and Bailey were assigned one-quarter each. Except for board and travel, none of the partners would receive salaries or compensation. Bailey and Hutchinson were meant to take the active roles in management. "The said Barnum," declared the contract, "shall use his influence and abilities" on behalf of the show, and "when able" would devote "his talents, knowledge and experience" to writing publicity. Barnum would also, "when he feels able and willing only, appear before the patrons of the same and address them; but nothing herein contained shall conflict with his visiting any part of the world."[26]

Obviously, all three of the partners recognized that Barnum was beginning to slow down and could not be expected to take an active role in the circus management. Shrewd businessman that he was, however, Barnum took precautions; he was permitted to choose "one or two intelligent, honest and well behaved persons, who shall be hired by said company," given a salary of fifty dollars a week and, more important, have access to all books and accounts. These men were to be "recognized and treated as representatives of said Barnum and have the comforts and traveling accommodations suitable and proper to their position." At his time of life Barnum was not willing to trust the honesty of his partners, or rely on good intentions, when so much money was at stake. But he recognized that the continuity of the enterprise was important. In the event of Barnum's death, the contract went on, all agreements would remain in force. His executors could dispose of his interest only after giving the first right of purchase to the other partners. His estate would not be charged, however, for the loss of his services.

Within a few months Barnum's foresight in acquiring active and able partners was validated, for in mid-November 1880, while in New York City, he fell seriously ill. He was not permitted out of the house for almost two months, and prayers were said in the Bridgeport churches for his recovery. Although his family feared for his life, and Bowser was shocked to discover his weight was down from a usual level of two hundred and fifteen pounds to one hundred and forty-three, by mid-December Barnum was making a two-hundred-thousand-dollar loan with the Emigrants' Industrial Savings Bank, and by January seventh was back in Bridgeport.[27] A Florida vacation and a trip to Europe that summer helped him regain his strength, and he had almost ten years of active life ahead of him.

The brush with death seemed to sober Barnum, and he began to grow more concerned about his will, his estate, and the faithfulness of his employees in protecting his various holdings. Bowser obviously enjoyed Barnum's confidence. His salary rose steadily from fifteen hundred dollars a year in 1879 to more than double that amount ten years later. In addition, Barnum left him a five-thousand-dollar legacy. "[His] honesty and diligence, [his] constant and intelligent regard and watch-fulness over every branch of my business interests" brought the showman's appreciation, and occasional presents.[28] The first year it was merely a morocco-bound edition of the autobiography *Struggles and Triumphs*, but subsequently Barnum's generosity advanced to presentation of a gold watch. Bowser took charge of a great deal of work. "I hope there won't be too much correspondence for me to wade through when I get home," Barnum wrote his secretary from England in 1881, "for I don't propose to work mentally or otherwise much more in this life. I feel my age some," he added.[29] A month before, in New York, he had been even more gloomy. "As my time for this life is but short at best," he wrote Bowser, "I am . . . anxious to have *two* clear heads (in case of accident to one) in full possession of all the details of my worldly affairs." He asked for "eternal vigilance" from his subordinates; "all who owe must be made to pay promptly, and nobody be permitted to cheat."[30]

The first year of the new show there were obvious tensions among the partners. C. P. Cary, secretary of the combined circus and Barnum's representative, complained of overwork and tyrannizing by "Lord Hutchinson."[31] Any departures from the wishes of Bailey and Hutchinson made his lot very unpleasant. When Barnum went abroad, Cary told Bowser that no respect was being shown his position or his need to do his duty to Barnum. The managers "seem fairly to hate the sight of a Barnum man." They claimed Barnum owned merely one-third, not one-half of the show, and put Cary to work selling tickets. Later on, one of his secretaries urged Barnum not to quarrel with Bailey over small things. "I think it is of greater importance to keep him good natured and good tempered with you and your servants than it is for you to lose a few dollars," was the wise advice.[32]

Actually, the show itself justified the tensions and difficulties. Entitled grandiloquently "P. T. Barnum's Greatest Show on Earth, Howe's Great London Circus and Sanger's Royal British Menagerie," it opened in New York in March 1881, and the torchlight parade surpassed any earlier circus spectacle. Open dens of wild animals, the "Car of Juggernaut," drawn by eight black horses, gilded chariots, torchbearers, stallions, and elephants paraded through the streets, along with zebras, camels, oxen, and four brass bands. Windows were sold along Broadway, so eager was the multitude to watch the pageant. Editors of newspapers in eastern cities were brought in to witness the parade and the opening performance at Madison Square Garden, lodged and fed at Barnum's expense. A "very costly piece of advertising," Barnum admitted, "which yet yielded us a magnificent return in the enthusiastic editorial endorsements of so many papers of good standing."

The circus foreshadowed the great combinations that would dominate the industrial world in the next twenty-five years. "Centralization of All That Is Great in the Amusement Realm," ran the early advertisements, "Trinity of the Three Grand Animal Collections of Earth — Eight Million Dollars Invested — Contemporaries Shrink Away As It Approaches — A Satiety for the Public Appetite — Each Individual Performer a Champion — To Behold This Repository of Sweeping Greatness Ends All Desire To See More, Since, of Its Genus, There Is Nothing Left To See."[33]

The size and expense of the show caused some to scoff. "All showmen down on P. T. B. because [he] threw up all old managers and foremen and took in new ones. Will be dead as a showman in two years!!!"[34] Rumors flew that the show would lose two hundred thousand dollars a season. "This city will receive its share of the losses on Monday, September 19th," the *St. Louis Post-Dispatch* wryly commented.[35]

In fact, the eighties were years of continuing prosperity. With his usual care, Bowser recorded the daily receipts of the circus for more than ten years, beginning with the Barnum-Hutchinson-Bailey trinity, continuing for a brief period in the eighties when Bailey retired for a time from the business, other men buying his share, and going on with Barnum and Bailey as equal partners, starting in 1887.

The first year set a pattern followed, with little variation, for the next decade. The circus opened its thirty-two-week season in New York in late March. The New York stands varied from three to six weeks. Then it toured the Pennsylvania–New Jersey area for several weeks, coming back for a one-week stand in Brooklyn, and moving, for eight weeks, through New England and New York State. July 11 it swung west, going through cities in Michigan, Indiana, Illinois, Ohio, Missouri, Iowa, Nebraska, and Kansas, and ending its tour in late October in Texas. The receipts for the season were $1,116,390, averaging some $5,864 each day and $34,887 each week (the circus normally played a six-day week, not showing on Sunday). The show cost $755,888 to put on, so the total dividend amounted to $360,510, a healthy thirty-one percent on the receipts, half the amount going into Barnum's coffers, the other half divided between Bailey and Hutchinson. In 1882 the show was even more successful, returning a profit of $607,000 on receipts of $1,333,787, despite the fact it ran for only thirty-one weeks, and in 1883, a thirty-week season produced receipts of $1,419,498, although the dividends amounted to only $560,000. The middle eighties saw the show's annual business drop below the million-dollar mark for three years in succession, only to pick up again in 1888 and never fall below a million so long as Barnum lived.

The enormous daily expenses of the circus meant that bad decisions about scheduling or mishaps on the road could be extremely costly. So bad was the brief Texas trip the circus took in 1881 that it did not return to the state for six years, and even then Ben Fish, a cousin of Barnum's wife and one of Barnum's representatives in circus matters, refused to go back, even if it meant one hundred thousand dollars.

After 1884, the routes were chosen so that the show did not duplicate all its engagements every year. In 1884, 1886, 1888, and 1890, the show visited western towns like Topeka, Leavenworth, Terre Haute, Council Bluffs, Lincoln, Grand Rapids, and Sedalia, along with larger cities like Chicago, Cincinnati, and Detroit. In 1885, 1887, and 1889, it confined its exhibitions to the East, spending several weeks also in some of the Canadian provinces. Weekly receipts varied widely; bad weeks might bring only twenty thousand dollars, but good weeks often tripled this amount.

Often Barnum traveled with the circus, since he formed one of its attractions. A St. Louis advertisement promised his appearance: "Wait and See the Old Hero About Whose Name Clusters So Much of Romantic Interest and Whose Brilliant Deeds Are Themes of Poetry and Prose."[36] Of course, this close identification sometimes created problems. In February 1883, Barnum received a misspelled and unpunctuated letter from Mrs. James Pendergrass in South Troy, New York. Angry and grief-stricken, Mrs. Pendergrass asked Barnum for some money. His circus had visited Troy the previous summer, with terrible results. "Mr. Barnum i had 5 of my girls up stairs with the type for fever from the feet of your elephant." Two of her daughters eventually died, and Mrs. Pendergrass, having heard that Barnum was "a kind man" and would hold himself responsible for "the effects of your elephant . . . coming to troy," begged for some relief. What Barnum eventually did in this case remains unknown, for he scrawled across the top of the letter, "I have not read this & dont wish to."[37]

With its three rings and two stages, the circus created an enormous impact wherever it went. Northampton, Massachusetts, tried prohibiting the Barnum and Bailey appearance on economic rather than religious or moral grounds. Because of the huge attendance the show gathered, natives complained that "for weeks after the circus has gone trade at Northampton languishes on account of the absence of the money which has been thus dissipated."[38] Critics answered that the thousands drawn from the countryside patronized Northampton tradesmen, and the board and lodging requirements of circus personnel provided additional cash, but the argument continued. In New York City many theater managers arranged to rent out their establishments during the circus engagement, because the ten thousand people Barnum could pack into Madison Square Garden cut down the business of New York's regular amusement places. Municipal governments also tried to get a piece of the profits. In 1883 St. Louis changed its licensing arrangements: where once a single fee of one hundred and fifty dollars covered shows for a six-month period, now circus owners were forced to pay fifty dollars a day for the main show and an additional ten dollars for their sideshows.[39]

The logistics of handling the eight hundred people who traveled more than ten thousand miles with the show each year Barnum left to the capable hands of quartermasters like James A. Bailey.[40] Bailey was undoubtedly the genius of the enterprise, aggressive, eager to take risks and spend money, restrained by a Barnum who had grown more cautious in his old age. Even the publicity, Barnum's area of true expertise, was assigned to an able corps of press agents, headed by the redoubtable "Tody" Hamilton. A "verbal conjuror," Hamilton's language was "so polysyllabic," according to "Uncle" Bob Sherwood, a famous circus clown, "that an Oxford professor would have found it difficult to understand."[41] Tody's rich words traveled "to the threshold of trembling tautology," commented an associate.[42]

But even in his old age Barnum retained his old touch on a number of important occasions, most notably in the episodes of Jumbo and the white elephant.

In 1881, the first year of the new combined shows, Jumbo was the pride of the Royal Zoological Gardens in London, and the largest elephant ever exhibited. He had come there some years before from a Paris zoo that did not realize the extraordinary size and value the animal would attain. Jumbo was idolized by the thousands of British schoolchildren whom he carried on his back. Despite the elephant's popularity, one of Barnum's agents was startled to discover in 1881 that the superintendent of the zoo was willing to sell Jumbo if the right offer arrived. He was concerned about the elephant's temperament

256

and feared that he might go wild someday. Because of his size the destruction he could cause would be catastrophic. Barnum cabled an offer of ten thousand dollars, convinced the zoo official would never accept, but the directors decided to make the arrangement. Jumbo was slated to go to America.

What happened next is unclear. "Uncle" Bob Sherwood charged later that Barnum himself assembled an enormous protest movement in England, starting with the schoolchildren, to fight Jumbo's departure.[43] Others maintained that the massive reaction was spontaneous and needed no encouragement. But whether natural or contrived, a wave of sentiment swept England and reached even into the Houses of Parliament and the royal family. Legal maneuvers were sought to keep the elephant in London by injunction, and the queen asked that the contract be broken. "No more quiet garden strolls, no shady trees, green lawns, and flowery thickets," moaned the *London Telegraph.* "Our amiable monster must dwell in a tent, take part in the routine of a circus, and, instead of his by-gone friendly trots with British girls and boys, and perpetual luncheon on buns and oranges, must amuse a Yankee mob, and put up with peanuts and waffles."[44] But neither threats nor pleas could stop the sale; Barnum responded to newspaper appeals describing the distress of British children by asserting that fifty-one million Americans were eagerly awaiting the beast's arrival. He made sure also that American newspapers covered the frantic last weeks of Jumbo's residence abroad and the thousands of visitors who came to say good-bye at the zoo; it was free publicity on a scale Barnum had not gotten since the drama of the Jenny Lind tour thirty years earlier.

Even more excitement flared at the departure. Jumbo refused to leave his surroundings and lay down in the street. While thousands of Englishmen protested the brutality of forced exile, Barnum got Matthew Scott, Jumbo's keeper, to lead the elephant for several days through a huge cage on the way to his exercise. One day, as he did so, the cage doors were shut, and, wrote Barnum, "Jumbo was mine." The elephant was taken aboard the *Assyrian Monarch*, loaded with his favorite buns, and accompanied by Scott. The ship arrived in New York on Easter Sunday, 1882, welcomed by huge crowds.

Jumbo quickly became the pride of the circus, earning, Barnum estimated, ten times his cost in the first six weeks he was on exhibition. Publicity pamphlets like *The Book of Jumbo* emphasized his great size with exaggerated woodcuts and inflated prose. "The Matchless Monarch of Over-Shadowing and Majestic Presence," "The Notorious International Character," whose purchase had caused an international incident, the target of poisoned buns by Englishmen determined he would never leave their island. Moreover, the elephant was still growing. Tody Hamilton, "who is a member of the YMCA and has never told a lie in his life," a *Times* reporter assured his readers, asserted in March 1883, that Jumbo had grown seven inches in the previous year and was thirteen feet, four inches high. "His trunk is the size of an adult crocodile, his tail is as big as a cow's leg, and he made footprints in the sands of time resembling an indentation as if a very fat man had fallen off a very high building."[45] In Barnum's circus procession Jumbo marched with a baby elephant, the better to emphasize his own size.

But Jumbo was not only large, he was gentle and benevolent. As such he suited the new American fascination with animal life. The growth of cities and interest in Darwinian theory helped create, in the late nineteenth century, municipal zoos, animal and bird protection leagues, and an enormous number of animal books. Some of these volumes were scholarly, but many more were popular and sentimental. Charles Roberts, Ernest Thompson Seton, William J. Long, and Jack London, among others, published novels and short stories about animal life that anthropomorphized their subjects, giving them wisdom, courage, compassion, and loyalty.[46] Debates about animal personality and intelligence filled popular magazines. The "Back to Nature" movement, which encouraged camping, hunting, fishing, and country living, supported a new sensitiv-

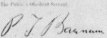

On the road

P. T. Barnum's Roman hippodrome, 1874

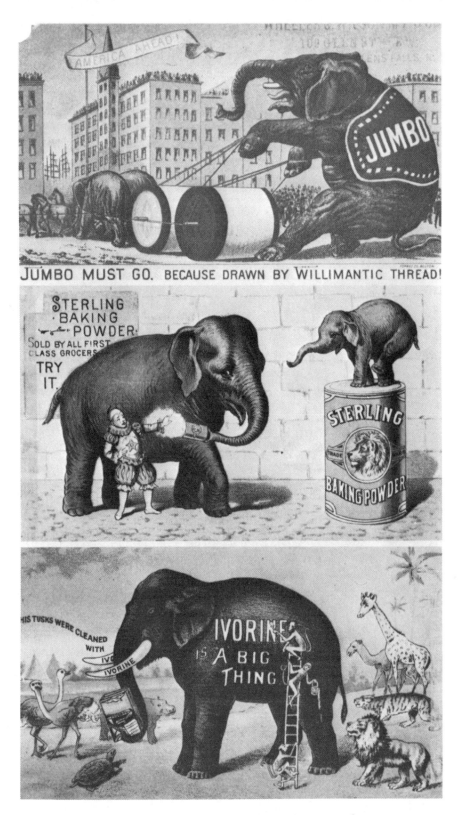

Jumbo: the advertisers' friend

Circus spectacular

eatest Show on Earth

MBUS AND THE DISCOVERY OF AMERICA.

COLUMBUS AT THE CITY OF BARCELONA. AMID BE-
ELS, IN FLASHING COSTUMES, WITH MYRIADS OF VARI-
ET BEFORE FERDINAND AND ISABELLA AT THE ROYAL PALACE.

EST, AMUSEMENT INSTITUTION.

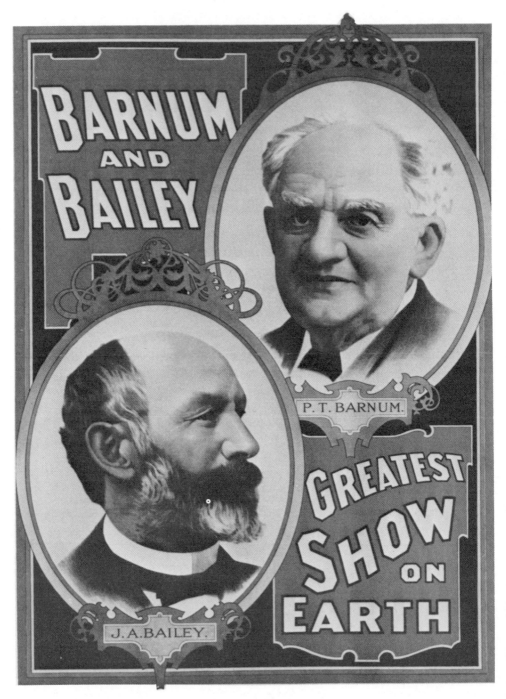

The circus men

ity to the suffering of domestic animals, especially horses, and focused attention on the plight of animals in the modern world of steel and concrete.

Cleverly appealing to this infatuation in his advertising Barnum, in 1885, got Matthew Scott, Jumbo's keeper, to bring out a biography of the elephant (and an autobiography of his own unique career). "Jumbo is a remarkably clean animal," Scott confided, "and he is mighty particular about his bed."[47] He loved music and little children. Barnum also arranged for Scott to lead Jumbo across the Brooklyn Bridge to test its strength; as thousands watched on the towers and the riverbanks, Jumbo marched from Manhattan to Brooklyn. The bridge stood the test, although Scott worried lest the elephant begin to dance, for each of his footsteps caused loud vibrations.

But Jumbo's American career was all too brief. In September 1885, while walking along a railroad track in St. Thomas, Ontario, he was hit by a freight train and killed. Circus and railroad blamed each other for the accident, and sightseers began to clip pieces of hair and hide from his body. Disheartened as he was, Barnum had been prepared. He had previously arranged for Professor Henry A. Ward of the Natural History Establishment in Rochester to stuff and mount Jumbo when he died. Ward was America's leading taxidermist, mounting birds and animals for museums throughout the country. Ward and two assistants reached the animal within forty-eight hours. They had an enormous task. Jumbo's hide weighed more than fifteen hundred pounds, and his bones were another twenty-four hundred. Ward received only twelve hundred dollars for the task and complained bitterly in letters to Barnum that this was trifling compared with his other commissions and the tremendous difficulties of hiding Jumbo's gashes and working with his tough skin.[48] But he did the job.

As soon as he could, Barnum displayed both the skeleton and the stuffed skin at the circus, and eventually the skeleton went to the American Museum of Natural History and the skin to the Natural History Museum at Tufts University, whose football team would later be known as the Jumbos. (Barnum made gifts to other universities as well: he once offered the afterbirth of a baby elephant to the Peabody Museum at Yale.)[49]

Nothing ever took Jumbo's place, although Barnum strove mightily for new exhibits. Anything rare, curious, or mysterious became a target for his collecting zeal. William A. Croffut, who served Barnum for a time as secretary, once asked him why he had never exhibited an Indian yogi. Barnum answered that he had in fact sent some agents to India to catch a live yogi: "I gave them all the money they needed . . . instructed them to bring me an assortment of yogis, and authorized them to make contracts to pay fifty dollars a night for each yogi for one year." The agents chased rumors to Calcutta, Bombay, Rangoon, and the Punjab, but they never laid eyes on a yogi; all they found were sleight-of-hand magicians. Barnum reluctantly concluded there were none to be found. "The reason I do not exhibit a yogi," he told Croffut, "is the same as the reason I don't exhibit Santy Claus. I can't catch him!"[50]

But with other treasures of the mysterious East Barnum had greater luck. For years he had longed to obtain a white elephant. These rare beasts were held sacred by many Buddhists, who believed that the spirit of Buddha inhabited them. White elephants were treated with respect and even adoration, housed in sumptuous stables, covered with jeweled ornaments and painted designs. To get one out of Thailand or Burma, their principal homes, was a formidable task.

Barnum, however, was insistent; the glory of exhibiting a pure white elephant filled him with anticipation, and he sent agents to the Far East who pursued their objective with intrigue and extravagance. Once, J. B. Gaylord, a Barnum agent, obtained a white elephant from a Siamese nobleman, but it was poisoned the day before he could place it on a steamer for England. At last, in late 1883, newspapers reported that an enormous bribe had induced King Theebaw of Burma to sell Toung Taloung, one of the sacred beasts. After "three years of patient persistence, and the exercise, on the part of half a score of our shrewdest agents, of wonderful tact, diplomacy and untiring energy, often at the peril of their lives, and the outlay of a quarter of a million dollars, our efforts were crowned with victory."[51]

There was, to be sure, one problem. The sacred white elephant was not very white. Correspondents in London who viewed Toung Taloung were startled by his appearance. "His outlines and proportions are really beautiful," wrote one of them, and he has "got a pair of splendid tusks, long and without a flaw. But as to his being, in any sense whatever, a 'white' elephant, this illusion had better be dispelled at once. From the tip of his trunk to the end of his tail, his skin is simply a rather dark slaty gray, except that his ears are fringed with pink, his toe-nails are ivory color, and the ridge of his proboscis is rather lighter than the rest of his body." Toung was "no more 'white' than the Black Sea is black or the Red Sea is red."[52] The best comment was offered by one of the employees of the London Zoo. "White, sir?" he said in response to a query. "Well, sir, not werry white, exactly; but, so I am given to understand, werry sacred, indeed, sir, — werry sacred."[53]

Cries of fraud began to be heard even before Toung Taloung arrived in New York in late March 1884. Some claimed there was no such thing as a white elephant; others that the Siamese did not worship it after all, and one New York clergyman insisted that Barnum was trying to palm off a leprous elephant on a gullible public.

When the *Lydian Monarch* steamed into the harbor, the New York press had a field day. Barnum heard of the news in his office. "Get me my hat!" he shouted, according to the *Times*. "Call a cab! Notify the President! Come on Hutchinson!" With Barnum were naturalists, diplomats, and business associates, all eager to see the animal. At the first sight of the *Lydian Monarch* there was a moment's anxiety; some in the party thought its flags were at half-mast, indicating the white elephant had died. Boarding the ship, however, they found Toung Taloung intact, but indisputably gray. We have all learned, Barnum lectured the press, "that there is no such thing as a really pure white elephant. This is a sacred animal, a technical white elephant, as white as God makes 'em."[54]

Like Jenny Lind, Toung Taloung was greeted by a poem written for the occasion. Joaquin Miller won the Prize Ode contest with his effort, which concluded:

> But welcome to the Christian's West,
>   From land of dreams to land of deed.
> You teach us much. Yet it were best
>   You pack this in your trunk to read
> To tyrants on returning East:
>   We worship neither man nor beast.[55]

Just as in the Jenny Lind contest thirty-four years earlier, there was a burst of parodies. The *New York Times* published a series of prize odes by Swinburne, Tennyson, Whittier, and Walt Whitman. Whitman's poem of four hundred lines was in his finest vein, said the *Times*; on reading it, a prominent estate lawyer telegraphed to the poet: "I greet you at the beginning of a grand career." It started:

> Beginning at a point on the northerly side of
>   West twenty-first street
> Distant six hundred and four feet westerly from
>   the point formed by the junction
> Of the westerly side of Fourth-avenue and the
>   northerly side of West Twenty-first street;
> Thence westerly along the said northerly side of
>   West Twenty-first street
> Twenty-five feet six and one-half inches; thence
>   northerly —[56]

But the hilarity of the newspapermen was not matched by public enthusiasm. Toung Taloung proved a disappointment to the public, who seemed more attracted to the white elephant belonging to a rival circus manager, Adam Forepaugh's "Light of Asia." Forepaugh's elephant was indeed creamy white and fulfilled the romantic expectations of Americans. Unfortunately, if he was white, the "Light of Asia" was also white-washed. George Gillespie of Liverpool, an animal trainer, swore in an affidavit in Philadelphia that he had, in obedience to his employer's orders, applied a composition of Paris white mixed with some other materials to an elephant named Tiny. The elephant had broken out in boils and sores, and Gillespie said it would die unless the treatment was stopped. The Pennsylvania Society for the Prevention of Cruelty to Animals became involved. Moreover, a clever reporter managed to brush some of the coloring off the "Light of Asia."

Barnum, meanwhile, surrounding Toung Taloung with Buddhist priests, distributed testimonials from naturalists, world travelers, diplomats, and others who might be considered to have some expert information, all to the effect that he was indeed exhibiting a genuine white elephant. He invited missionaries and oriental scholars to a conference in Madison Square Garden one morning in early April 1884, along with celebrities like Theodore Thomas, the conductor; Mrs. Frank Leslie, the publisher; Carl Schurz, Civil War veteran and political reformer; and the winning poet, Joaquin Miller. The group inspected Toung Taloung and declared him, or at least those of them who had ever seen a white elephant, to be genuine. Then they went on to inspect Barnum's "Ethnological Congress," a part of the circus that featured representative Zulus, Nubians, Afghans, and Sioux.

Adam Forepaugh was not through. He published a fourteen-page pamphlet entitled *Too White for Barnum. . . . Forepaugh's Sacred White Elephant the "Light of Asia" Proved by the Highest of Scientific Authority to Be Genuine and Barnum's "Sacred White?" Elephant and All Its Surroundings a Rank Fraud.* On his side Forepaugh ranged Professor William S. Forbes of the Jefferson Medical College, Dr. Joseph Leidy, a professor of anatomy at the University of Pennsylvania, and several others, all of whom insisted that Forepaugh's beast was a sacred white elephant. He charged that Barnum had bribed witnesses to lie; and the Philadelphia reporter who claimed to have rubbed paint off had also been bribed by Barnum. The bill of sale Barnum offered to prove that he had indeed imported Toung Taloung from Burma was also fraudulent, said Forepaugh, for there was no written Burmese language.[57] Moreover, the idols, banners, and umbrellas that Barnum surrounded his elephant with were manufactured by a New York theatrical-goods maker. Affidavits and charges flew back and forth between the two circuses.

The rivalry was worthy of Barnum's early days, except that now he was placed in the unprecedented position of having the real article but combating a fake that met public expectations better. "Desirable as knowledge is," wrote the *New York Times* sadly, "we cannot without regret lose our inherited belief in the sacred white elephant of Siam. Who is there who has not, in fancy, seen a Siamese state procession headed by a white elephant as pure as porcelain in tint . . . a spotless and seraphic beast living upon the choicest bread and the golden fruit of the Kalibichromagunga tree? To exchange this vision for that of a wretched little sand-papered beast, revelling in cheap brandy and as devoid of dignity as a pig, is indeed a blow to the romance of the remote and mysterious East."[58] The choice lay between a handsome fake and a disappointing reality. The American public chose the fake, and the "Light of Asia" remained more popular than Toung Taloung.

And Toung Taloung did not remain Barnum's for long. In November 1887, another disastrous fire struck Barnum's Bridgeport winter quarters. Most of the elephants and one lion escaped the flames, but the rest of the menagerie was consumed. Barnum estimated his loss at a quarter of a million dollars. Once again, reporters indulged their imagination and sense of humor. "A choicer selection of howls, roars, and screams, and a subtler combination of all three was never heard in Africa, Asia, Europe, or Australia than was produced here last night," wrote one. "Bridgeport's Chief of Police says that he has never heard anything to equal it in his life, and he has travelled extensively in Connecticut and Rhode Island."[59]

Barnum himself was so cheerful that some found it hard to believe his optimism could be impromptu. "We spurn the hypothesis that Barnum set the fire, made his way to New York by milk train, ready to talk to reporters at the Murray Hill Hotel," the *Times* editorialized; "his alibi is complete."[60] But among the four elephants lost was Toung Taloung who, wrote Barnum, "determinedly committed suicide," rushing back into the flames from the keepers who were trying to save him. One reporter suggested that the elephant was despondent because of public rejection. That, of course, was never Barnum's fear.

Although his Far East adventure had not turned out well, and some thought he would finally decide to retire, Barnum began immediately to collect another menagerie. He wrote, "I am not in the show business alone to make money. I feel it my mission, as long as I live, to provide clean, moral, and healthful recreation for the public to which I have so long catered." And the circus was soon bigger than ever.

During the circus years Barnum crossed swords a number of times with Henry Bergh, the founder of the American Society for the Prevention of Cruelty to Animals.[61] Bergh fought, unsuccessfully, to prevent Barnum from feeding his pythons live rabbits; Barnum had to produce a letter from famed naturalist Louis Agassiz, arguing that the snakes would starve without live prey. Bergh protested the use of the iron prod by elephant trainers; Barnum countered that the elephant's hide was two inches thick, and the goad did not inflict much pain. Bergh pointed to Barnum's firetrap museums and circus buildings; Barnum installed more safety equipment. Bergh complained about horses jumping through flaming hoops; Barnum jumped through one himself, followed by half the circus. The two, nevertheless, became friends. In March 1884, Bergh wrote Barnum, noting "the vast amount of pleasure and instruction" he had afforded humanity and wondering whether Barnum had "remembered in his will, the poor dumb animals from whom he has derived so large a share of his splendid fortune?"[62] Barnum remembered Bergh, at any rate, leaving money for a monument to the philanthropist, as well as a legacy to the Bridgeport Society for the Prevention of Cruelty to Animals.

More serious, at least temporarily, was Barnum's clash with Elbridge Gerry's Society for the Prevention of Cruelty to Children.[63] The society was concerned about Barnum's use of the Elliott children in a bicycle-riding act and warned him he might be violating the law. The six children ranged in age from six to sixteen. Addressing an open letter to Gerry, Barnum insisted that it was rather late in life for him to begin violating the law. He and his wife were both members of Gerry's society, and the two men had lectured from the same platform. "I yield not even to you in affection and consideration for children," wrote Barnum. "Millions of the little ones and their parents call me, as did the late President Garfield, the 'Kris Kringle of America.'" The Elliott children did "nothing that is not healthful, invigorating, and within the bounds of law and propriety, and that which I would permit my own children or grandchildren to do." Gerry's response was that if the penal code was being violated, he would take action.

Barnum continued to show the Elliott act. "I love law and will abide by it," he told the press, insisting the performance was legal. But on March 2, 1883, Barnum, along with his partners and the children's father, was arrested following an affidavit made by a society officer, who charged that using children as gymnasts, contortionists, riders, and acrobats was illegal. Arranging a special exhibition for lawyers and doctors, Barnum came in to court in early April with a good deal of supporting testimony. Although the SPCC said the children appeared exhausted by the act, physicians argued that the performance benefited their health, and a police captain found the children simply amused. The court decided the case did not fall within the bounds of the statute and found the defendants not guilty.

But Barnum could not leave the issue at that. After the verdict he walked up to Mr. Jenkins, the superintendent of the SPCC "and offered him two hundred dollars a week to exhibit himself as 'the man who wanted to take the bread out of those children's mouths.'" Jenkins only stared and growled, "Go away, sir, go away." Almost seventy-three years old, Barnum could still handle himself well when the object was publicity.

Not all the publicity, of course, was beneficial. As a loyal Republican Barnum brooded about the chances of Grover Cleveland in the 1884 election. November 3 of that year he sent a letter to the *Tribune* pledging himself to sell all he possessed of his Bridgeport real estate "for one-quarter less than its present acknowledged value *if the Democrats elect their President.*" He continued, "Every taxpayer and every workingman and woman will see business permanently palsied if the South gets into the saddle. It will establish free trade, get pay for its slaves, and obtain pensions for all rebel soldiers."[64] After Cleveland's election, Barnum said nothing more, nor did he sell off any property, but rival circuses posted ads quoting Barnum's promise when touring the South, hoping to cut into his ability to attract cutomers.

Four years later, Barnum was at it again. He declared he would put up fifty thousand dollars in cash, binding himself to sell every building and piece of land he owned in Bridgeport for twenty-five percent off its market value if Cleveland was reelected with a Democratic Congress.[65] He had become more cautious, for the chances of Democrats obtaining control of the Senate were extremely slight. In any event, Harrison's election relieved Barnum of responsibility.

The circus, to be sure, went on and on. Although first Coup, and then Bailey, were the animating spirits, the public identified only Barnum with the enterprise. "There are things so mighty, so awful, so truly gigantic," wrote the *Saturday Review* in 1884, "that the mind of man shrinks before them and shrivels. . . . One of these things is Barnum's One and Only Greatest Show on Earth. . . . As Mont Blanc is the monarch of mountains, and as the Pacific is the vastest of oceans, so is Barnum's alone in its glory. . . ."[66] Barnum got credit for the three rings, the two menageries, the hippodrome, and the museum of curiosities. He was acclaimed for his clever juxtaposition of Jumbo with the tiny elephants and for darkening the herd to make Toung Taloung look a little whiter. And it was Barnum who asked praise for "the greatest and most daring undertaking that was ever before ventured upon by individuals in the line of public exhibition," the transport of "The Greatest Show On Earth," its animals, costumes, equipment, and performers, to London for a triumphal appearance at the Olympia. But the show went to Europe at the urging of Bailey, who realized that the American circus had become more spectacular than any in the Old World and that the profits of a European tour would be enormous.

Bailey was right. European circuses still retained one ring, and with only a few exceptions operated on a much smaller scale than "The Greatest Show On Earth." "Americans have a boundless admiration of everything big," one chronicler of the circus lectured his British countrymen. "Circus proprietors bring their establishments before the public, not by vaunting the talent of the company, or the beauty and sagacity of the horses, but by announcing the thousands of square feet which the circus covers, the thousands of dollars to which their daily or weekly expenses mount, and the number of miles to which their parades extend."[67] Earlier American circuses had toured Europe (the great Seth Howes took his show abroad in 1857 and stayed for seven years), but they were puny compared with the Combined Shows of Barnum and Bailey. For more than three months the circus delighted capacity crowds. Along with the receipts of more than five hundred thousand dollars came a series of personal triumphs for Barnum. Members of the royal family joined the audience, some more than once, and W. E. Gladstone watched one performance with Barnum in the royal box. At every performance he attended, Barnum's open carriage was driven round the arena, the showman, like a crowned head, accepting the homage of the crowd by rising and lifting his hat.

The London *Times* caught the essence of the show and its reduction of spectators to a state of passive wonder. The newspaper was reminded of another institution that overpowered observers, "some vast factory, with its endless spindles and revolving shafts and pulleys." There was unending movement, universal activity. "It is precisely in the immensity, the complexity, the kaleidoscopic variety, and, to use the word in its strict etymological sense, the incomprehensibility of the show that Mr. Barnum's genius is displayed." By placing all these marvels into "one bewildering heap," the circus not only dazzled the visitor, but placed him "under the necessity of coming again and again."[68] Amplitude had replaced humbug as the vital attraction.

Even more satisfying to the old showman than his box-office conquests was a banquet held in his honor at the Hotel Victoria. Lords "were as thick as blackberries" among the guests. Londoners had been disappointed that Barnum had not been permitted to contribute his elephants and giraffes to the procession for the lord mayor, Sir Aaron Isaacs, but the banquet compensated wonderfully.[69] Those attending included the Earl of Kilmorey, who presided, Viscount Bury, Lord Randolph Churchill, R. D. D'Oyly Carte, W. P. Frith, William Howard Russell, and more than a dozen members of Parliament. They heard George Augustus Sala, the toastmaster, compare Barnum with Caesar, Napoleon, and Nero, to the American's advantage. All were entertainers, at least in part, but Barnum had shed no blood.[70]

There was one final gesture to be made. In the eighties and early nineties, Edison's new phonograph was attracting universal admiration. The chance for vocal immortality was exciting. Celebrities determined to make wax cylinders for the benefit of posterity, and Barnum was among them. Before leaving London he consented to record his voice. In strong, deep tones (which didn't fit the "squeaky" label some contemporaries fixed on his speech), Barnum thanked the British public for their kindness and hospitality. But he was never one to rest content with the ordinary. In typical Barnum fashion he added one last thought. "I thus address the world through the medium of the latest wonderful invention," he went on, "so that my voice, like my great show, will reach future generations, and be heard centuries after I have joined the great, and as I believe, happy majority."[71] To the end, Barnum could not resist the chance for advertisement or the opportunity for philosophizing.

The successful London trip over, Barnum arrived home in March 1890. It was his last European journey, and later that year his health began to worsen. He had moved with his wife into a last house, Marina, adjacent to Waldemere but smaller and easier to manage. He spent some time adding codicils to his lengthy and complicated will, instructing Bowser to subtract various gifts to relatives from their future legacies. By the early part of 1891 it was clear that he would not recover. Choosing his funeral hymns and clergymen, Barnum prepared for the end. To cheer him up, the *New York Evening Sun* printed some obituary notices, giving him the chance to see what his career would look like to newspaper readers. But his energy could not be rallied, and on the evening of April 7, 1891, in his eighty-second year, Barnum died. The city of Bridgeport went into mourning, and his portrait could be seen everywhere; most stores and his favorite charities draped themselves in black, their flags at half-mast. On Friday, April 10, a cool, dark day, funeral services were held, the Reverend Dr. Collyer giving the prayer and the address. The coffin was taken to Mountain Grove, and Barnum was buried in the cemetery he helped establish. "The foremost showman of all time," as the *Boston Herald* put it, was gone.

TEN

The Compleat Showman

Even in death Barnum did not quietly glide from public attention. Details of ritual and interment, ordinarily quiet and solemn, were, like most other things, exceptional for the showman. The funeral crowd, for example, was so large at the church that a pickpocket was arrested trying to practice his craft. And seven weeks after burial, early on May 29, 1891, an attempt was made to steal Barnum's body from the vault in Mountain Grove.[1] Grave-robbing and holding the body for ransom were not uncommon in late-nineteenth-century America, and the Barnum family had hired two guards to watch the vault; the robbers were interrupted in their work, but not before they had dug a hole four feet long and two feet deep in their effort to reach the body. Nothing about Barnum was ever quite final.

The newspapers, in this country and abroad, greeted his death with expressions of sadness and long accounts of his career. The tone was universally one of awe for his achievements and admiration for even those methods of exaggeration criticized by an earlier generation. The *New York Times*, asserting that "since the beginnings of history there has been no showman to be compared to him," admitted that Barnum's methods involved humbug, but argued that this was not the dominant theme of his contributions: "What distinguished Barnum from other public entertainers of equal or nearly equal conspicuousness was really the absence of humbug. Poetical statements about particular objects are by no means so mischievous, either to him who makes them or to him who accepts them, as a deceptive statement about the character of an entertainment in general. . . . Barnum was never under any illusions, nor did he ever encourage any illusions, about the nature of his function. He did not pretend to be an evangelist or an artist, but simply a showman."[2]

In terms of his career, this last sentence is inaccurate. Barnum claimed to be both evangelist and artist; he insisted he had redeemed entertainment from the control of the wicked. *Harper's Monthly* paid him at least this compliment: "The late Mr. Barnum, a generation ago, in his American Museum showed that a theatre could be as innocent as a concert-room. Barnum practically bowdlerized the play-house. He eliminated the wickedness. He provided a family theatre, a purged play-house, in which even the clergy could sit harmless, even the cloth could be unsoiled."[3] And the *New York Recorder* concluded that "there has been no one who did more to preserve the circus from vulgarity, and to hold it to its proper province of instructing and edifying, while it amuses."[4]

The European press was even more complimentary, its death notices "punctuated with admiring phrases, somewhat astonishing but nonetheless gratifying to Americans," as the *Times* noted.[5] French newspapers called him "a great benefactor of humanity," "the character of our century, the creator of discoveries, and the king of advertising," "the incomparable," whose "name is immortal." Even the London *Times* had softened. "His death removes an almost classical figure, and his name is a proverb already, and a proverb it will continue until mankind has ceased to find pleasure in the comedy of the show-man and his patrons — the comedy of the harmless deceiver and the willingly deceived." Americans praised his benevolence, admired his techniques, and were grateful for his amusements; Europeans made him a symbol of an international era, the dispenser of amusements for the mass audience produced by democracy and industrialization. What had once been feared and loathed was now accepted as a fact of cultural life: the taste of the mob as a standard of certification.

And while Barnum sought always to purify and instruct, he accepted mass verdicts as legitimate. If an exhibit did not draw well, or proved positively unpopular, Barnum did not blame the public for failing to measure up to his own fine sensibilities; he blamed the exhibit, or the advertising, or the management. His artistry was a servant, not a molder of popular preferences, and he sought primarily the distinction that wealth and respectability could bring — great houses, rich furniture, eminent friends — not the distinction of being recognized as an original genius whose opinions were more refined and cultivated than those of the vulgar herd.

Certainly, Barnum never kept his opinions to himself. On almost every issue he had something to say, and in the last twenty years of his life he achieved the status of an oracle, dispensing his wisdom at every opportunity. He commented on international relations and national character; he gave advice about the Columbian Exposition (it should be held in New York and feature the mummy of Rameses II, Pharoah of the Israelite exodus); he detailed his travels abroad for various periodicals; and he delineated his political positions.[6] When General Grant faced bankruptcy toward the end of his life, Barnum offered to pay him one hundred thousand dollars down and one hundred thousand dollars in commissions for the privilege of exhibiting his many medals and gifts, hoping to turn a profit and be a patriot at the same time.[7] And in 1877 Barnum entangled himself in one of the most memorable crimes of the late nineteenth century, the kidnapping of little Charley Ross.[8] Barnum offered a reward of ten thousand dollars for the boy's return, and newspapers throughout the country printed his public statement promising not to prosecute the criminals if they got in touch with him. Barnum's only condition was the right to exhibit the child after he had been found. The hard-pressed family was horrified by the thought and by Barnum's audacity, but agreed finally either to reimburse Barnum for his ten thousand dollars or place Charley on exhibition. Because not even Barnum's fame sufficed to recover the boy, this choice never had to be made.

Barnum's reputation seemed never to diminish. Presidents and ex-presidents told him he had become the most famous American in the world, eclipsing even generals, statesmen, and inventors. And his life story was anthologized along with biographies of Carnegie, Rockefeller, and Vanderbilt, self-made men who had gathered their fortunes with luck and pluck.[9] Although he never matched these titans, Barnum's fortune at one point was estimated to come close to ten million dollars, and his actual estate was almost half that sum. And finally, additional proof of his public position, there were the letter writers, hundreds annually asking for aid to retire church debts, money to buy livestock, contributions to antitobacco leagues — or offering to sell three-legged hens, self-inking presses, six-legged pigs, monster twins, almost anything that was exotic, curious, or memorable. Barnum had become the national clearinghouse for the bizarre and the grotesque.[10]

By the end of his life, his preeminence as an American institution was challenged by only one other man and the two lived not many miles apart, in Connecticut. Only Mark Twain, resident of Nook Farm in Hartford, could match the showman's reputation — at home and abroad — as a quintessential American. The two men were, in fact, friendly correspondents, each recognizing in the other a prolific contributor to national mythology and a figure of major significance. Their families exchanged visits, while Barnum sought, unsuccessfully but persistently, to get a Twain testimonial for "The Greatest Show On Earth."

Twain became fascinated with the requests for aid and money Barnum received, his "queer letters," as the two called them, and toyed with the idea of publishing the most interesting.[11] "The symbol of the race ought to be a human being carrying an ax," Mark Twain had written, "for every human being has one concealed about him somewhere, and is always seeking the opportunity to grind it."[12] Barnum's correspondence offered a wonderful opportunity for Twain to make this point, and Barnum eagerly saved the letters for Twain to see, although the scheme never materialized.

Their relationship did not begin on a happy note. There was Twain's rather caustic prediction of Barnum's congressional speech, and a description of the museum he wrote for the *San*

Francisco Alta California in March 1867. "There is little or nothing in the place worth seeing," Twain complained, "and yet how it draws! It was crammed with both sexes and all ages. . . . Barnum's Museum is one vast peanut stand now, with a few cases of dried frogs and other wonders scattered here and there, to give variety to the things." He called for "some philanthropist" to burn the museum again.[13]

If Barnum was angered by these early writings, he never let on. Any publicity was better than none, and Twain gradually became more friendly. In *Following the Equator* Twain related rumors that Barnum had once thought of purchasing the Nelson Column, and more seriously, of buying Shakespeare's house in Stratford and setting it up in New York. If Barnum had failed to get Jumbo, Twain wrote, he would have caused his designs on the column to find their way into print, get hundreds of pages of free advertising, and then in a blundering but warm letter of apology let the monument go in exchange for Stonehenge. Barnum believed that such a letter, "written with well-simulated asinine innocence and gush, would have gotten his ignorance and stupidity an amount of newspaper abuse worth six fortunes to him, and not purchasable for twice the money."[14] Twain also worked for a time on a magazine sketch entitled "Personal Habits of the Siamese Twins," a commentary on Chang and Eng, one of Barnum's more profitable exhibition items.

And finally Twain, like Barnum, was fascinated by the issue of duplicity. Through his work, believes Malcolm Bradbury, there runs a deep sense "that in America imposture *is* identity; that values are not beliefs but the product of occasions; and that social identity is virtually an arbitrary matter, depending not on character nor on appearance but on the chance definition of one's nature or colour." Thus Twain's obsession, for example, with the case of two exchanged infants in *Pudd'nhead Wilson*, one white, the other black, and all the paradoxes that mistaken identity inevitably raises. In an analysis that brings to mind the concerns of such older American writers as Melville and Hawthorne, Bradbury argues that Twain created a world "in which no one can be sure, literally or figuratively, of his own whiteness or blackness, though totally different lives are laid down for those who are socially recognized to be one or the other."[15]

Barnum's own experiences could have been used in *Pudd'n-head Wilson*. There were some stories he never described in his autobiography, one of which came from the pen of a critic, Thomas Low Nichols, who left America for voluntary exile when he found some contradictions too unbearable. Nichols wrote his own memoirs during the Civil War and recalled the moment when Barnum suddenly needed a blackface entertainer. His own singer had left and all he could find was a genuine Negro. The boy sang and danced exceptionally well, but it was impossible to present him as he was. So Barnum "blacked and wigged" him so "as to pass for a make-believe one, because the New Yorkers who applauded what they supposed was a white boy in a blackened face and woolly wig, would have driven the real Negro from the stage and mobbed his exhibitor."[16] This extraordinary commentary on illusion and prejudice would have appealed to Twain's sense of irony; Barnum simply discarded the story, if he ever thought about it at all.

Despite all their mutual interests, and a curious set of parallels in their personal lives, the two men were strikingly different. The parallels include fathering three girls, with premature death among them, loss of a wife, financial bankruptcy and personal crisis from careless business transactions, religious heterodoxy, love of gadgetry, and extravagant house-building.

But Twain and Barnum reacted to problems in contrasting ways. Barnum's religious dissent was optimistic and benevolent; Twain's was tinged with terror, so dark and foreboding that he postponed publication of some of his convictions. Barnum's bankruptcy was only a pause in his frantic career from which he rebounded energetically; Twain's bankruptcy was catastrophic, and he was never able entirely to recover. Barnum's family problems were considerable.[17] His daughter Pauline died in 1877, at age thirty-one; her children included two boys, Clinton and Herbert, who, if they had possessed the ability, might have succeeded to Barnum's business enterprises. But although Clinton proved more capable than his brother Herbert, Barnum was disappointed with both, and the Barnum connection with the circus disintegrated shortly after P. T.'s death. Another daughter was divorced, and various relatives embarrassed Barnum with dishonest financial transactions, but all of these complications never affected him in the paralyzing and self-tormenting fashion grief did Twain. Not for Barnum was the agonizing nihilism and cynicism about human nature and the fate of the world that Twain expressed. To the end, Barnum's remained a positive, contented, and blandly optimistic vision of existence: difficulties existed only to be surmounted, life was an encounter that could be won by calculation and industry. The world of nightmare and despair lay beyond his senses.

Barnum's affirmative, noncritical stance was best shown by his attitude toward children. His biographers and obituaries stressed his devotion to the interest (and company) of youngsters, his concern with their pleasure and reaction to his entertainments. When Barnum attends the circus, noted the *New York Sun*, "he does not concentrate his attention on any of the numerous performers. He is waiting for the children to tell him what they think of his great show. When the hosts of funny clowns tumble into the rings the face of the Showman begins to radiate with delight, for then he floats into an earthly paradise on the ripples of unrestrained childish laughter." Unveiling Thomas Ball's statue of Barnum on July 4, 1893 (presented to Bridgeport by his partners and widow), the eulogist argued that of all Barnum's admirable qualities "the first was his fondness for children. He always seemed delighted in their presence, and treated them as though they were spirits sent from above."[18]

Barnum himself declared that there was "no picture so beautiful as ten thousand smiling, bright-eyed, happy children; no music so sweet as their clear-ringing laughter. That I have had power, year after year, by providing innocent amusements for the little ones, to create such pictures, to evoke such music, is my proudest and happiest reflection." Reporters described his diversion of a circus route in order to pass a house where a little boy lay sick. He even entertained at children's gatherings, doing a little juggling and telling some of his famous stories. "A happy smile on a child's face acted like a tonic on the old man," wrote the *New York Times* in its obituary. "He loved them all, black and white, homely and pretty, so long as there were smiles on their faces."[19]

During his career Barnum had continually surrounded himself with appeals to the childlike: Tom Thumb, Lavinia Warren, Admiral Dot, Commodore Nutt, Cordelia Howard, Jenny Lind, Jumbo, the beautiful baby contests — so many of his greatest exhibits represented either the innocence of the child and the naïf, or exploited the sense of lost innocence in adults. The nineteenth-century stage, in England and America, worshiped infant phenomena, precocious children like the Batemans (whom Barnum took to England), Mary Gannon (who appeared in the American Museum), Clara Fisher (another museum performer), the Marsh Juvenile Troupe, and Master Burke.[20] Barnum had almost a monopoly on child stars and child customers.

In contrast, Twain's use of children, as theme and as audience, revealed greater ambiguities and complexities. In his stories, the role "boys and girls are called upon to play is moral commentator on adult society." The passivity so many of Twain's fictional children display was a way of expressing his belief that life itself was rigidly determined. Twain often enveloped the world of childhood with nostalgia, but he also made it " a frightening nightmare. . . . His neophyte is typically an innocent strippling, just old enough to know what evil is but seldom evil himself. Menacing the inexperienced child is an adult environment apt to explode into violence at any moment.

Such grim possibilities are always realized and the innocent is made to experience, forcibly and suddenly, the stupidity, cruelty, and destructiveness of human nature and, by extension, of the universe."[21]

No such rites of initiation took place in Barnum's entertainments. Twain's double-edged vision throws the simpler posture into contrasting relief. Nightmares were banished from the circus. There were no intimations that the delight of childhood was destined to end in disappointment. Like a later master of American entertainments, Walt Disney, Barnum grew into childhood, matured into a universe of dreams that became steadily richer and more fabulous. Their boyhood illusions ended so early that life thereafter had room for newer, more romantic mysteries. Born poor both became rich; growing up obscure both died famous after applying their brilliant organizational skills toward creating landscapes of fantasy. The scale of Barnum's own success molded his opinions of others. His universe had one dimension, and that was good.

Most of Barnum's affirmations came from the era that formed him; good Jacksonian that he was, his targets and opponents were clearly identified, and his political sentiments retained some of the brashness of that egalitarian era. Delighted by the praise of noblemen and royalty, living in the style of a grandee, Barnum nonetheless was not troubled by the changes of identity and loyalty that tormented Mark Twain. No feelings of social discomfort ever afflicted him; confidence in his social mission and a reputation for outrageousness made possible his maintenance of the same personality in every situation. His own brief entries into society, as in the Tom Thumb tour, seemed designed to humiliate, or at least to conquer, foreign nobility, rather than advance his own social standing. Only rarely did Barnum break down and show his fatigue at the hard-fought, moneymaking race he ran. He was content with the temper of his age and the character of his countrymen. They had always been an appreciative audience, and no showman could ask for more.

Henry E. Bowser, the faithful secretary

The Great Man's stationery

To Mrs H.E. Bonner
Compliments of
June 1885   PT Barnum

Barnum: the last years

Barnum's skill in making the transition from one era of American culture to another was impressive. But he had always managed to adopt his advertising to prevailing modes of taste. In the forties and fifties he moved between high and popular culture with consummate ease, combining the operational aesthetic and the high-minded simplicity of Jenny Lind. When he transferred his attractions to the Old World he demonstrated his ability to adapt his rhetoric and methods to different values and conditions.

But the Kris Kringle, Father Christmas figure that Barnum presented to the postwar generation ("to every American child his name has been a compeer of that of Santa Claus himself") was in some ways a less imaginative if more benevolent symbol than that of earlier days. Before the war American entertainment made a virtue of necessity, exploiting native themes and local exotica in ways that actively involved their audiences. No one saw Barnum as a Kris Kringle then; he was a clever competitor, a brilliant innovator, an aggressive impostor, and quite possibly a scoundrel. The museum was large and variegated, its wonders must have seemed infinite to the country folk who thronged it. But its emphasis lay not on dazzling but on diverting and instructing. Case after case of stuffed animals and relics, all carefully cataloged and numbered, filled most of the building, and the "moral" melodramas praised honest virtue while they condemned cruel vice. The circus, on the other hand, partook of the American genius for organization on the largest scale and reduced its spectators to passive bedazzlement. Its curiosities were less comprehensively selected, for its arrangements suited dramatic rather than pedagogic needs. The three rings could not possibly be enjoyed simultaneously; instead, they glutted the taste for splendor and heroics.

By the late nineteenth century the thrust toward the spectacular had taken over mass entertainment. Stage productions featured glitter and verisimilitude, and football crowds grew as gargantuan as their new arenas. Plenitude replaced cleverness as the current taste. The impresario became the beneficent supplier, the wizard who could always top one season's amplitude with another. Circus chariots grew larger and more encrusted, acrobats and elephants multiplied, pageantry became more breathtaking. Barnum's generation of circus managers opened the cornucopia of wonders wider and wider, as if to belie the increasing grimness of the industrial civilization that they served.

Illusion was no longer a subject for debate. The austerity of the old republic had been eclipsed by the trappings of a new empire. If McKinley's America paid lip service in its hagiography and colonial revivals to the pieties of an older day, it supplemented them with a taste for pomp and power that would endure for many generations. Critical, doubting voices were raised in the eighties and nineties, but Barnum's was not among them. His own brand of hedonism fitted the national temper even better in the postwar era, when it became popular, than in the forties and fifties, when it still represented a minority view of the conduct of life.

The issues of illusion and deceit, of social confidence and political democracy, of beauty as process or disguise, were not resolved by Barnum or his audiences. The controversy continues today in arguments about the function of popular culture. Barnum's career, with all its self-conscious strategies and elaborate justifications, fails to present any final solution, but it does point up the antiquity of dilemmas we tend to localize as agonizingly modern. In itself, this is no small comfort. Barnum was not simply the Prometheus of the Pleasure Principle, as his admirers portrayed him. Nor was he a "damaged soul," as some of his detractors argued. He began his career, as his society began its own existence, as an act of criticism; he ended it as a yea-sayer. If the transformation was inevitable, few carried it off with so much enjoyment, or demonstrated so conclusively the involvement of the politics of entertainment with the politics of life.

Acknowledgments

I T IS A PLEASURE to thank some of those who helped me with my work. Walter M. Whitehill kindly provided me with a typed transcript of the Barnum-Kimball Letters and gave me permission to quote from them. Mr. and Mrs. Granville J. Wood of Middletown, New York, permitted me to examine their superb collection of Barnum materials and were generous and hospitable during one summer weekend. I am grateful for the suggestions of Kenneth Holmes, the curator of the Barnum Museum at Bridgeport, and for the aid of Alexander Clark of the Firestone Library of Princeton University. Thomas Parkinson sent me some excellent suggestions for circus research — I wish I could have followed more of them up. Professor Louis Budd offered material concerning Mark Twain's relations with Barnum, and James H. Kettner did some fine on-the-spot research in Boston. I appreciate the aid of Helen Smith and Robert Rosenthal of the University of Chicago Library; Archie Motley of the Chicago Historical Society; Mr. Robert Sokan of the Illinois State University at Normal; Mary Ann Jensen of the Theater Collection at Princeton University; Frederick Anderson, editor of the Mark Twain Papers at the University of California, Berkeley; and staff members at the Bridgeport Public Library, the Historical Society of Pennsylvania, the Newberry Library, the New York Public Library, the New-York Historical Society, and the Widener and Houghton libraries of Harvard University. The Social Science Divisional Research Fund at the University of Chicago helped defray typing costs, and four secretaries worked ably on the manuscript's preparation at various times: Marnie Deering, Margaret Fitzsimmons, Helen Little, and Harriet Pearl. I am grateful to my Chicago colleagues, John G. Cawelti, Barry Karl, and Donald M. Scott, for their readings of the manuscript. Most of all I wish to thank Oscar Handlin and Arthur Mann for their tactful, encouraging, and extremely helpful comments on an earlier version of this book.

Bibliographic Essay

For a man of his extraordinary achievements and active business interests, P. T. Barnum has left a surprisingly small store of manuscript records. The principal repository for Barnum's letters and memorabilia is the Bridgeport Public Library. Nelle Neafie, "A P. T. Barnum Bibliography" (Lexington, Ky., 1965) is a mimeographed description of the holdings of this library. Various historical societies, notably the New-York Historical Society, the Historical Society of Pennsylvania, and the Massachusetts Historical Society, hold Barnum letters, and so do the New York Public Library, the Library of Congress, and libraries at Tufts University, Cornell University, Harvard University, and Princeton University. The fine circus collection at the Illinois State University at Normal contains an interesting group of Barnum letters. The Westervelt Collection at the New-York Historical Society is an important source for materials pertaining to Jenny Lind, and the McCaddon Collection at Princeton is invaluable for the history of the circus. The Boston Athenaeum possesses a large and hitherto unpublished group of letters between Barnum and Moses Kimball, to which many references have been made in the text of this book. Mr. and Mrs. Granville J. Wood of Middletown, New York, own a fascinating collection of letters, photographs, contracts, and memorabilia, originally gathered by Henry Eugene Bowser, Barnum's private secretary. And other libraries and collectors have more materials. Nevertheless, the bulk of Barnum's enormous correspondence has disappeared, presumably destroyed sometime after his death.

But if the manuscript sources are disappointing, the published sources are not. The first place to look, of course, is Barnum's famous autobiography. The history of this remarkable book has been described in the text. The first *Life of P. T. Barnum* (New York, 1855) has unfortunately never been fully reprinted; editors of composite editions have felt it desirable to omit some of the anecdotes, anecdotes which reveal much of Barnum's temperament and philosophy. The 1869 edition, *Struggles and Triumphs; or, Forty Years' Recollections of P. T. Barnum* (Hartford, 1869), has been reprinted by Arno Press (New York, 1970) and is a useful guide to the middle years, particularly the Civil War experiences, Barnum's legislative service, and the fight back from bankruptcy. The last phase of Barnum's career is described in an edition of thirty years later, *Struggles and Triumphs; or, Sixty Years' Recollections of P. T. Barnum* (Buffalo, 1889). These three editions (with some deletions) were assembled in an annotated version by George S. Bryan, ed., *Struggles and Triumphs; or, The Life of P. T. Barnum, Written by Himself,* 2 vols. (New York and London, 1927). This handsome set is now out of print, but Bryan's introduction gives an excellent guide to the labyrinthine history of the book. The autobiography has not been analyzed by literary historians to any great extent, and indeed the whole genre of American autobiography deserves further study.

There is one other place a student of Barnum can begin to look for information, and this is in the monumental work of R. Toole Stott, *Circus and Allied Arts: A World Bibliography, 1500–1971,* 4 vols. (Derby, England, 1857–1971). Barnum, as one of the great celebrities of the circus world, is given a special section in vol. 2 of Stott, and the indices in vols. 3 and 4 note the dozens of references to Barnum in books listed under other categories. Most published commentary on Barnum is included in Stott's references. And this bibliogrpahy, of course, is the logical place to begin further investigation of the circus.

Barnum has also been the subject of a number of biographies and biographical essays. The earliest, Joel Benton, *Life of Honorable Phineas T. Barnum* (Philadelphia, 1891), is the least useful for, while it adds some information, it relies principally on the autobiography. The major biography, M. R. Werner, *Barnum* (Garden City, N.Y., 1927), is an evocative, balanced, and well-researched portrait, still extremely useful, Like most of Barnum's biographers, Werner was highly sympathetic. Harvey W. Root, *The Unknown Barnum* (New York and London, 1927), less original and incisive than Werner, is nonetheless important for Barnum's activities as mayor of Bridgeport and Connecticut legislator.

The decade of the twenties, with its glorification of advertising and the businessman, its application of Freudianism, and its anti-Puritan crusades, was especially hospitable to Barnum scholarship. Besides the Werner and Root biographies and the Bryan edition of the autobiography, there is the superb chapter on Barnum in Constance Rourke, *Trumpets of Jubilee* (New York, 1927), the most subtle attempt to make historical sense of Barnum's career and personality. Where I find the Rourke analysis most wanting is in its failure to periodize Barnum's achievements which, I have argued, change in character from the Jacksonian era to the late nineteenth century. Harvey O'Higgins and Edward H. Reede, M.D., *The American Mind in Action* (New York and London, 1924); and Gamaliel Bradford, *Damaged Souls* (Boston and New York, 1922, 1928), exemplify the perils and pleasures of applying Freudian models (of a highly simplified type) to historic figures, but their essays on Barnum are readable and provocative. Chapter 25 of Frank Presbrey, *The History and Development of Advertising* (Garden City, N.Y., 1929) is an intelligent (and profusely illustrated) narrative of Barnum's contribution to that craft.

Since the 1920s there has been little serious writing on Barnum. The exceptions are chapter 6 in Hamilton Basso, *Mainstream* (New York, 1943); John R. Betts, "Barnum and Natural History," *Journal of the History of Ideas* 20 (June–September 1959), pp. 353–368; and Irving Wallace, *The Fabulous Showman: The Life and Times of P. T. Barnum* (New York, 1959), a book that offers new information about Barnum's family life and presents a well-rounded assessment of his show business triumphs. I have profited from reading all these books and essays; those interested in more bibliographical details about Barnum would do well to consult them.

The notes to this book contain references, when appropriate, to secondary sources that touch on individual Barnum exhibits; it should not be necessary to repeat them here. Jenny Lind, Tom Thumb, and the Siamese twins have their own literature. On the larger issues of American entertainment as an art form there is a growing body of commentary, but large gaps remain. This literature has tended to polarize. One group of books, aimed at a popular audience, has produced helpful narratives (often lavishly illustrated) that do not move too far beyond surface details. Another group of writings has been the work of antiquarians, concerned with technical details to the exclusion of larger issues. This polarization has been present in American theater history and has spilled over into the history of the circus. The latter is treated in George L. Chindahl, *A History of the Circus in America* (Caldwell, Idaho, 1959); John and Alice Durant, *Pictorial History of the American Circus* (New York, 1957); Charles P. Fox and Tom Parkinson, *The Circus in America* (Waukesha, Wis., 1969); Earl Chapin May, *The Circus from Rome to Ringling* (New York, 1932); R. W. G. Vail, *Random Notes on the History of the Early American Circus* (Worcester, Mass., 1934); and Leonidas Westervelt, *The Circus in Literature* (New York, 1939), but important questions concerning the circus's audiences, recruitment patterns, rural and/or urban appeal, and comparative development (so far as it related to the European circus) remain largely untreated.

Similarly, although the visits of European artists are described in Milton Goldin, *The Music Merchants* (New York 1969), and Henry Knepler, *The Gilded Stage: The Years of the Great International Actresses* (New York, 1968), they raise unanswered, indeed unasked questions. Further bibliography, as well as comprehensive narratives, can be found in Foster Rhea Dulles, *A History of Recreation: America Learns to Play*

(New York, 1940, 1965), and Russel B. Nye, *The Unembarrassed Muse* (New York, 1971).

In recent years some books have attempted to strike out and ask hard questions about the form, as well as the content, of American popular culture and have moved beyond anecdote and detail to new levels of argument. Among those I have found most useful are Carl Bode, *The Anatomy of American Popular Culture, 1840–1861* (Berkeley and Los Angeles, 1960); Reuel Denney, *The Astonished Muse* (Chicago, 1957); David Grimsted, *Melodrama Unveiled: American Theater and Culture, 1800–1850* (Chicago, 1968); Francis Hodge, *Yankee Theatre: The Image of America on the Stage, 1825–1860* (Austin, 1964); John A. Kouwenhoven, *The Arts in Modern American Civilization* (New York, 1967); Kenneth S. Lynn, *Mark Twain and Southwestern Humor* (Boston, 1960); and Albert F. McLean, Jr., *American Vaudeville as Ritual* (Lexington, Ky., 1965). Finally, discussions of recreation and samples of the materials that can still be exploited are found in two anthology series, one edited by Hennig Cohen and John William Ward, *Documents in American Civilization Series* (Garden City, N.Y., 1967–), and Neil Harris, ed., *The American Culture*, 8 vols. (New York, 1970–1973).

Notes and Index

Notes

When the principal source of information or quotation is Barnum's autobiography, no citation will be given.

ONE

(7–30)

1. For further information see Eben Lewis Barnum and Reverend Francis Barnum, S.J., *Genealogical Record of the Barnum Family: Presenting a Conspectus of the Male Descendants of Thomas Barnum, 1623–1695* (Gardner, Mass., 1912), and William Richard Cutter, et al., *Genealogical and Family History of the State of Connecticut*, 4 vols. (New York, 1911), 1. Letters from various relatives responding to P. T.'s request for genealogical information can be found in the Barnum Letters, Bridgeport Public Library (hereafter BPL). Connecticut newspapers announced in early 1882 that P. T. was preparing a history of the Barnum family, and in his name requested information.
2. Charles T. Barnum to P. T. Barnum, Wilkes-Barre, January 29, 1882, Barnum Letters, BPL.
3. *Genealogical Record of the Barnum Family*, passim. Barnum's Hotel in Baltimore, and Barnum's Hotel in St. Louis, both nationally known hostelries, were established by members of the family.
4. See Michael Zuckerman, *Peaceable Kingdoms: New England Towns in the Eighteenth Century* (New York, 1970); Richard L. Bushman, *From Puritan to Yankee: Character and the Social Order in Connecticut, 1690–1765* (Cambridge, 1967); Charles S. Grant, *Democracy in the Connecticut Frontier Town of Kent* (New York, 1961); and Kenneth A. Lockridge, *A New England Town: The First Hundred Years* (New York, 1970).
5. Herzen is quoted by George S. Bryan in his lively introduction to the modern, composite edition of Barnum's autobiography, George S. Bryan, ed., *Struggles and Triumphs; or, The Life of P. T. Barnum, Written by Himself*, 2 vols. (New York and London, 1927), 1:lv.
6. John Samuel Ezell, *Fortune's Merry Wheel: The Lottery in America* (Cambridge, 1960), discusses techniques of lottery management and the intervention of state governments.
7. Barnum to Henry Eugene Bowser, Southport, England, June 20, 1881, Granville Wood Collection, Middletown, N.Y.
8. Although he often employed relatives to help in business matters — uncles, cousins, and in later life, Benjamin Fish, the brother of his second wife — Barnum rarely mentioned them in his published writings. He was one of nine siblings, four the children of Thomas Barnum's first wife, and five the product of his second marriage. There has survived almost no correspondence between Barnum and any of his sisters and brothers, although he seems to have been in contact with nieces, nephews, and cousins.
9. Connecticut ended her church establishment in 1818, followed by New Hampshire in 1819 and Massachusetts in 1833.
10. P. T. Barnum to Gideon Welles, Danbury, October 7, 1832, Barnum Letters, BPL. "The bar and seat of the judge was filled with *priests*," Barnum noted derisively, "there being no less than eight present."

11. Fisk quoted in newspaper, Barnum Clipping File, BPL.

12. For descriptions of New York in the Jacksonian period see Robert Green-halgh Albion, *The Rise of New York Port, 1815–1860* (New York, 1939); Robert Ernst, *Immigrant Life in New York City, 1825–1863* (New York, 1949); and James F. Richardson, *The New York Police, Colonial Times to 1901* (New York, 1970).

13. One of the places where Barnum denied manufacturing the Joice Heth episode was in a letter to a friend of Lindsay's after Lindsay had fallen on hard times. Enclosing one hundred dollars to help him, Barnum insisted that he had purchased Joice Heth in good faith. He argued that Lindsay had falsely represented her as "the Nurse of Washington," presenting *"a forged Bill of Sale purporting to have been made by the father* of George Washington. I honestly *believed* all this and exhibited accordingly as Lindsay had done for months previously — finally she died, and the imposition became manifest and *I* have ever since borne the stigma of *originating* that imposture. I never denied it before — but I ought to have done so truly." Barnum to Baker, n.p., n.d., Ford Collection, New York Public Library (hereafter NYPL). The Granville Wood Collection contains a contract made between James S. Bowling and Lindsay, in which they agree to share profits and losses for twelve months. This was the agreement that Barnum bought from Lindsay; it was dated June 10, 1835. Despite her great age, Joice Heth was evidently considered to be lively. One clause of the contract bound Lindsay to join Bowling in pursuit "if the said Joice Heth should escape at a distant city or town. . . ."

14. William G. B. Carson, *Managers In Distress: The St. Louis Stage, 1840–1844* (St. Louis, 1949), pp. 144–146. According to Smith, Barnum gained almost two thousand dollars from the arranged contest. Smith, nonetheless, remained an admirer of Barnum, dedicating his own autobiography to him. "I honor you, oh! great Impresario, as *the* most successful manager in America, or any other country. Democrat as you are, you can give a practical lesson to the aristocrats of Europe, *how to live.*" *The Theatrical Journey-Work and Anecdotal Recollections of Sol Smith* (Philadelphia, 1854), p. 9.

15. See J. W. F. White, "The Judiciary of Alleghany County," *Pennsylvania Magazine of History and Biography* 7 (1883), p. 176. There are other versions of this episode, including a description in *Managers In Distress,* and in Maria Ward Brown, *The Life of Dan Rice* (Long Branch, N.J., 1901), but White's version seems most convincing.

TWO

(31–57)

1. Henry P. Tappan, *A Step from the New World to the Old, and Back Again,* 2 vols. (New York, 1852), 1:100.

2. As quoted in Daniel J. Boorstin, *The Lost World of Thomas Jefferson* (Boston, 1963), p. 239. Chap. 1, "The Supreme Workman," presents a fine synthesis of Jeffersonian natural philosophy.

3. As quoted in Charles Coleman Sellers, *Charles Willson Peale* (New York, 1969), p. 333. The sentences are taken from Peale's *Discourse Introductory to a Course of Lectures,* published in 1800. Chaps. 17 and 24 of Sellers's book include an evocative history of Peale's Museum.

4. For more on some of these early museums, including institutions in Philadelphia, Cincinnati, and St. Louis, see *A Cabinet of Curiosities* (Charlottesville, 1967).

5. I am indebted in this discussion to Gordon S. Wood, ed., *The Rising Glory of America, 1760–1820* (New York, 1971), pp. 14–18.

6. *Charles Willson Peale,* p. 350.

7. Thomas Fitzgunne, "A Flying Shot at the United States," *Dublin University Magazine* 40 (1852) p. 590, quoted in Blanche Muldrow, "The American Theatre as Seen by British Travellers, 1790–1860" (Ph.D. diss., University of Wisconsin, 1953), p. 465.

8. William K. Northall, *Before and Behind the Curtain; or, Fifteen Years' Observations Among the Theatres of New York* (New York, 1851), pp. 6–7.

9. The variety of New York's entertainments, along with the specific shows being presented in the city's museums, can be found in the appropriate volumes of George C. D. Odell, *Annals of the New York Stage*, 15 vols. (New York, 1927–1949).

10. Information on Moses Kimball can be found in the *National Cyclopedia of American Biography*, 53 vols. to date (New York, 1893–), 20:70; Claire McClinchee, *The First Decade of the Boston Museum* (Boston, 1940); and William W. Clapp, Jr., *A Record of the Boston Stage* (Boston and Cambridge, 1853). Kimball (1809–1895) had a career that resembled Barnum's. Like Barnum he participated in politics, serving as a Boston alderman, and in the Massachusetts legislature, and was active in various philanthropies and businesses, besides his museum interests.

11. *A Record of the Boston Stage*, p. 471.

12. Barnum to Kimball, New York, January 30, 1843, Barnum-Kimball Letters, Boston Atheneum (hereafter BA). All these letters are from New York unless otherwise noted.

13. Barnum detailed the expenses of operating Peale's in a letter to Kimball, February 5, 1843, Barnum-Kimball Letters, BA. Barnum had only contempt for Rubens Peale's business ability. Apparently Peale had written him "to ask if I could not send him a Tom Thumb — or a two headed man." Barnum replied that he could furnish him with a "beast with 7 heads and 10 horns, at short notice, or any other that he ordered — that Tom Thumb was made to my order six [months] ago — and being now *nearly new* and without a rival, he was [very] *valuable.*" He demanded at least half the receipts if Peale exhibited him.

14. Aside from the many publicity pamphlets that appeared during Tom Thumb's lifetime, the best description of his career is Alice Curtis Desmond, *Barnum Presents General Tom Thumb* (New York, 1954). There is room for more work on this extraordinarily popular nineteenth-century phenomenon.

15. The promotional literature distributed for Tom Thumb at his exhibitions gave capsule histories of famous giants and dwarfs, and emphasized not only his small size but his pleasant and unblemished appearance. The literature on giants, dwarfs, and other human curiosities, is sparse and nonanalytical. Walter Bodin and Burnet Hershey, *It's A Small World: All About Midgets* (New York, 1934), while it is garrulous, repetitive, and occasionally appeals to salacious tastes (it spends a good deal of time on the sexual habits and potency of midgets), is nonetheless the only popular modern survey of the subject. Chaps. 2 and 3 discuss the glandular basis for stunted growth and describe the various categories of midgets and dwarfs. Other even more anecdotal works include Edward J. Wood, *Giants and Dwarfs* (London, 1868), and Colin Clair, *Human Curiosities* (London, New York, Toronto, 1968). Raymund Fitzsimons, *Barnum in London* (London, 1969), also presents some information on the history of dwarfism and its glandular basis. Finally, see Irving Wallace, *The Fabulous Showman: The Life and Times of P. T. Barnum* (New York, 1959), pp. 73–76, for a discussion of Barnum's use of historical precedents in exploiting Tom Thumb.

16. A copy of the agreement can be found in the Granville Wood Collection. The tutor who accompanied Tom Thumb, "Parson" Fordyce Hitchcock, received twelve dollars a week, more than the boy did. "Hitchcock's wages may seem high," Barnum wrote Kimball from New York

on January 30, 1843, "but he is genteel, industrious and knowing the way of the boy well." Barnum-Kimball Letters, BA.

17. Barnum to Kimball, February 5, 1843, Barnum-Kimball Letters, BA.
18. Barnum to Kimball, March 8, 1843, Barnum-Kimball Letters, BA.
19. Barnum to Kimball, May 15, 1843, Barnum-Kimball Letters, BA.
20. Barnum to Kimball, May 24, 1843, Barnum-Kimball Letters, BA.
21. Barnum to Kimball, October 12, 1843, Barnum-Kimball Letters, BA.
22. Barnum to Kimball, September 1, 1843, Barnum-Kimball Letters, BA.
23. Barnum to Kimball, October 26, 1843, Barnum-Kimball Letters, BA.
24. Barnum to Kimball, September 24, 1843, Barnum-Kimball Letters, BA. Despite Barnum's complaints, he was doing rather well. While showing the Indians, he was averaging about one hundred and twenty dollars a day and Peale's was bringing in another forty dollars daily. See Barnum to Kimball, September 29, 1843, BA. The first week in October he was up to seven hundred and four dollars, with Peale's adding four hundred dollars, although by this time Kimball was showing the Indians in Boston. See Barnum to Kimball, October 8, 1843, BA. Some weeks he might take in as much as fifteen hundred dollars, although on occasions his receipts fell to one-fifth of that amount. In this early stage of his career it was difficult to predict which attractions would draw well, and Barnum did not yet possess the reputation or the permanent collection that guaranteed the steady trade he produced in the late 1840s and 1850s.
25. Spirit of the Times, March 29, 1843, p. 2.
26. Barnum to Kimball, March 20, 1843; March 21, 1843; March 26, 1843, Barnum-Kimball Letters, BA.
27. Barnum to Kimball, March 22, 1843, Barnum-Kimball Letters, BA. Barnum advertised that tickets might be bought personally from Grace Darling at the museum offices. "I think that will help some," he wrote Kimball, "as I am not the only one who thinks her a 'saint' a vestal in fact. [However, I] expect she will sell most of her tickets to those who hope she is not quite a saint."
28. Barnum to Kimball, Paris, April 30, 1845, Barnum-Kimball Letters, BA.
29. John Delaware Lewis, Across the Atlantic (London, 1851), p. 24, quoted in "The American Theatre as Seen by British Travellers," pp. 440–441. A similar sentiment was expressed sixteen years later by an American, Richard Grant White. He observed, in his pseudonymous satirical treatment of the British tourist in America, that Mr. Barnum "is the representative man, and his museum is the representative 'institootion' of this country. . . . And I should like to know, if the British Museum is to be taken as an index of the state of civilization, why the American Museum is not to be looked upon in a similar light as regards America? And, if not, I ask again why the government don't disavow the place, and cause it to be shut up until the name is changed. . . . If the majority did not consent that Mr. Barnum should set his place up as 'The American Museum,' of course he could not do it." [Richard Grant White] The Adventures of Sir Lyon Bouse, Bart., in America, During the Civil War (New York, 1867), p. 30.
30. "A Flying Shot at the United States," "The American Theatre as Seen by British Travellers," p. 465.

THREE

(59–89)

1. A copy of the contract is located in the Granville Wood Collection.
2. The best account of this debate, and an analysis of Nott's position, can be found in William Stanton, The Leopard's Spots: Scientific Attitudes toward Race in America, 1815–59 (Chicago, 1960). Stanton also discusses the Charleston scientists, and John Bachman in particular.

3. Barnum to Kimball, September 4, 1843, Barnum-Kimball Letters, BA.
4. Barnum to Kimball, February 5, 1843, Barnum-Kimball Letters, BA. The complicated story of Taylor's southern tour, along with discussion of the projected libel suit and the newspaper debate, has been pieced together from letters and newspaper clippings in the NYPL, along with the correspondence now located in the BA.
5. Barnum to Kimball, February 13, 1843, Barnum-Kimball Letters, BA. Actually, the mermaid was not yet on her way to New York, because Taylor tried to continue the tour some time longer.
6. Bachman wrote as "No Humbug" to the *Charleston Mercury* in January 1843. The mermaid was exhibited at the Masonic Hall in Charleston from January 17 to January 21, along with an orangoutang, some fancy glassblowing "by Belzoni Davidson, the ornighotyncus," an exhibition by a ventriloquist and magician, and an automaton. In short, this was an early Barnum road show.
7. Taylor wrote as "The Man Who Exhibits the Mermaid," *Charleston Mercury*, January 21, 1843, promising to pay five hundred dollars to any one who produced a monkey or baboon with a head and shoulders like those of the mermaid. He further implied that "No Humbug" could not be a scientist or a physician and suggested that he might have served a term in jail. To cap things off, Taylor insisted that the mermaid could not be taken out of the glass case nor cut in any way. John Bachman wrote to the *Mercury*, February 7, 1843, identifying himself as "No Humbug," and insisted that the affair was a vile imposition. The letter of the Charleston scientists appeared in the *Mercury*, February 5, 1843. It stated: "Regarding as we do the exhibition of such a deformity, an injury to natural science — as calculated to perpetuate on the minds of the ignorant an absurd fable, and to extract money from the public under false pretenses, we feel it our duty to expose this vile deception." For more on the Gibbes family and Charleston science see Richard M. Jellison and Philip S. Swartz, "The Scientific Interests of Robert W. Gibbes," *South Carolina Historical Magazine* 66 (April 1965), pp. 77–97. Jellison and Swartz describe another dispute involving Bachman and Robert W. Gibbes, a cousin of Lewis R. Gibbes. This centered on the discoveries of Albert Koch, a remarkable pseudoscientific charlatan who claimed to have discovered a new genus of sea serpent. This time, Bachman defended the exhibitor.
8. *Charleston Courier*, February 6, 1843. Lewis R. Gibbes replied, February 13, in a letter that asserted once more the superiority of scientific judgment, even without examining the mermaid. Is it right, he asked, that "gentlemen, who, by study and long practice, have acquired a power of discrimination in these matters, that may appear surprising to those unaccustomed to them, should be 'held of no authority,' because they are able to decide without the removal of a glass case." Yeadon answered the attack in the *Charleston Courier*, February 15, 1843.
9. *Charleston Mercury*, March 29, 1843.
10. Barnum to Kimball, February 21, 1843, Barnum-Kimball Letters, BA. Charleston newspapers referred to the expected court fight. See *Charleston Mercury*, March 29, 1843. In connection with later southern hostility to Barnum and his autobiography, it might be noted that the *Courier*, which supported Barnum's side, was a Unionist newspaper in the great South Carolina nullification controversy, while the *Mercury*, which published many of the attacks of Bachman, Gibbes, and the scientists, was one of the leading southern-rights newspapers. However, so many personalities and local issues were involved in the newspaper fight that it may be impossible to discover any logic in their opposed positions on this particular dispute.
11. Barnum to Kimball, March 27, 1843, Barnum-Kimball Letters, BA. Barnum was angered at Yeadon's "impudence" in bringing up the sub-

ject of fees. On April 4 Barnum wrote Kimball urging that they keep up the excitement, but not go to the law. In this way they would reap the benefits of publicity. As noted previously, rumors of a twenty-thousand-dollar lawsuit had been given press attention by late March. Gibbes welcomed the lawsuit, promising to apologize publicly if found to be in error. Meanwhile, Barnum piously denied he was the mermaid's owner (Kimball remained the legal proprietor), but also welcomed a legal battle. Using language similar to Yeadon's, Barnum declared that the results of a trial "will discomfit a number of two-penny self-dubbed 'scientific' wiseacres, whose optics, like those mentioned by the poet, can discover 'things not to be seen.' I imagine further, that the sage and sagacious Charleston D.D.'s and M.D.'s must each possess a pair of Sam Weller's 'patent double million gas microscopes of hextra power,' instead of eyes, to enable them to see the pretended 'seams,' through a glass case. . . . It is an easy thing to LOOK WISE, and raise learned 'doubts' without examination of the thing criticized, but in this instance I opine that it will require something more than senseless innuendos, to prove the falsity of what no naturalist dare swear is not genuine." This letter to the *New York Sun* was reprinted in the *Charleston Courier*, March 20, 1843.

12. Locke's hoax is described in Robert Silverberg, *Scientists and Scoundrels: A Book of Hoaxes* (New York, 1965), pp. 34–50, as well as in many other places. See also Curtis D. MacDougall, *Hoaxes* (New York, 1940, 1958), chap. 27.
13. Quoted in *Hoaxes*, p. 230.
14. Edgar Allan Poe, "The Balloon-Hoax," *The Works of Edgar Allan Poe*, 20 vols., ed. Edmund Clarence Stedman and George Edward Woodberry (New York, 1894, 1914), 2:207, 217. More than one critic has pointed out that Poe filched much of his text from two pamphlets by Monck Mason. For more on Poe's balloon hoax see Harold H. Scudder, "Poe's 'Balloon Hoax,'" *American Literature* 21 (May 1949), pp. 179–190; Ronald S. Wilkinson, "Poe's 'Balloon-Hoax' Once More," *American Literature* 32 (November 1960), pp. 313–317; T. N. Weissbuch, "Edgar Allan Poe: Hoaxer in the American Tradition," *New-York Historical Society Quarterly* 45 (July 1961), pp. 291–309; and Burton R. Pollin, *Discoveries in Poe* (Notre Dame, London, 1970), chap. 10.
15. "Diddling Considered as One of the Exact Sciences," *Works of Poe*, 4:234–248. In "The Business Man," 4:158–170, Poe outlines other variations of sharp practices. For an interesting interpretation of Poe's hoaxing, which I do not agree with but find stimulating, see Michael Allen, *Poe and the British Magazine Tradition* (New York, 1969).
16. For a summary of British views see Max Berger, *The British Traveller in America, 1836–1860* (Gloucester, Mass., 1964), especially chap. 3. Allan Nevins, *America Through British Eyes* (New York, 1948), anthologizes excerpts from British travel writings and includes such authorities as Charles Dickens, Alexander Mackay, and Captain Marryat.
17. Mrs. Frances Trollope, *Domestic Manners of the Americans*, ed. Donald Smalley (New York, 1949), pp. 278–279.
18. Charles Dickens, *Works of Charles Dickens*, 36 vols. Centenary edition (London, 1910), vol. 32, *American Notes*, p. 292. "You will strain at a gnat in the way of trustfulness and confidence, however fairly won and well deserved," Dickens told Americans, "but you will swallow a whole caravan of camels, if they be laden with unworthy doubts and mean suspicions." See also Harriet Martineau, *Society in America*, 3 vols. (London, 1837), 3:34–37.
19. *Domestic Manners of the Americans*, p. 209. See also, in the same work, pp. 86, 305. So prevalent was this sense of American gravity that Englishmen who disagreed with the generalization could refer to it as a platitude. See Thomas Colley Grattan, *Civilized America*, 2 vols. (London, 1859), 2:336.

20. See Constance Rourke, *American Humor: A Study of the National Character* (New York, 1931) and *The Roots of American Culture* (New York, 1942); Kenneth S. Lynn, *Mark Twain and Southwestern Humor* (Boston, 1960); and Richard Chase, *Herman Melville: A Critical Study* (New York, 1949).

21. *Herman Melville*, p. 80.

22. Some of the sources elaborating on American concern with technology in the nineteenth century are Marvin Fisher, *Workshops in the Wilderness: The European Response to American Industrialization, 1830–60* (New York, 1967); H. J. Habakkuk, *American and British Technology in the Nineteenth Century: The Search for Labour-Saving Inventions* (New York, 1962); John A. Kouwenhoven, *Made in America: The Arts in Modern Civilization* (Garden City, N.Y., 1962); Leo Marx, *The Machine in the Garden: Technology and the Pastoral Ideal in America* (New York, 1964); Hugo A. Meier, "American Technology and the Nineteenth-Century World," *American Quarterly* 10 (Summer 1958), pp. 116–130, and "Technology and Democracy, 1800–1860," *Mississippi Valley Historical Review* 43 (March 1957), pp. 618–640; and Perry Miller, *The Life of the Mind in America: From the Revolution to the Civil War* (New York, 1965), Part 3.

23. Harriet Martineau, *Retrospect of Western Travel* (London, New York, 1838), 2:90–91. Sixty years later, Americans were still debating the problem of scientific hoaxing. See "Dangers of Scientific Joking," *Literary Digest* 13 (October 3, 1896), p. 719.

24. This was the Reverend Ezra Stiles Gannett, quoted in *The Life of the Mind in America*, p. 308.

25. Joseph Atterley, *A Voyage to the Moon* (New York, 1827), pp. 10–11.

26. Bird is quoted in Richard Rudisill, *Mirror Image: The Influence of the Daguerreotype on American Society* (Albuquerque, 1971), p. 51.

27. Edward P. Hingston, *The Genial Showman: Being Reminiscences of the Life of Artemus Ward and Pictures of a Showman's Career in the Western World*, 2 vols. (London, n.d.), 1:166–173.

28. Carl Bode, *The Anatomy of American Popular Culture, 1840–1861* (Berkeley and Los Angeles, 1960), p. 130. Chap. 9 of Bode's book, pp. 119–130, is entitled "Manuals for All Things."

29. See, for example, Orson S. Fowler, *A Home for All; or, A New, Cheap, Convenient, and Superior Mode of Building* (New York, 1848), and Z. Baker, *The Cottage Builder's Manual* (Worcester, Mass., 1856).

30. C. W. Elliott, *Cottages and Cottage Life* (Cincinnati, 1848), passim.

31. Richard Henry Dana, Jr., *Two Years Before the Mast* (New York, 1964), pp. 32–33.

32. J. E. Hilary Skinner, *After the Storm; or, Jonathan and His Neighbours in 1865–6*, 2 vols. (London, 1866), 1:9. Skinner was impressed with the variety. "Allow an expert cracksman six companies and thirty minutes' time to plunder the Brompton Boilers, ten minutes at Madame Tussaud's, twice as long at the British Museum (stuffed animal department), and an hour for removing some choice specimens from Regent's Park Zoological Gardens; then take a few articles from the Polytechnic, with a lecturer to explain them, and collect all the human oddities on view in London." This, plus an orchestra, theater, shooting gallery, and refreshment room, would reproduce Barnum's museum on July 4. Skinner, of course, was describing the museum more than twenty years after Barnum had taken it over.

33. Charles Godfrey Leland, *Memoirs* (New York, 1893), pp. 112–113.

34. For more on American attitudes toward art in the antebellum era see Neil Harris, *The Artist in American Society: The Formative Years, 1790–1860* (New York, 1966), passim.

35. Ralph Waldo Emerson, "Art," *The Complete Works of Ralph Waldo Emerson*, 12 vols. Centenary edition (Boston and New York, 1903–1904), vol. 2, *Essays*, 1st ser., p. 362. For more on Transcendentalist aesthetics see

Vivian C. Hopkins, *Spires of Form: A Study of Emerson's Aesthetic Theory* (Cambridge, 1951); F. O. Matthiessen, *American Renaissance, Art and Expression in the Age of Emerson and Whitman* (London, Toronto, New York, 1941); Charles R. Metzger, *Emerson and Greenough, Transcendental Pioneers of an American Aesthetic* (Berkeley, 1954); and Robert B. Shaffer, "Emerson and his Circle: Advocates of Functionalism," *Journal of the Society of Architectural Historians* 7 (July–December 1948), pp. 17–20. Emerson's comments on Barnum are brief and uncomplimentary. Travel with Horace Greeley, for example, Emerson found a trying experience because of the newspaperman's restless activity. "He is an admirable editor, but I had as lief travel with an Express man or with Barnum." Emerson to Lidian Emerson, Syracuse, N.Y., January 17, 1857, *The Letters of Ralph Waldo Emerson*, 6 vols., ed. Ralph L. Rusk (New York, 1939), 5:56. A sharper note had been struck earlier. In the winter of 1855 Emerson learned of Barnum's bankruptcy. I see "that P. T. Barnum has assigned his property, — which is what old people called — the gods visible again." Emerson to Lidian Emerson, Chicago, December 30, 1855, *The Letters of Ralph Waldo Emerson*, 4:541.

36. Journal entry for October 9, 1857. Henry David Thoreau, *The Writings of Henry David Thoreau*, 20 vols., ed. Bradford Torrey (Boston and New York, 1906), 10:80.

37. *Works of Emerson*, 2:367.

38. George William Curtis to John S. Dwight, New York, December 22, 1843. George William Curtis, *Early Letters of George William Curtis to John S. Dwight*, ed. George Willis Cooke (New York, 1898), pp. 139–140.

39. *Made in America*, passim. The sheer delight in machine movement can be found in hundreds of comments, but none more striking than the description of a cotton mill by Samuel Goodrich, an author and publisher, in 1845: "The ponderous wheel that communicates life and activity to the whole establishment; the multitude of bands and cogs, which connect the machinery, story above story; the carding engines, which seem like things of life, toiling with steadfast energy; the whirring cylinders, the twirling spindles, the clanking looms — the whole spectacle seeming to present a magic scene in which wood and iron are endowed with the dexterity of the human hand — and where complicated machinery seems to be gifted with intelligence — is surely one of the marvels of the world." Quoted in *The Life of the Mind in America*, p. 300.

40. Nathalia Wright, *Horatio Greenough, the First American Sculptor* (Philadelphia, 1963), is the only modern biography. Writing to William Cullen Bryant from Washington, December 27, 1851, Greenough argued that "we have developed in our ships, our carriages and engines a new style . . . the Yankee Doric . . . strictly in harmony with the great primal law of God's own structures. . . . It is high time to rouse the country to introduce in structures of a civil character, the sound logical doctrine embodied in the engine." Horatio Greenough, *Letters of Horatio Greenough*, ed. Nathalia Wright (Madison, Wis., 1972), p. 399.

41. Harold A. Small, ed., *Form and Function: Remarks on Art, Design, and Architecture by Horatio Greenough* (Berkeley and Los Angeles, 1962), p. 61.

42. Ibid., p. 111.

43. [Theodore Dwight Weld], *American Slavery As It Is — Testimony of a Thousand Witnesses* (New York, 1839), pp. 7–8.

44. David B. Davis has explored this theme on a number of occasions, most effectively, perhaps, in "Some Themes of Counter-Subversion: An Analysis of Anti-Masonic, Anti-Catholic, and Anti-Mormon Literature," *Mississippi Valley Historical Review* 47 (September 1960), pp. 205–22.

45. Captain Frederick Marryat, *A Diary in America (1837–1838)*, ed. Jules Zanger (Bloomington, 1960), p. 78, quoted in Fred Somkin, *Unquiet*

314

Eagle: *Memory and Desire in the Idea of American Freedom, 1815–1860* (Ithaca, 1967), p. 125. Somkin's discussion of American notions of space and privacy is a brilliant analysis.

46. "Barnum and Mrs. Stowe," *Writings of Severn Teackle Wallis*, 4 vols. (Baltimore, 1896), 2:69–84. This review of Barnum's *Life* and *Sunny Memories of Foreign Lands* by Mrs. Stowe appeared originally in the *Southern Literary Messenger*.

47. There is a large literature on the history of the detective novel, and some interesting analyses of Poe's contribution to the genre. I have found the following to be helpful: Howard Haycraft, "Murder for Pleasure," ed. Howard Haycraft, *The Art of the Mystery Story* (New York, 1946), pp. 158–177; A. E. Murch. *The Development of the Detective Novel* (London, 1958); Carolyn Wells, *The Technique of the Mystery Story* (Springfield, Mass., 1913); and most recently, Daniel Hoffman, *Poe Poe Poe Poe Poe Poe Poe* (Garden City, N.Y., 1972), chap. 4. See also the brief but provocative remarks of Siegfried Kracauer, *From Caligari to Hitler: A Psychological History of the German Film* (Princeton, 1947, 1966), pp. 19–20, treating the relationship between liberal democracy and the detective hero.

48. *Works of Poe*, 3:65.

49. *Works of Poe*, 3:220.

50. [Evert A. Duyckinck, ed.], *Tales by Edgar Allan Poe* (New York, 1845). Among those stories that Duyckinck left out and Poe thought well of were "William Wilson," "Ligeia," and "The Tell-Tale Heart."

51. W. D. Howells, *A Life of Abraham Lincoln* (Columbus, O., 1860; Springfield, Ill., 1938), pp. 31–32. Various historians of the detective story have referred to the statement, including A. E. Murch, *The Development of the Detective Novel*, p. 78.

52. W. K. Wimsatt, Jr., "What Poe Knew About Cryptography," *Publications of the Modern Language Association* 58 (September 1943), p. 779. For more on "The Gold Bug" see J. Woodrow Hassell, Jr., "The Problem of Realism in 'The Gold Bug,'" *American Literature* 25 (May 1953), pp. 179–192.

53. W. K. Wimsatt, Jr., "Poe and the Chess Automaton," *American Literature* 11 (May 1939), pp. 138–151, remains useful.

54. The best study of American science fiction is still unpublished: Thomas Dean Clareson, "The Emergence of American Science Fiction: 1880–1915; A Study of the Impact of Science upon American Romanticism" (Ph.D. diss., University of Pennsylvania, 1956). H. Bruce Franklin, *Future Perfect: American Science Fiction of the Nineteenth Century* (New York, 1966), anthologizes the work of some writers of science fiction and contains some interesting commentary.

55. Sir Arthur Conan Doyle was one of those who handsomely acknowledged his debt to Poe. See *The Development of the Detective Novel*, pp. 81, 83.

56. Jean Eugene Robert-Houdin, *Memoirs of Robert Houdin, Ambassador, Author, and Conjuror: Written by Himself*, 2 vols. (London, 1859), 1:194.

57. Ibid., 1:235.

FOUR

(91–109)

1. *Sketch of the Life, Personal Appearance, Character and Manners of Charles S. Stratton* (New York, 1862), p. 5.

2. Quoted from the *Literarian*, May 5, 1857, in *Sketch of the Life of Charles S. Stratton*, p. 25.

3. Fred Bridges, "The Phrenological Development of General Tom Thumb," in *Sketch of the Life of Charles S. Stratton*, p. 19. The analysis examined, among more than forty separate qualities, Tom Thumb's amativeness,

philoprogenitiveness, acquisitiveness, combativeness, preservationess, secretiveness, firmness, hope, ideality, and benevolence. Phrenologists frequently approximated the role of modern vocational guidance counselors; this particular summary indicated Tom Thumb was in the right field. See Allan S. Horlick, "Phrenology and the Social Education of Young Men," *History of Education Quarterly* 11 (Spring 1971), pp. 23–38.

4. Quoted in Alice Curtis Desmond, *Barnum Presents General Tom Thumb* (New York, 1954), p. 67.
5. Barnum to Kimball, Norwich, England, July 29, 1844, Barnum-Kimball Letters, BA.
6. Barnum to Kimball, Norwich, July 29, 1844, Barnum-Kimball Letters, BA.
7. Barnum to Kimball, Bristol, England, August 18, 1844, Barnum-Kimball Letters, BA.
8. Barnum to Kimball, Kidderminster, England, October 18, 1846, NYPL.
9. Barnum to Kimball, London, January 30, 1845, Barnum-Kimball Letters, BA.
10. Barnum to Kimball, Bordeaux, August 26, 1845, Barnum-Kimball Letters, BA.
11. Barnum to Kimball, Bordeaux, August 26, 1845, Barnum-Kimball Letters, BA.
12. Barnum to Kimball, Brighton, England, August 18, 1846, NYPL.
13. Barnum to Kimball, Kidderminster, England, October 18, 1846, NYPL.
14. And it inspired the opening of Mark Twain's *A Connecticut Yankee in King Arthur's Court*. See Hamlin Hill, "Barnum, Bridgeport and the Connecticut Yankee," *American Quarterly* 16 (Winter 1964), pp. 615–616.
15. Barnum brought his baby show up to Boston, giving five hundred dollars to the winner. See Alfred Pairpoint, *Uncle Sam and his Country: Or, Sketches of America, in 1854–55–56* (London, 1857), pp. 41–43. It was in the 1840s also that Barnum exhibited the great circus clown and gymnast Dan Rice, advertising him as "The Young American Hercules" and boasting that Rice could support a pipe filled with one hundred and twenty-six gallons of water while two men stood on his chest. The huge puncheon had only half a dozen gallons in it, however, and when it fell to the floor the fifth night of Rice's appearance, the amused audience discovered the imposture and Rice's engagement came to an end. See Maria Ward Brown, *The Life of Dan Rice* (Long Branch, N.J., 1901), pp. 70–73.
16. Barnum to Kimball, February 2 [1848], NYPL.
17. Maud and Otis Skinner, *One Man In His Times: The Adventures of H. Watkins Strolling Player, 1845–1863, from his Journal* (Philadelphia, 1938), p. 232. The change in Barnum's programming is outlined in George C. D. Odell, *Annals of the New York Stage*, 15 vols. (New York, 1927–1949).
18. Walter Thornbury, *Criss-Cross Journeys*, 2 vols. (London, 1873), 1:175, quoted in Blanche Muldrow, "The American Theatre as Seen by British Travellers, 1790–1860" (Ph.D. diss., University of Wisconsin, 1953) pp. 520–521.
19. William K. Northall, *Before and Behind the Curtain* (New York, 1851), p. 166.

FIVE

(111–141)

1. Fanny Elssler's American tour is described in Ivor Guest, *Fanny Elssler* (Middletown, Conn., 1970), and Duncan Crow, *Henry Wikoff, the American Chevalier* (London, 1963). For some indication of her earnings see

William W. Clapp, Jr., *A Record of the Boston Stage* (Boston and Cambridge, 1853), p. 370. In thirteen nights in Boston Fanny Elssler's receipts totaled $14,166, considered a fabulous sum. Ten years later Jenny Lind would surpass that amount in a single concert.

2. The American tours of European artists are described in Milton Goldin, *The Music Merchants* (New York, 1969). Henry Knepler, *The Gilded Stage: The Years of the Great International Actresses* (New York, 1968), concentrates on the post–Civil War period, but analyzes the trip of the great Rachel in the 1850s.

3. The official source for Jenny Lind's life is H. S. Holland and W. S. Rockstro, *Memoirs of Madame Jenny Lind-Goldschmidt: Her Early Art-Life and Dramatic Career, 1820–1850* (London, 1891). Joan Bulman, *Jenny Lind* (London, 1956), is an informative biography but does not spend too much space on the American years. Gladys Denny Shultz, *Jenny Lind: The Swedish Nightingale* (Philadelphia and New York, 1962), is the most complete modern work in English and devotes more than half its space to the American tour.

4. Quoted in *Jenny Lind*, p. 105.

5. Max Maretzek, *Crotchets and Quavers; or, Revelations of an Opera Manager in America* (New York, 1855, 1966), p. 121.

6. G. G. Foster, *Memoir of Jenny Lind* (New York, 1850), p. 3.

7. Quoted in N. Parker Willis, *Memoranda of the Life of Jenny Lind* (Philadelphia, 1851), p. 217.

8. London *Times*, Sept. 24, 1850, quoted in *Jenny Lind*, a broadside published in Boston during her tour. A copy of the broadside is in vol. 1 of "Barnum's Enterprises," a collection of manuscripts, clippings, and pamphlets at the New-York Historical Society (hereafter NYHS).

9. *Memoranda of the Life of Jenny Lind*, p. 159.

10. Ibid., p. 145.

11. [William Butler], *Barnum's Parnassus; being Confidential Disclosures of the Prize Committe on the Jenny Lind Song*, 2nd ed. (New York, 1825), pp. 17–18. *The Jenny Lind Comic Almanac* (New York, 1851) also contains several short poems and satirical pieces on Lindomania. See William Allen Butler, *A Retrospect of Forty Years, 1825–1865*, ed. Harriet Allen Butler (New York, 1911), pp. 234–236.

12. See Daniel J. Boorstin, *The Image: Or What Happened to the American Dream* (New York, 1962), chap. 1.

13. Thatcher Taylor Payne to Lizzie Payne, New York, September 11–12, 1850, Jenny Lind Mss., NYHS.

14. Shultz, *Jenny Lind*, writes, p. 197, "Just what Barnum meant by this remark is not quite clear," but the Thatcher Taylor Payne letter, which adds Barnum's previous words about sinking into insignificance, makes his intentions quite obvious.

15. George Templeton Strong, *The Diary of George Templeton Strong*, 4 vols., ed. Allan Nevins and Milton Halsey Thomas (New York, 1952), 2:20–21.

16. See *Memoranda of the Life of Jenny Lind*, pp. 94–96, for a report of London reactions to the American reception.

17. Ibid., pp. 102–104.

18. Ibid., p. 94.

19. Ibid., p. 181.

20. Morris J. Raphael to A. Hart, New York, September 27, 1850, Simon Gratz Collection, Historical Society of Pennsylvania (hereafter HSP).

21. Josiah Foster Flagg to father, November 6, 1850, "A Philadelphia Forty-Niner," *Pennsylvania Magazine of History and Biography* 70 (October 1946), p. 407. The Lind sensation was quickly satirized in two farces. One was a skit produced at Burton's Theater, *She's Come! Jenny's Come*, which included among its characters Mr. Blarneyem, Mr. von Humbug, and The Anaconda. *Jenny-phobia* opened at the Olympic Theater on September 18, 1850. See George C. D. Odell, *Annals of the New York*

Stage, 15 vols. (New York, 1927–1949), vol. 6. Barnum had already been the subject of some other stage productions.

22. C. G. Rosenberg, *Jenny Lind in America* (New York, 1851), p. 44. Rosenberg's book is a major source for descriptions of the Lind tour, for he accompanied the soprano on her travels. Contemporaries charged that Barnum's behavior at the auctions was dishonest and unfair. Stung, Barnum wrote angrily to James Gordon Bennett promising a reward of five thousand dollars "to any person who shall prove by respectable authority, that I was ever directly or indirectly in the remotest degree interested with any person in bidding for a purchasing ticket at auction for the concerts of Mlle. Jenny Lind, as stated by your New Orleans correspondent. . . . I assert positively that this was *never* the case." Barnum to Bennett, New Orleans, March 4, 1851, Special Collections, Illinois State University Library, Normal.

23. Asmodeus (Thaddeus W. Meighan), *Jenny Lind Mania in Boston; or, A Sequel to Barnum's Parnassus* (n.p., n.d.), p. 40.

24. *Mahomet; or, The Unveiled Prophet of Inistan: A Boquet for Jenny Lind* (Boston, 1850), pp. 6–7.

25. Quoted in *Memoranda of the Life of Jenny Lind*, pp. 15–16. The *Herald*, Sept. 14, 1850, argued that "the voice that could produce the 'Herdsman's Song,' never could be fed on anything warmer than cold air. It never could be so clearly and so purely brought out, with bell-like precision, except upon the refinement which nature itself has instituted. . . . Hence it is . . . that Jenny Lind will become the most popular vocalist that has ever visited this country. Her organization is suited to please the people of our cold climate. She will have triumphs here that never would attend her progress through France or Italy." Quoted in *Annals of the New York Stage*, 6:87.

26. Quoted in *Memoranda of the Life of Jenny Lind*, p. 123.

27. Quoted in *Memoir of Jenny Lind*, p. 50.

28. Henry T. Tuckerman, "Jenny Lind," *Essays, Biographical and Critical; or, Studies of Character* (Boston, 1857), pp. 223–236.

29. *Harper's New Monthly Magazine* 1 (October 1850), p. 704.

30. *Essays, Biographical and Critical*, p. 234.

31. Quoted in *Memoranda of the Life of Jenny Lind*, p. 39.

32. Ibid., p. 141. Later recollections also emphasize the naturalism and spotless variety of Jenny Lind's performances. See Sir Julius Benedict, "Jenny Lind," *Scribner's Monthly* 22, (May 1881), pp. 120–123, and Fanny Morris Smith, "What Jenny Lind Did for America," *Century Magazine* 54 (August 1897), pp. 558–559. For a summary of American musical sentiments at the time, see Joseph A. Mussulman, *Music in the Cultured Generation: A Social History of Music in America, 1870–1900* (Evanston, Ill., 1971), p. 66. And for more comments on Jenny see Kenneth Rose, "Jenny Lind, Diva," *Tennessee Historical Quarterly* 8 (March 1949), pp. 34–48, and Emmett Robinson, ed., "Dr. Irving's Reminiscences of the Charleston Stage," *The South Carolina Historical and Genealogical Magazine* 52 (1951), pp. 31–32. Jenny Lind's execution, wrote Dr. Irving in the late 1850s, "constituted the difference between that which can be acquired and that which is *from above* — a bird sings without an effort, by the aid of that Power alone, that gave it power — it is Nature, not Art — God made the bird vocal, and so He did this wondrous creature, Jenny Lind."

33. There is an immense literature on American attitudes toward Nature. For some general ideas and bibliography see Wilson O. Clough, *The Necessary Earth: Nature and Solitude in American Literature* (Austin, 1964); Arthur A. Ekirch, Jr., *Man and Nature in America* (New York, 1963); Neil Harris, *The Artist in American Society* (New York, 1966); Hans Huth, *Nature and the American: Three Centuries of Changing Attitudes* (Berkeley, 1957); Leo Marx, *The Machine in the Garden* (New York, 1964); Roderick Nash, *Wilderness and the American Mind* (New Haven

and London, 1967); Sherman Paul, *Emerson's Angle of Vision: Man and Nature in the American Experience* (Cambridge, Mass., 1952); and Stephen E. Whicher, *Freedom and Fate: An Inner Life of Ralph Waldo Emerson* (Philadelphia, 1953).

34. *Jenny Lind*, in vol. 1 of "Barnum's Enterprises." In keeping with Transcendentalist tenets, observers found that Jenny Lind's power lay in her ability to lose herself in her work, to transcend the boundaries between her ego and her singing. "The peculiar charm of Jenny Lind, as an artist, is her unconsciousness. We are disposed to regard this as one of the most reliable tests of superior gifts. It at least proves the absorption of self in what is dearer — a condition essential to all true greatness." *Essays, Biographical and Critical*, p. 231. The Reverend Mr. Peabody of Boston observed, "In the case of the great singers whom we have heard, they have always appeared to be artists. The art was the prominent thing. In this case we forgot art, we lost all idea of criticism, and leaned back and abandoned ourselves. . . . It was a beautiful, happy-hearted girl, full of unconscious genius, singing without pretension or effort." Quoted in *Memoranda of the Life of Jenny Lind*, p. 195.

35. *Memoranda of the Life of Jenny Lind*, p. 217.

36. Ralph Waldo Emerson, *Journals of Ralph Waldo Emerson*, 10 vols. ed. Edward Waldo Emerson and Waldo Emerson Forbes (Boston and New York, 1909–1914), 7:129, 247, 443.

37. These poems can be found in "Lindiana," an anthology of Lind appreciations compiled and edited by William Augustus Hildebrand, Cheatham Collection, NYHS.

38. Henry Tuckerman, "To Jenny Lind," "Lindiana."

39. *Memoranda of the Life of Jenny Lind*, pp. 174–5. Max Maretzek, inspired perhaps by prose like this, called Willis a "Master of Ceremonies" with "a highly refined language, a style of extreme elegance and finish, but a wonderful paucity of striking ideas. Like the banquet set before the Barmecide, there are splendid China dishes and gold spoons. Vases of silver and a profusion of flowers abound, but unfortunately there is *no* meat." *Crotchets and Quavers*, p. 84.

40. Alfred Bunn, *Old England and New England, in a Series of Views Taken on the Spot*, 2 vols. (London, 1853) 2:93. Another complaint came from the managers of Rachel's tour in the 1850s, who were bitter about the great actress's failure to match Jenny Lind's receipts. See Léon Beauvallet, *Rachel and the New World* (New York, 1856), passim, and the comparative figures, pp. 368–370.

41. *A Peep Behind the Curtain, by a Supernumerary* (Boston, 1850), p. 68. One of Barnum's advance pamphlets warned nervously, "It is evident to us that in respect to the concerts of Mlle. LIND, all our present notions of prices must be swept away. . . . If we will be satisfied with nothing short of artists of European reputation, we must pay European prices for them." Quoted in *Memoir of Jenny Lind*, p. 64.

SIX

(143–181)

1. *Harper's New Monthly Magazine* 4 (May 1852), p. 844. See also *Harper's New Monthly Magazine* 5 (June 1852), p. 127.

2. This was Max Maretzek's charge in *Crotchets and Quavers; or, Revelations of an Opera Manager in America* (New York, 1855, 1966), p. 31.

3. See Barnum to Bayard Taylor, New York, December 16, 1852. Barnum Misc. Mss., NYHS. The weekly ran up a circulation of seventy thousand before its demise.

4. For more on this subject see Richard Rudisill, *Mirror Image: The Image of the Daguerreotype on American Society* (Albuquerque, 1971), pp.

156–157. A prospectus for the contest can be found in the Chicago Historical Society.

5. George Templeton Strong, *The Diary of George Templeton Strong*, 4 vols., ed. Allan Nevins and Milton Halsey Thomas (New York, 1952), 2:177.

6. Barnum to Kimball, Bridgeport, July 14, 1854, NYPL.

7. For the history of Bridgeport, and Barnum's involvement with it, see Reverend Samuel Orcutt, *History of the Old Town of Stratford and the City of Bridgeport, Connecticut*, 2 vols. (New Haven, 1892), and George C. Waldo, Jr., ed., *History of Bridgeport and Vicinity*, 2 vols. (New York and Chicago, 1917).

8. Chauncey Jerome, *History of the American Clock Business for the Past Sixty Years, and Life of Chauncey Jerome* (New Haven, 1860), p. 111.

9. *Frank Leslie's Illustrated Newspaper*, March 29, 1856.

10. In the 1880s the *New Haven Register* charged that Barnum had promised to pay his creditors in full but suddenly "packed his grip sack and took sail for Merrie England." In the Granville Wood Collection there are letters between Barnum and Professor Charles Ritchell about the articles, which were actually written by Julian Sterling, a distant relative and foe of Barnum who made several clumsy attempts to blackmail the showman late in his life and who conducted some vitriolic correspondence with him, both privately and publicly.

11. Kenneth S. Lynn, *William Dean Howells, an American Life* (New York, 1971), p. 162.

12. Barnum to Fields, Osgood & Co., New York, November 22, 1870, Barnum Letters, NYHS.

13. Ralph Keeler, *Vagabond Adventures* (Boston, 1872), pp. 123–124.

14. George C. D. Odell, *Annals of the New York Stage*, 15 vols. (New York, 1927–1949); 7:337–338. Two years later Barnum wrote Anderson to find out if he possessed the American flag that flew over Fort Sumter and requesting permission to exhibit it. Barnum to Robert Anderson, Lindencroft, September 16, 1863, Robert Anderson Mss., Library of Congress. When patriotism damaged profits, however, it was another story. On April 21, 1865, the *New York Times* announced its shock on discovering that Barnum, alone among New York theater managers, opened his establishment during the city's period of mourning for the assassination of Lincoln. "Whilst the city was humbled in prayer on one side of the street, Mr. Barnum's players were mouthing it on the other." *New York Times*, April 21, 1865, p. 4.

15. Six thousand applied in vain for tickets to the reception. See letter of Barnum, February 7, 1863, Simon Gratz Collection, HSP.

16. "Cymon," *The Pigmies and the Priests: Showing How Some Dismal Pagans Were Converted to a Lively Faith* (New York, 1863).

17. The following description is taken from an exhibition catalog published at the time. A copy is located in the Theater Collection, Firestone Library, Princeton University. *An Illustrated Catalogue and Guide Book to Barnum's American Museum* (New York, n.d.).

18. *New York Times*, July 14, 1865, p. 1.

19. *Diary of George Templeton Strong*, 3:31.

20. Barnum to Oliver Wendell Holmes, July 29, 1862, Houghton Library, Harvard University. Twenty years later Barnum was at it again. "I take the liberty of sending you my autobiography," he began, and ended, "I wish you could see Jumbo, my 26 elephants, 12 giraffes, 12 ostriches and the whole great menagerie in its shirt sleeves, at our winter quarters here." Barnum to Oliver Wendell Holmes, Bridgeport, December 22, 1882, Houghton Library, Harvard University. Even in private correspondence Barnum remained the active promoter.

21. *Barnum's American Museum Illustrated* (New York, 1850), p. 2.

22. The story was told by J. F. B. Marshall, and clippings that describe it are found in the Henry Eugene Bowser scrapbook, Granville Wood Collection.

23. *Annals of the New York Stage*, 7:577.
24. *Diary of George Templeton Strong*, 3:598.
25. *New York Tribune*, quoted in Joel Benton, *Life of Hon. Phineas T. Barnum* (n. p., 1891), pp. 551–552.
26. *New York Times*, July 14, 1865, p. 1.
27. *Diary of George Templeton Strong*, 4:18.
28. Ibid., 4:86. Barnum's feelings about Bennett had, of course, been bitter for many years. He wrote Bennett from New York, April 28, 1854, asking for a truce in Bennett's newspaper attacks. "Don't you think it is time to let me drop? I mean, as a *target* for ridicule. I decidedly think *it is*, and respectfully request you to do so. Myself personally, I don't care two straws for all the newspaper squibs that could be written in a century. But I am now engaged in managing a public enterprise which I hope and believe will be made highly conducive to the interests and reputation of this city. . . .

   Second, I have a family growing up around me — am myself not quite as young as I once was, and all things considered, I have to request that you will hereafter *not* speak of myself or my actions in a spirit of ridicule. . . ." Special Collections, Illinois State University Library, Normal. Bennett did not let up, and Barnum's anger was finally vented by the sale of his lease.
29. See for example, Daniel M. Fox, *Engines of Culture: Philanthropy and Art Museums* (Madison, Wis., 1963); and Neil Harris, "The Gilded Age Revisited: Boston and the Museum Movement," *American Quarterly* 14 (Winter 1962), pp. 545–566.
30. The Cornell University Library owns ten letters from Barnum to Bayard Taylor, which expose not only this scheme but Barnum's elaborate concern with details of every sort, especially the naming of his various houses. On April 13, 1861, Barnum sent a long letter to Taylor thanking him for suggestions about a house name; this residence became Lindencroft. On May 28, 1869, he wrote Taylor asking advice on the spelling of Waldemere. The letters in which Barnum outlined his plans for a new American Museum, to be subsidized by the government, were both written from Bridgeport and dated July 16, 1865, and July 22, 1865.

SEVEN

(183–204)

1. Barnum to Thomas Ritchie, Baltimore, December 14, 1850, Simon Gratz Collection, HSP. The *Washington Union*, at the time, was a major Democratic newspaper.
2. The three substitutes were James Burton, Philo Morris, and Henry Stein, according to notes in the Granville Wood Collection.
3. Harvey Root, *The Unknown Barnum* (New York and London, 1927), pp. 294–298, tells the story with unalloyed admiration. Root's book is invaluable for information about Barnum's political activities and service as mayor of Bridgeport.
4. Ibid., p. 187. Chap. 12 describes Barnum's career as a Connecticut legislator.
5. Barnum to Theodore Tilton, Bridgeport, May 29, 1865, Barnum Mss., NYHS.
6. William H. Barnum later served in the United States Senate, became chairman of the Democratic National Committee, and directed the successful 1884 campaign of Grover Cleveland.
7. *Bridgeport Evening Standard*, April 2, 1867.
8. "The Two Hundred Thousand and First Curiosity," the *Nation* 4 (March 7, 1867), pp. 190–192. The *Nation* was particularly aroused by the election of John Morrisey, a speculator, gambler, and prizefighter, as a con-

gressman from New York. Morrisey was a Democrat, and while the *Nation* saw Tammany as beyond redemption, it felt the Republican party should not be permitted to descend to this level.

9. See the letter from J. B. in the *Nation* 4 (March 28, 1867), p. 259, and the counter editorial, "Scratching," the *Nation* 4 (April 11, 1867), pp. 295–297.

10. *New York Evening Express*, March 5, 1867. I am indebted to Professor Louis Budd for sending me a copy of this rare piece.

11. Quoted in David Montgomery, *Beyond Equality: Labor and the Radical Republicans, 1862–1872* (New York, 1967), p. 298.

12. George Templeton Strong, *The Diary of George Templeton Strong*, 4 vols., ed. Allan Nevins and Milton Halsey Thomas (New York, 1952), 4:86.

13. Major J. B. Pond, *Eccentricities of Genius: Memories of Famous Men and Women of the Platform and Stage* (New York, 1900), passim.

14. Ibid., pp. 350–354.

15. *Bridgeport Daily Standard*, April 6, 1875. Barnum obviously received many Democratic votes, for Bridgeport had a normal Democratic majority, and for weeks before the election letter writers claiming to be Democrats urged Barnum's candidacy. See, for example, letter to the editor, *Bridgeport Daily Standard*, March 30, 1875.

16. "Honor to Whom Honor is Due," *Bridgeport Daily Standard*, April 21, 1875, reprinted the comments of newspapers throughout the country.

17. *New York Times*, April 16, 1875, p. 8, reprinted most of the speech.

18. "Out of Work — Nothing To Do," *New York Times*, April 19, 1875, p. 4.

19. *Proceedings of the Common Council*, 1875–1876 (Bridgeport, 1882), p. 134. This was at the last meeting over which Barnum presided. In his early messages Barnum urged, in addition to the enforcement of liquor and sabbath laws, beautification of the city, prevention of the sale of adulterated food, and general retrenchment. At one point he asked for an across-the-board fifteen percent reduction in salaries of all municipal employees. This did not, of course, endear him to city workers. See *Proceedings of the Common Council*, April 12, 1875, p. 2.

20. Messrs. Sailer and Stevens appeared before the police commissioners and told Barnum that he couldn't decide "what we shall eat and drink." They insisted that he carry out all his laws, not select certain ones to enforce, and argued that "Mayor Barnum showed disrespect for the Germans by speaking against selling liquor." *Bridgeport Daily Standard*, September 4, 1874.

21. *Bridgeport Daily Standard*, June 7, 1875.

22. *Bridgeport Daily Standard*, July 10, 1875. On July 21, Oskar Kohn of New York wrote to the *Standard* to say that Barnum had no prejudices at all.

23. *Bridgeport Daily Standard*, September 13, 1875. "In the nature of things," Barnum continued, "it is almost impossible for a man to serve others as faithfully as he serves himself. . . . Now I by no means say or think that all men are dishonest . . . but I do say that if men are honest, they are less liable to be tempted if they know that their actions are under continual surveillance. . . . Honest men do not fear investigations." Barnum was defending the snooping of his retrenchment committee.

24. Laura C. Holloway, *Famous American Fortunes and the Men Who Have Made Them* (Philadelphia . . . San Francisco, 1885), p. 505, mentions the incident.

25. Julian Sterling to Barnum, Bridgeport, January 18, 1890, NYHS. Sterling was replying to a letter from Barnum, London, December 31, 1889, BPL, in which Barnum tried to make peace between the two of them. The Seaside Club of Bridgeport had refused to accept Sterling's application, said Barnum, because many Bridgeport people had been hurt by his attacks in the *New York World* and did not want to open good society to him. Sterling was bitter in his reply. He accused Barnum, among other things, of dishonest business transactions and of having fathered

a bastard. "Pray tell me, Dear Mr. Barnum, what you really know of 'Society'? Were you ever admitted to the exclusive inner circle of well bred society to study the ways of 'Society'?" Sterling also implied that Barnum was suffering from softening of the brain.

26. *The Unknown Barnum*, chap. 15, details the cemetery fight. Barnum's letter is quoted from pp. 233–235.
27. Ibid., pp. 235–236.
28. Ibid., pp. 236–240.
29. Ibid., pp. 240–243.
30. This rumor was mentioned in a pamphlet by Charles F. Greene and Walt Kelly, *P. T. Barnum's Life in Pictures and Prose*, a copy of which is owned by the BPL.

EIGHT

(205–231)

1. Barnum to A. B. Norton, New York, October 17, 1854, Robert G. Caldwell Collection, Firestone Library, Princeton University.
2. A copy of the agreement can be found in the Barnum Misc. Mss., NYHS.
3. In his introduction to the composite edition of the autobiography, George S. Bryan gives a helpful history of the book. See George S. Bryan, ed., *Struggles and Triumphs: or, The Life of P. T. Barnum, Written by Himself*, 2 vols. (New York and London, 1927), 1:xi–lxii.
4. The phrase is William Dean Howells's and is quoted in Mary Sue Carlock, "I Celebrate Myself and Sing Myself: Character-Types in Early American Autobiographies, 1840–1870" (Ph.D. diss., Columbia University, 1958), p. 5.
5. Ibid., p. 8.
6. Charles Godfrey Leland, *Memoirs* (New York, 1893), pp. 211–212.
7. For more on the Yankee type as Americans conceived it see Kenneth S. Lynn, *Mark Twain and Southwestern Humor* (Boston, 1960); Constance Rourke, *American Humor: A Study of the National Character* (New York, 1931); and William R. Taylor, *Cavalier and Yankee: The Old South and American National Character* (New York, 1961).
8. Thomas Colley Grattan, *Civilized America*, 2 vols. (London, 1859), 2:94.
9. Daniel Owen Madden, *Wynville*, 3 vols. (London, 1852), 2:72, quoted in Myron F. Brightfield, "America and the Americans, 1840–1860, as Depicted in English Novels of the Period," *American Literature* 31 (November 1959), p. 313.
10. For Hackett, Yankee Hill, Dan Marble and other interpreters of the Yankee onstage, see Francis Hodge, *Yankee Theatre: The Image of America on the Stage, 1825–1850* (Austin, 1964).
11. Lady Emmeline Stuart-Wortley, *Travels in the United States, etc. during 1849 and 1850* (New York, 1851), p. 73.
12. "The Lesson of Barnum's Life," *Littell's Living Age* 44 (January 1855), p. 150.
13. Alexis de Tocqueville, *Democracy in America*, 2 vols., ed. Phillips Bradley (New York, 1954), 2:130.
14. P. T. Barnum, *The Humbugs of the World* (New York, 1865), p. 159.
15. David M. Reese, *Humbugs of New York: A Remonstrance Against Popular Delusion, Whether in Philosophy, Science, or Religion* (New York, 1838). See the approving review in the *Southern Literary Messenger* 5 (June 1839), pp. 380–383. This generous reaction contrasted with the hostility the *Messenger* showed Barnum's autobiography sixteen years later.
16. P. T. Barnum to Thomas Wentworth Higginson, Bridgeport, n.d., Barnum Letters, BPL.
17. *The Humbugs of the World*, p. 102.

18. For more on this see Neil Harris, *The Artist in American Society: The Formative Years, 1790–1860* (New York, 1966), chap. 2.
19. [Thomas Hamilton], *Men and Manners in America* (Philadelphia, 1833), pp. 28–29.
20. Horace Mann, "The Necessity of Education in a Republican Government," excerpted in Edwin C. Rozwenc, ed., *Ideology and Power in the Age of Jackson* (Garden City, N.Y. 1964), p. 45.
21. For more discussion on the use of didacticism to legitimize art in America see *The Artist in American Society*, passim.
22. *American Whig Review* 1 (January 1845), p. 98, reprinted in *Ideology and Power in the Age of Jackson*, p. 54.
23. *Democracy in America*, 2:106.
24. Quentin Anderson, *The Imperial Self: An Essay in American Literary and Cultural History* (New York, 1971), p. 60.
25. Nathaniel Hawthorne, *The House of the Seven Gables* (New York, 1961), p. 119.
26. A. N. Kaul, *The American Vision: Actual and Ideal Society in Nineteenth-Century Fiction* (New Haven, 1963), p. 149.
27. Harold Kaplan, "Hawthorne: The Need to Become Human," chap. 5 in *Democratic Humanism and American Literature* (Chicago and London, 1972), contains an illuminating discussion of this issue; indeed the entire book examines American writers as they confront the themes of personal freedom and human community.
28. Marvin Meyers, *The Jacksonian Persuasion: Politics and Belief* (New York, 1960), chap. 4, has an interesting discussion of Cooper's conservatism, and references to other commentaries.
29. Richard Chase, "Melville's Confidence Man," *Kenyon Review*, 11 (Winter 1949), p. 136.
30. See Richard Chase, *Herman Melville: A Critical Study* (New York, 1949), pp. 75–77. Hershel Parker has edited an authoritative edition of *The Confidence-Man* and brought together background sources, reviews, and some important critical essays. References to Barnum are scattered through the volume. See Herman Melville, *The Confidence-Man: His Masquerade*, ed. Hershel Parker (New York, 1971).
31. *Democratic Humanism and American Literature*, pp. 250–251.
32. Fish, who first met Barnum in 1858, called one of his engines Barnum, and another Charity.
33. *Knickerbocker Magazine* 45 (January 1855), p. 80.
34. For these quotes and more on the use of the term "confidence man" see Johannes Dietrich Bergmann, "The Original Confidence Man," *American Quarterly* 21 (Fall, 1969), pp. 560–577.
35. Severn Teackle Wallis, "Barnum and Mrs. Stowe," *Writings of Severn Teackle Wallis*, 4 vols. (Baltimore, 1896), 2: 69–84.
36. [William H. Hurlburt], "Barnum's and Greeley's Biographies," *The Christian Examiner and Religious Miscellany* 58 (March 1855), pp. 245–264.
37. *The Autobiography of Petite Bunkum, the Showman* (New York, 1855), pp. 5–6. Parodies were appearing as late as 1889. Two years before Barnum's death, *Auto-Biography of Barnum; or, The Opening of the Oyster* (Danbury, Conn., 1889), was published. In this sixteen-page parody, which measures two by one and a half inches, dedicated "To the Bearded Lady and her hairs," Barnum's indifference to his immediate family is aptly satirized. "According to the best authority I had a father, but no matter about him; and a mother, but that's of no consequence," p. 3. A copy is located in the Beinecke Library, Yale University.
38. "Revelations of a Showman," *Blackwood's Edinburgh Magazine*, American edition, 40 (February 1855), pp. 187–201.
39. "Barnum," *Fraser's Magazine* 51 (February 1855), pp. 213–223.
40. "Barnum for President," *Punch* 29 (September 1, 1855), p. 89.
41. See Raymund Fitzsimons, *Barnum in London* (London, 1969), chap. 6, for the Haydon episode and fears about the Americanization of England.

42. "Revelations of a Showman," *Blackwood's Edinburgh Magazine*, p. 193.
43. Roger D. Abrahams, "Trickster, the Outrageous Hero," *Our Living Traditions: An Introduction to American Folklore*, ed. Tristram Peter Coffin (New York, 1968), pp. 171–172.

NINE

(233–276)

1. For the early history of the American circus see George L. Chindahl, *A History of the Circus in America* (Caldwell, Idaho, 1959); Earl Chapin May, *The Circus from Rome to Ringling* (New York, 1932); Gil Robinson, *Old Wagon Show Days* (Cincinnati, 1925); and R. W. G. Vail, *Random Notes on the History of the Early American Circus* (Worcester, Mass., 1934).
2. M. Willson Disher, *Greatest Show On Earth* (London, 1937), recounts the history of Astley's.
3. Philip Graham, *Showboats, the History of an American Institution* (Austin, 1951), discusses the early circus boats. The first showboat deliberately built as such was launched in the summer of 1831.
4. W. C. Coup, *Sawdust and Spangles: Stories and Secrets of the Circus* (Chicago, 1901), p. 7. *Old Wagon Show Days* also contains reminiscences of circus violence.
5. John R. Betts, "Barnum and Natural History," *Journal of the History of Ideas* 20 (June–September 1959), pp. 353–368, explores Barnum's plans for a zoo, and his benefactions to scholarly and philanthropic institutions.
6. Coup describes his various innovations in *Sawdust and Spangles*, but he doesn't mention the inclined planes. Chindahl, in *A History of the Circus in America*, speculates on their origin, p. 116, but there is a good possibility that Coup developed them.
7. Dexter W. Fellows and Andrew A. Freeman, *This Way to the Big Show: The Life of Dexter Fellows* (New York, 1936), p. 220. Fellows was a publicity agent who worked for the Buffalo Bill Wild West Show, Barnum, and finally, the Ringling Brothers. "The enemy that is to be considered," Fellows continued, "is adverse economic conditions which may exist in certain parts of the country. It would be poor policy for the circus to tour the South before the cotton crop is picked and likewise to play the great midwestern wheat belt before harvesting is started. . . . For this reason the circus heads into New England a month or so after it leaves New York, goes west in midsummer, and swings into the South late in the fall."
8. Cleveland Moffett, "How The Circus Is Put Up and Taken Down," *McClure's Magazine* 5 (June 1895), pp. 49–61. Military imagery dominated the articles that stressed the precision of circus movements. See, for example, "Circus Hands," *Harper's Weekly* 37 (April 22, 1893), p. 377, where circus hands are described as "a great 'show family,' possessed of a discipline and an *esprit de corps* that appear quite military — very foreign indeed to the atmosphere of the old-time circus." Circus publicists, of course, were eager to present the circus performers as clean-living, moral, and industrious workers to allay the suspicions of middle-class readers who dreamed of orgies and wild behavior among them. See also Ralph Bergengren, "Taking the Circus Seriously," *Atlantic Monthly* 103 (May 1909), pp. 672–679.
9. Cleveland Moffett, "Behind the Scenes in the Circus," *McClure's Magazine* 5 (August 1895), pp. 277–278.
10. W. C. Thompson, *On the Road with a Circus* (New York, 1905), p. 18. Thompson's book contains excellent descriptions of many aspects of circus management.

11. *Sawdust and Spangles*, p. 63.
12. E. S. Hallock, "The American Circus," *Century Magazine* 70 (August 1905), pp. 568–585, describes the decline of the talking clown. Another reason for his decline was suggested by the *Nation* 35 (August 3, 1882), p. 83. The culprit was popular journalism. "The press make a business of supplying daily just such jokes as the circus used to provide, and ambitious humorists, who would formerly have worn stripes and spangles in the ring, now entertain the public through a newspaper." The press, of course, did not stop vaudeville comedians, who also used topical humor, so Hallock's explanation, resting on the growth in size of the circus, makes more sense.
13. *New York Times*, December 25, 1872, p. 4.
14. *New York Times*, March 29, 1873, p. 12.
15. Details of the hippodrome are given in the *New York Times*, February 12, 1874, p. 8. The fears of property-owners are discussed in the *Times*, February 11, 1874, p. 8.
16. See for example, *New York Times*, April 25, 1874, p. 7; and April 28, 1874, p. 5. For later pageants see the *Times*, November 24, 1874, p. 4; and December 24, 1874, p. 4.
17. Programs for some of these spectaculars can be found in the McCaddon Collection, Firestone Library, Princeton University. J. T. McCaddon was manager of Adam Forepaugh's circus for a time, Barnum's great rival, and eventually became associated with the Ringling brothers. The McCaddon Collection contains important materials on the history of the circus, but mainly for the years after Barnum's death.
18. The very different emphases of hippodrama are well described in A. H. Saxon, *Enter Foot and Horse: A History of Hippodrama in England and France* (New Haven, 1968). Further evidence of the turn to the spectacular is provided by Richard Moody, *America Takes the Stage: Romanticism in American Drama and Theatre, 1750–1900* (Bloomington, Ind., 1955), pp. 206–207, 222. Men like Augustin Daly and Steele MacKaye experimented in the eighties and nineties with sensational new scenic effects. MacKaye planned a Spectatorium for the Chicago World's Fair of 1893, an enormous building with twenty-five telescope stages and all the latest machinery, devoted entirely to dramatic presentations. Unfortunately, it was never built. For different but applicable material concerning the glitter and magnificence of vaudeville palaces and their shows, see Albert V. McLean, Jr., *American Vaudeville as Ritual* (Lexington, Ky., 1965), passim.
19. *New York Times*, July 8, 1874, p. 4.
20. For more on Barnum's balloon projects see the *New York Times*, September 18, 1873, pp. 4–5; July 3, 1874, p. 5; and May 2, 1874, p. 5.
21. *New York Times*, May 2, 1874, p. 5.
22. "An Alarming Sacrifice," *New York Times*, December 2, 1875, p. 4.
23. W. C. Crum, *History of Animals and Leading Curiosities Contained in P. T. Barnum's World's Fair and Colosseum of Natural History and Art* (New York, 1873), pp. 11–12.
24. "Barnum Strikes Back," *New York Times*, August 26, 1890, p. 4.
25. The Bowser materials, consisting of a diary, ledger books, correspondence, contracts, photographs, and memorabilia, are in the possession of Mr. and Mrs. Granville J. Wood of Middletown, New York, who have the most important privately owned group of Barnum materials. The collection has not been cataloged, but the circus figures are taken from Bowser's own notations. Mr. and Mrs. Wood have kindly given me permission to quote from their materials.
26. This contract, dated August 26, 1880, is in the Granville Wood Collection.
27. Bowser diary, December 3, 1880; December 12, 1880; December 16, 1880, Granville Wood Collection.

28. Barnum to Bowser, Block Island, R.I., July 30, 1884, Granville Wood Collection. Barnum vacationed on Block Island for several summers.
29. Barnum to Bowser, Southport, England, June 20, 1881, Granville Wood Collection.
30. Barnum to Bowser, New York, May 1, 1881, and November 28, 1881, Granville Wood Collection.
31. C. P. Cary to Bowser, April 25, 1881, and July 5, 1881, Granville Wood Collection.
32. ? to Barnum, n.d., Granville Wood Collection.
33. An 1881 advertisement in the Granville Wood Collection.
34. Bowser ledger, March 9, 1881.
35. *St. Louis Post-Dispatch*, September 1, 1881.
36. The advertisement ran alongside the news item about losses. *St. Louis Post-Dispatch*, September 1, 1881.
37. Mrs. James Pendergrass to Barnum, South Troy, New York, February 5, 1883, Special Collections, Illinois State University, Normal. By this time Mrs. Pendergrass had become involved with several lawyers who were not entirely sympathetic with her case. One of them insisted that a daughter who died had consumption and had suffered from it long before Barnum's elephant ever arrived in Troy. Her letter continues: "Mr Barnum this is not a lawyers letter but from my self there is lawyers wanted to take this from me but I do not like law business i do not want to draw the dead up out of the grave in the court house i would go and see you my self but money is so scarce with me. . . ." Mrs. Pendergrass suggested the experience had cost her at least eight hundred dollars, in addition to her grief. The amount Barnum was to repay her she did not specify.
38. *St. Louis Post-Dispatch*, June 1, 1882, reprinted the story from the *New York Times*.
39. *St. Louis Post-Dispatch*, May 30, 1883.
40. Bailey's remarkable career, summarized by every circus historian, has been analyzed in an interesting pamphlet, Richard E. Conover, *The Affairs of James A. Bailey* (Xenia, O., 1957). Conover based his narrative on the McCaddon Collection at Princeton.
41. Robert E. Sherwood, *Here We Are Again: Recollections of an Old Circus Clown* (Indianapolis, 1926), p. 195.
42. *This Way to the Big Show*, p. 195. The phrase came from a speech given by Whiting Allen, a colleague of Hamilton's. Allen tried to mimic Tody's manner. "Tall and towering Tody! 'Tis his transmutation transmitted and translated into tens of thousands of tongues that tell thrilling titillating tales to towns that teem with thousands and that transform things trite and thin into tremendously thick and telling truths that terrify timorous teachers, transfigure terms and take a thundering tough trip to the threshold of trembling tautology."
43. Robert E. Sherwood, *Hold Yer Hosses! The Elephants Are Coming* (London, 1932), pp. 66–71.
44. *London Telegraph*, February 22, 1882, quoted in *The Book of Jumbo*, a Barnum publicity release, which apeared in June 1882.
45. *New York Times*, March 22, 1883, p. 3. Describing the procession greeting Jumbo, the *Times*, March 25, 1883. p. 2, declared that there was more excitement in New York "than there would be in London if Queen Victoria's imperial knee was swelled to twice its royal size." Bowery toughs, swells, crooks, and detectives watched the procession, "and the multitude burst into a roar of applause which almost shook the City to its foundations and caused the cobble-stones to grind against each other in the streets." In this golden age of American journalism, ordinary news stories were treated with the loving care that Barnum lavished on his advertisements and announcements.
46. For more on these nature writers see Peter J. Schmitt, *Back to Nature: The Arcadian Myth in Urban America* (New York, 1969), especially

chaps. 3–4, 12. *American Vaudeville as Ritual*, chap. 7, has a provocative interpretation of the Jumbo incident, which McLean links to a new late-nineteenth-century totemism. The circus does not quite fit his conception of urban entertainments in the period (it was popular in both rural and urban areas), and he argues, erroneously I believe, that "although the circus still maintained its strength into the twentieth century, it revealed none of vaudeville's capacities for growth, and characteristic of most amusements in their declining stages, it became thought of as a diversion for children." The clown's pantomime, McLean continues, "ran counter to the dominant verbalism of the new entertainment and his brand of whimsy seemed old-fashioned for the machine age" (p. 28). Because this observation generalizes about a period in which the silent films captivated the mass urban audience, it seems out of place. The pantomime clown, as noted in the text, was a late invention, replacing a more purely verbal performer. And the pleasure adults have taken in entertainment labeled as "children's" from the nineteenth century onward suggests that a more complex division than juvenile versus mature, or adult versus child is needed to categorize entertainment forms.

47. Matthew Scott, *Autobiography of Matthew Scott* (Bridgeport, Conn., 1885), p. 55. Scott, whose father was brewer to the Earl of Derby, began his career tending to the earl's bird collection. When the birds were bequeathed to the London Zoological Society Scott accompanied them.
48. The Barnum-Ward relationship is described by John R. Russell, "Jumbo," *University of Rochester Library Bulletin* 3 (Autumn 1947), pp. 12–20.
49. Bowser ledger, February 4, 1882, Granville Wood Collection.
50. William A. Croffut, *An American Procession 1855–1914: A Personal Chronicle of Famous Men* (Freeport, N.Y., 1968), p. 290. Croffut published his book in 1931. Barnum and Croffut's father had known each other as children, and Croffut served as Barnum's private secretary in the mid-1860s, when Barnum was running for Congress.
51. For more on the negotiations, see the *New York Times*, June 9, 1883, p. 5, and December 6, 1883, p. 5.
52. *New York Times*, February 9, 1884, p. 2.
53. Ibid., p. 2.
54. *New York Times*, March 29, 1884, p. 1. Greeting the animal along with Barnum were Daniel Sickles, ex-consul to Siam, Professor Frederick Holder, a naturalist, and many press agents. New York newspapers were filled with stories about the elephant's role in Buddhism and arguments about the true appearance of white elephants in their natural habitat.
55. With his usual care, Barnum supervised the contest. He wrote one of the contestants that his poem was "cute" but could not be published "unless the lines about Patrick and Norah were changed — for the Irish element is a *live* one and you can judge how that class would regard the big show if I endorsed the sentiment alluded to." Obviously, Barnum had learned from his mayoralty about the sensitivity of ethnic groups. He offered the poet twenty-five dollars to change the lines. See Barnum to Mr. Cornell, New York, June 4, 1884, Barnum Misc. Mss., NYHS.
56. "The Prize Odes," *New York Times*, June 1, 1884, p. 8.
57. The McCaddon Collection at Princeton has this rat sheet by Forepaugh. Forepaugh and Barnum combined their shows in 1887 for a stupendous spectacle in New York, and later divided their territories so as not to cut into one another's profits. Forepaugh died one year before Barnum, in January 1890.
58. "White Elephants," *New York Times*, March 22, 1884, p. 4.
59. *New York Times*, November 22, 1887, p. 4.
60. *New York Times*, November 22, 1887, p. 4.
61. For more on Bergh and his relationship to Barnum see Alvin F. Harlow, *Henry Bergh: Founder of the ASPCA* (New York, 1957), passim.

62. Henry Bergh to Barnum, New York, March 22, 1884, Granville Wood Collection.
63. The story can be followed in the *New York Times*, March 31, 1883, p. 2; April 3, 1883, p. 8; April 5, 1883, p. 8. Barnum's open letter of protest to Gerry was published in the Times, March 30, 1883, p. 8.
64. Barnum's letter was reprinted in the *New York Times*, November 4, 1888, p. 4.
65. *New York Times*, September 24, 1888, p. 4. For the actions of rival circus owners see the *Times*, February 2, 1885, p. 2.
66. "Barnum's," *Saturday Review* 57 (April 26, 1884), p. 539.
67. Thomas Frost, *Circus Life and Circus Celebrities* (London, 1881), pp. 223–224.
68. London *Times*, November 12, 1889, included in vol. 5 of "Barnum's Enterprises," NYHS.
69. See the *New York Times*, November 10, 1889, p. 1.
70. Sala is quoted in the London *Times*, November 11, 1889, included in vol. 5 of "Barnum's Enterprises."
71. Barnum's recording has been reproduced in a retrospective glance at the history of recording, *The Wonder of the Age: Mr. Edison's New Talking Phonograph*, Argo ZPR 122–3.

TEN

(277–292)

1. *New York Times*, May 30, 1891, p. 1.
2. "Barnum," *New York Times*, April 8, 1891, p. 4.
3. *Harper's New Monthly Magazine* 83 (October 1891), pp. 797–798.
4. "P. T. Barnum," *Literary Digest* 2 (April 11, 1891), p. 670. This was reprinted from the *New York Recorder*, April 8, 1891.
5. Along with its own comments the *New York Times* reprinted the observations of European newspapers, April 28, 1891, p. 9.
6. See, for example, P. T. Barnum, "Do Americans Hate the English?" *Independent* 26 (April 9, 1874), p. 3; "What the Fair Should Be," *North American Review* 150, (March 1890), pp. 400–401; "A Trip Abroad," *North American Review* 152 (June 1891), pp. 696–703. The chauvinism of Barnum's youth had given way to a tolerant internationalism.
7. William A. Croffut, *An American Procession, 1855–1914: A Chronicle of Famous Men* (Freeport, N.Y., 1968), pp. 292–293.
8. For Barnum's involvement see Norman Zierold, *Little Charley Ross: America's First Kidnapping for Ransom* (Boston, Toronto, 1967), pp. 275–277, and the *New York Times*, May 20, 1877, p. 7.
9. An example is Laura C. Holloway, *Famous American Fortunes and the Men Who Have Made Them* (Philadelphia . . . San Francisco, 1885).
10. Many of these letters are listed and summarized in Nelle Neafie, "A P. T. Barnum Bibliography" (Lexington, Ky., 1965), a mimeographed pamphlet. The letters described are all in the collection of the BPL.
11. See, for example, Barnum to Clemens, Bridgeport, January 27, 1876, Mark Twain Papers, University of California, Berkeley, California.
12. Twain quoted in Albert Bigelow Paine, *Mark Twain, a Biography: The Personal and Literary Life of Samuel Langhorne Clemens*, 4 vols. (New York and London, 1912), 2:564.
13. Letter XI, New York, March 2, 1867, Franklin Walker and G. Ezra Dane, eds., *Mark Twain's Travels with Mr. Brown* (New York, 1940), pp. 116–118. Twain's first travel letter, written to his mother from New York, August 24, 1853, and published in the *Hannibal Journal*, September 8, 1853, described some of the exhibits at the American Museum, although he did not mention it by name. See Minnie M. Brashear, *Mark Twain, Son of Missouri* (New York, 1964), p. 154.

14. Mark Twain, *Following the Equator: A Journey Around the World*, 2 vols. (New York and London, 1897, 1899) 2:312–317.

15. Mark Twain, *Pudd'nhead Wilson* (Baltimore, 1969), introduction by Malcolm Bradbury, p. 24.

16. Thomas Low Nichols, *Forty Years of American Life, 1820–1861* (New York, 1864, 1937), p. 70.

17. I wish to thank Mr. Kenneth Holmes of the Barnum Museum for originally suggesting the personal parallels between Barnum and Twain. References to Barnum's family problems are scattered through his correspondence, particularly in the Bowser papers. For the questionable financial practices of some of Barnum's relatives (from which he occasionally bailed them out), see Barnum's statement concerning his cousin, E. T. Nichols, in the Barnum Collection, BPL; and Mary Ammerman to Barnum, Brooklyn, January 28, 1891, Granville Wood Collection, concerning Barnum's nephew, Charles Benedict, one of the family's black sheep. Clinton H. Seeley, one of Barnum's grandsons, changed his name to C. Barnum Seeley to gain a legacy, but P. T. wrote Bowser on April 12, 1889, that he didn't expect "to give him any power whatever in regard to my affairs." Clinton was left three percent of the annual net profit of the circus on condition that he travel with it, but this codicil led to a court fight. The other partners thought little of Clinton's work. In the end the Barnum heirs sold out to Bailey for a much smaller sum than they might once have received. Irving Wallace, *The Fabulous Showman: The Life and Times of P. T. Barnum* (New York, 1959), especially chap. 7, undertakes the most extensive examination of Barnum's family life.

18. This statement by the Honorable William B. Hurd of Brooklyn, can be found quoted in the clipping file, Granville Wood Collection.

19. *New York Times*, April 12, 1891, p. 17. See also Joel Benton, "P. T. Barnum, Showman and Humorist," *Century Magazine* 64 (August 1902), pp. 580–592, for Barnum's delight in entertaining children.

20. See Laurence Hutton, "Infant Phenomena of America," *Curiosities of the American Stage* (New York, 1891), pp. 207–254, for the cult of the child stars.

21. Albert E. Stone, Jr., *The Innocent Eye: Childhood in Mark Twain's Imagination* (New Haven, 1961), p. 274.

Index

333

336